YEAR OF PLAGUES

YEAR OF PLAGUES

A MEMOIR OF 2020

FRED D'AGUIAR

HARPER

An Imprint of HarperCollins*Publishers*

"Black Lives Matter" was first published in a slightly different form in *A Restricted View from Under the Hedge*, no. 3 (Autumn 2018), edited by Mark Davidson (www.hedgehogpress.co.uk/arfur).

The memoir essay, first published as "A Son in Shadow" in *Harper's Magazine* (March 1999), appears here in a revised form.

"I Wake with His Name on My Tongue" was first published, in a slightly different form, in the Summer 2021 issue of *Poetry London*.

HarperCollins books may be purchased for educational, business, or sales promotional use. For information, please email the Special Markets Department at SPsales@harpercollins.com.

FIRST EDITION

Designed by Leah Carlson-Stanisic

Library of Congress Cataloging-in-Publication Data has been applied for.

ISBN 978-0-06-309153-5

21 22 23 24 25   LSC   10 9 8 7 6 5 4 3 2 1

For Debbie Dalton and our Christopher, Nicholas,
and Liliana, lockdown strong, no matter how long

I cannot, for the present, express my meanings more clearly.

—Spinoza

Beware the terror of not producing

Beware the urge to justify your decision.

Watch out for the kitchen sink and the plumbing and that painting that always needed being done. But remember the body needs to create too.

Beware feeling you're not good enough to deserve it

Beware feeling you're too good to need it

Beware all the hatred you've stored up inside you, and the locks on your tender places.

—Audre Lorde, from *Sister Love: The Letters of Audre Lorde and Pat Parker, 1974–1989*

CONTENTS

ACKNOWLEDGMENTS

My heartfelt thanks go to Jonathan Burnham for his editorial "Edward Scissorhands" genius and the team at Harper, Jackie, Gabe, Kim, and copyeditor Douglas Johnson. Also, to André Naffis-Sahely who read like a critic with a poet's eye and grace. And to Geoff Hardy and his husband, Peter Roscoe, for confirming aspects of my past, as did my brother, Gregory D'Aguiar and his partner, Maria, and Patrick D'Aguiar living his dream with Tanawan. For Andrew D'Aguiar who found love in Milton Keynes with two-*t*'s Nattasha. In memory of Grace Theriault, who honored her first name in the way she lived her life. In admiration of Matthew Kay: son, your wise words and films gave me strength. To Cameron, your struggles brought much needed perspective in my fight, while your children, Dylan and Aniyah, turned me into a granddad. To Elliot and Antonia for their little miracle, Cruz, who brought me joy. And for my mother, Kathleen Cadogan, whose spirit presides over all. Last and most crucial, to the doctors, nurses, and staff in oncology at the UCLA medical center.

YEAR OF PLAGUES

OUT OF THIS TIME

Good morning, cancer. How are you? You must have been there that balmy night in Atlanta in the early nineties. At that sports bar. A group of us poets decompressing with quick rounds of drinks and propelled into a state of collective foolhardy bravery, decided, while we faced the long trough of the urinal and watched the small TV screens mounted directly in front of us at eye level, to aim our various streams up at those screens.

We had rushed to the bar after a day of all things to do with poetry, from readings and performances to panels on poetics and the future of poetry books in light of the digital revolution. We wanted nothing more to do with poetry that day though everything about us reeked of our poetry personas, our berets, fedoras, long scarves, pebble spectacles, handlebar moustaches, excessive beards, tweeds, corduroy, you get the picture.

There was no *Ghostbusters* crossing of streams as we stood shoulder to shoulder at the urinal. This was strictly parallel play. We blurred the images flickering at us and cheered. We were a testament to the power of the body over technology. For as long as we peed and in our state of blissful inebriation there would not be any diminishing of this strength. Posers. We were young. We toasted afterward to our experience already consecrated to mythic memory.

In the three decades that followed my night at the bar I took my excretions for granted. If I went out for any length of time,

I never wondered about the location of the next public convenience. I could hold it. In fact, if someone polite and considerate asked me if I needed to go, I invariably said no, without having to think if I needed to relieve myself right then, because I would have to empty at some point soon. All of the above was true for me until the fall of 2019.

Around October I began to notice that I had to concentrate to pee. I seemed to be in possession of a shy bladder even though I stood there in response to an urge that I had to attend to immediately. No more texting with one hand as I directed my stream with the other, no more playing the partial absentee from the job at hand. I strained a little and the result was a desultory trickle that barely registered against the porcelain. What happened to the comforting noise of my piss forcibly trained at porcelain or into toilet water, that sound of mounting relief that is the liquid waste equivalent of exhaling?

There was synergy that night in Atlanta for all of us at that time in that place. If synergy teaches anything, it is this: that it holds a plurality of things together for a moment and one moment only before those things disperse into their chaotic patterning of our reality. I heard this anecdote from a drunken poet: he said with glazed eyes and through splattering, beery saliva, that in a certain martial arts movie, the hero runs from a group of ninjas chasing him toward a river. The camera shows the audience that the river, with its traffic of junks, presents the final roadblock for our hero on the run. As the ninjas draw near we see they are dripping with nunchucks and other deadly implements. They close in on our hero and the real estate runs out for him as he looks at the river and again clocks the surface teeming with junks. Just as we think the chap has to stand his ground and perish against overwhelming odds, the camera pans to the river once more, and that chaotic scene of junks on the water switches to elegance and order with the junks all lined up in a row as they pass each other. The star spots his escape route and he hops from one junk to the next until he reaches the far shore of the river. Just as he leaps ashore we see the ninjas arrive at the opposite bank and prepare to follow the same route across the river. But the junks immediately fall apart and resume their chaotic commerce of navigating the river, and the ninjas tumble into the water.

That moment when the junks aligned for the hero may be the moment of synergy that we captured fleetingly that evening in that sports bar. We knew from instinct that our young bodies had reached their zenith. Our flesh-and-blood awareness was primed for decline from that night onward. We acted in a ritual that marked that threshold with gratitude for the unaccountable privilege of having reached that moment in our episodic lives. For we deemed life to be fragile and ruled by chance, full of accidents, if not plain disaster, and liable to be taken from us without notice or, if with notice, then with added pain and dread.

I owed this awareness of a temporary harmony with forces beyond my control to my emergence as a poet. Poetry primed me for insecurity and chance. Poetry's knack for forging relationships among unconnected things chimed with my penchant for sound, rhythm, and image of words as tantamount, a way to make sense of the world. My nervous system seemed predisposed to insecurity as bedrock for belonging to the world of disparate elements and chance occurrences. That night in the sports bar crowned my belief that knowledge would be mediated by the body's unquestioning sensory reception of the world.

All this expansive sense switched its focal point from the world at large to my bladder. A weight and pressure in my loins cancels my heart and pulse as twin guards of my hours. Those twins are replaced by the liquid hourglass of my bladder. An announcement of some imminent threat to my life calendar surges in me. Without knowing what could be wrong, I feel this burgeoning fear that something most definitely is not right. I take several days to focus any language to formulate what I am feeling, since the heightened emotions generated by the new sensations result in confusion, in incapacitating alarm.

From fall 2019 I began to think about input and output. Not

just in terms of the age-specific need to be aware that if I drank *X* amount of beer I would have to urinate *Y* number of times but of how everything I took into my body would be registered by the Geiger counter of my bladder. Whereas before my gut told me when I was hungry, or my sluggishness or dry mouth said that I should drink some water, this new time device behaved like supersensitive radar for all my consumption, and sprang up in my crotch.

I planned my socializing as a meticulous robber might a heist. Where was the nearest gents in this building or that mall, or park? I began to think like an off-duty fire marshal who enters every structure with a mindset that clocks all the hazards and exits. I could not relax. I invariably devoted a portion of my awareness to the demands of my bladder. Every time I embarked on a task—it could be anything, a meeting or car journey or shopping expedition—I wondered when my bladder would announce its presence. And what an announcement: a twisting of my innards located in the area behind my pubic bone, a sharp sense of a wild flame from a naked torch deliberately glanced against my body but improbably from inside my body, a burst of this sharp feeling that radiated down my legs and up my back and spread to the ends of my fingers that made me clench my teeth and narrow my eyes.

When did I think something was definitely wrong and I needed to do something about it rather than accommodate it? I wish I had a precise date. I have only this Southern California season, late autumn into winter. There never was for me a where-were-you-when moment of realization. Instead it dawned on me, imperceptibly. The kind of thing people said about a stoic toad in a pot of water gradually brought to the boil. I sensed the need to act one day and put it into words the next and made inquiries on yet another day.

I felt my scrotum for any sign of change. Nothing. I looked long and hard at my crotch to see if the area at my pubic bone showed any alteration. Nothing. I went so far as to crouch over my plate-size concave shaving mirror to see if the place under my scrotum and around my rectum had changed in some way. Nothing.

I turned to Google and YouTube. The two search engines supplied a cornucopia of alarming statistics and graphics all pointing to cancer of the prostate. On the one hand, people testified to my symptoms as indicative of "the good cancer" as a thing to live with, rather than die of. On the other, at fifty-nine, as I was at the time of the discovery, I learned that I could die from the probable cause of this obstruction to my free flow. If the web were true, I would suffer a rapid demise of the body and matching depletion of the spirit, and no shortage of pain along the way. The beast of the thing would take over my body from the inside and shut down each function of it like the flight of businesses from a dying mall.

I was born in 1960, which the Chinese zodiac tells me is the year of the metal rat: a good year for London's Notting Hill Carnival, for which the radical thinker Claudia Jones* (expelled from the United States) serves on the carnival's steering and planning committee; Chubby Checker's "The Twist" begins the dance craze; JFK wins the US presidential election; Hitchcock's *Psycho* premieres in New York; Harper Lee's *To Kill a Mockingbird* is published; in South Africa the Sharpeville Massacre of schoolchildren launches the armed resistance of the African National Congress (ANC) to apartheid symbolized by the leadership of Nelson Mandela; Cassius Clay (later Muhammad Ali) wins his first professional fight; the soap *Coronation Street* premieres on the UK's Independent Television (ITV) network; Wilson Harris publishes his seminal first novel (his third in terms of composition) titled *Palace of the Peacock*, with its ecological dismantling of the idea of the colony; and many colonies continue breaking free of

---

* Carole Boyce-Davies, *Left of Karl Marx: The Political Life of Black Communist Claudia Jones* (Durham, NC: Duke University Press, 2008).

their European masters—Benin, Chad, Nigeria, Senegal, Cameroon, Mali, Niger, Somalia.

Conjecture is everything. February 2, a Tuesday, early evening, I am born. Redheaded and anemic, dropped off with a nanny during the week, while my parents slaved away on the buses as driver and conductress (as my mother was called back then) with her nifty ticket machine whose noise I clocked as Mum's freeze-dried heart (for her ability to leave my older brother and me in care all week). As for Dad, his ticker was destined to stop, aged fifty-three, the same number as his bus that he aimed down Blackheath Hill into the sprawling capital. 1960 was not as cold as feared. The London Carnival was only two and the 1950s gave up its signs, NO BLACKS, NO IRISH. My parents bought a two-up, two-down redbrick terrace.

Worse than my advanced middle age was the statistical liability credited to my race. As a Black man, the degree of equity in the dire stock of the disease multiplied. Black skin, whose penalty was not only a history of enslavement and its epidemiology of distress, but biology as well, gifted me certain predispositions. Of course, I put it down to statistical social design rather than any objective ability of science to examine Black people. Science cannot help itself when it comes to Black bodies. Science exercises a shamefully high degree of subjectivity. Blacks always look worse than everyone else under the outright hostility or, at best, indifferent profit rubrics of the White gaze. To escape that incapacitating gaze that literally drains the color out of a Black body (a seemingly desirable condition, non-Black, though, in fact, a state of living death that robs the person of any memory of Black vitality and Black being), the Black person must be twice as healthy, virile, fashionable, inventive, funny, and tragic.

Do I feel pain more acutely than Whites on account of a history of hurt? Is a White prostate any less invasive of bladder function than a Black one? Of course not, fool. The thought that this bias might be the case is a cause of some concern to me and my psyche, a suspicion that I am inclined to think neurotically as if primed by a history of oppression to react in this way. I don't know enough about what it is like to feel a serious pain emanating from inside me. (You never gave birth, my wife, Debbie, says to me.) Apart from stomach and muscle soreness from exercise, the feeling of pressure around my bladder area feels different. It is pain and not painful. It is a history of pain that I should recognize, and nothing like it at all, something altogether new. I do not suffer as a Black individual. I suffer as a person afflicted by a condition that is a new experience. I do not worry as a Black man. I worry as a man not accustomed to worrying about his body.

I am not lonely as an artist because I am Black. My loneliness may be a precondition of my art and has no bearing on my sense of being Black. If anything, I feel alone with my symptoms, private even, thanks to a predilection of mine to keep things to myself. I do not wish to bother or burden people, so I live with things alone in my heart and head and work them out until they lessen in urgency. My bladder would not allow me to be lonely. Information about it brought me up against the fact of how alone I felt and how singular the experience would be for me. Even though men everywhere suffered from it (one out of every four), this experience would be mine, a solo rendition of my sense of limited time in my life. I had to share my problem with Debbie.

My mortality concerned me not because I am a Black man prone to neurosis, but thanks to my predisposition toward conjecture (speculation is not neurotic). I read that my prostate cancer may have spread to other parts of my body, which made me worry along a curve extrapolated from that point of information as a part of the function of my imagination. I do not think this is Black or White. It is just human. It may be overthink and undue worry. It may just be me. I am I (not wishing to channel Popeye!) if I concede a unitary being bearing my name launched into the flux of this world (an artistic loner), rather than a brief span of history with a specific heredity (a communal loner).

Nevertheless I made the appointment. I combed my workplace web pages for names and reviews, videos and articles about oncology. I found other experts near and far to compare with my university. I made the call based on excellent appraisals for the oncology group at University of California, Los Angeles (UCLA). I asked the phone attendant for someone experienced, or someone who had masses of experience operating on this very thing. The last thing my crotch area needed was a novice.

The fact that it was a teaching hospital bypassed me. I was not in the frame of mind to be anyone's guinea pig or dummy practice patient. I wanted the expert with the most experience. It seemed to me that there was no room for error. To further medical knowledge was one thing, but not on my vanishing body. I wished them luck without any personal commitment to their need for experimentation. I said as much in several conversations that ran in my head in advance of my taking the leap into action. All of which may be testament to my anxiety about the whole enterprise, one in which all roads of thinking led back to my prostate dilemma.

I began to worry, in advance, about things going wrong. I figured that my block and tackle (a teen term), my waterworks (from my prepubescent years), my pleasure principle nerve center (those satirical twenties and thirties), required expert attention with a minimum of risk. I imagined a posttreatment reality of improved function: a return to a powerful, noisy stream, to forgetfulness when it came to all things urinary, to feeling more than ten years younger again, a pictograph of my body in which the ink dried somewhere in my early to midforties.

Ah, to forget about my bladder, to consign its forefront status in my mind to the back burner of inattention. Memory and attention have powered me to this point in my life. I lived up to this point in the solid conviction that I was against forgetting, that to forget was to be negligent of a writer's responsibility to history and to the art of remembering by imaginative design. I never dreamed that forgetting could be a psychological condition of peace in waking life, of contentment with the frailties of an aging body. It would be a case of one part of my body acting in the interest of the whole by selectively removing itself from the arena of my attention.

I had to fix what was wrong with my body if I wanted it to work judiciously for and with me. At the moment it behaved like the enemy who had slipped past the ramparts to wage a guerrilla campaign from inside. I felt pressured onto my back foot, always reacting to some new action by my bladder and never able to catch up or anticipate what it would do next to keep me off balance. Now at the front of my mind, now dictating the geography of my diary with regular bathroom pit stops, now waking me up twice a night, now pushing me to the edge of almost afraid to drink. What a song and dance (my mum said this about any aspect of life that gave her the runaround) my bladder led me in.

I needed to break the partnership with my conundrum and become in effect a solo dancer in charge of all the choreography. I needed someone like the legendary Mr. Bojangles, someone able to move and invent the next move and the next in fluid motion (he tried to patent his dance up and down stairs, and failed, though succeeded in inventing the word *copacetic*) and make it look not just easy, but good. Or else a Billy Cobham figure with drums, a one-man orchestra, many-limbed like a spider, playing his *Total Eclipse* extravaganza. Or the anarchic inventions of a cut-to-pieces and scrambled then reassembled modern mind like Jean-Michel Basquiat. You cannot look for long, and you cannot look away for too long either without feeling impoverished.

Debbie, my wife, had noticed my symptoms some time ago and mentioned it to me, but I was casual in my response to her (not ready to hear her) until now. I told her my suspicions and she grew alarmed. Her response heightened my own sense of doom nursed quietly by me as I sought to protect the children from anxiety over me. Debbie always presented as someone in touch with her feelings in a way that left me in awe and in horror: awe at her facility with difficult emotion, horror that it might be contagious and leave me at the mercy of something out of my control. In contradiction to this taciturn approach of mine on the emotional front, I championed methods like meditation and yoga, and writings about mind and body unity—all disciplines invested in a life of emotional intelligence.

My ideal for coping with the materialist treadmill turned out to be a pinch of the anarchist with chunks of socialism and utopianism. Blake's *Jerusalem* meets Octavia Butler's Afrofuturism. I really wanted everyone to know themselves and to get along with one another and hug trees too, all in a garden where it was cool to eat the fruit and be naked without compromising the right to be there. As if the garden were an invitation to experiment in community that could never be revoked. No pre-, no post-, just perpetual current good standing.

And for poise under bladder pressure I conjure Emma Goldman on Ellis Island in December 1919, on the eve of her deportation to Russia for her "un-American" anarchistic activities. She makes sure everyone around her is settled and calm and able to write last messages of hope to loved ones whom they are about to leave behind with no inkling of when they might return and be reunited, messages that she hides in her dress. Her enormous sacrifice for her beliefs turned into a life practice as she tends selflessly to the needs of others in true enactment of her equitable ideals. As with everyone else whom she helps, she too faces the fate of being cast out of her adopted country because of her politics.

I made the call to see an oncologist. The receptionist asked me a few pertinent questions and I answered as tersely as I could, not knowing to whom I was talking, and not wanting my business out there. At last she said that she needed to ask these things to be sure she matched me with the right person. How long had I been experiencing difficulty urinating? How many times at night did I go to the bathroom? Was it painful to urinate? Did it alter my bowel movement? Could I refrain from sex two days before seeing the doctor? No problem on that last count, I joked. My sexual appetite had waned considerably. She asked me where I worked, and when I said at the university, she piped up, sounded more animated, and wanted to know what I did, and when I said that I was a professor she became positively gleeful, personable, much more accommodating and even said that she would do everything she could for me since I belonged to the UCLA "family."

I attended that first appointment alone. Debbie had to be somewhere else and the time was in the middle of my teaching day. I put her off coming with me in the belief that this first meeting was preliminary and I would need her further down the road of the progress of the doctor investigating what was going on with me. How odd to turn up to a waiting room full of people with the same malady. All men. The only difference was that everyone seemed so much older and when someone younger-looking turned up everyone gawked at him with a mix of pity and alarm that so young a body might be facing such an affliction reserved for senior bodies. No one spoke. We sat and waited for our names to be called. And when that happened the person answered quickly but took quite a while to lever the ailing body out of the comfortable chair and catch up with his name.

The doctor, a retired oncologist who worked part time, put me at ease immediately by acting as if he were a plumber who needed to examine my faulty fixtures and offer his diagnosis. He asked me to drop my trousers and underpants. He stared for a long moment at the distribution and arrangement of my genitalia. He focused the way I do when I visit a gallery and stare for ages at a painting that I close my eyes to see in my mind's eye, and look at again to augment my memory of it, and again close my eyes to add to what I remember and so on before I build a story about how it works on me, and what I think and feel about those influences. I had showered longer than usual that morning for this very reason—his face was close to my crotch—and picked my newest pair of underpants. He pulled on a pair of gloves. There was an immediate pungent smell of rubber as if I had woken on the inside of an inner tube, like the gigantic one for the rear wheels of the tractor that cruised the farm of my paternal grandparents in Guyana.

Next he slapped on copious amounts of what looked like jelly onto his fingers. He asked me to lean over by resting my elbows on the chair and he unceremoniously stuck his index and middle finger into my anus and up my rectum, and swiped along the tube as if to wipe my interior clean. That was a new feeling, of some blind, double-proboscis creature released in my rectum and bumping into its architecture to forge deep into me. To cope with my shock of his prodding around inside me I visualized my arm wiping the steamed-up inside of the car windscreen on a winter morning in South London, or on the East Coast, say, Massachusetts or Virginia, a crucial act to see where I was driving, just as he needed to know what was happening to my body.

I felt shock at the intrusion and a modicum of discomfort, it must be said, not pain exactly but the start of a painful procedure if it continued unchecked. He worked swiftly, deeply, knowledgeably. Mercifully, he extracted his fingers in a deft move and wiped them and dispensed with his glove, rolled it off his hand by pulling it inside out. He informed me as I wiped myself and pulled up my underpants and trousers that my prostate was more than twice as large as it should be. Instead of roughly walnut size, it was two and a half walnuts.

I could visualize that. Most mornings since around 2005 I'd been eating a little helping of walnuts—enough to cover the palm of my hand—in the sound belief that their high quotient of antioxidants and omega-3 fatty acids (good guys) strengthened my aging heart. I hardly ever ran out of them, because I bought the walnut halves in bulk and filled a tall jar with them. I wondered if that two and a half was with or without the pesky shells, whose pieces sometimes stole into the shelled batch and shocked teeth that clamped down and experienced a shard. Two and a half times bigger than the usual outcrop of prostate growing inside me. Conjoined twins fused to another single; sick little triplets; a ballooning time bomb; a crab growing in a shell it cannot jettison and so destined to meet some impasse with; something I never gave a second thought to before, now center stage in my life as if to tax me for my neglect of it.

The doctor ordered a blood sample—two ampoules of the bright-red stuff—and a nurse drew it from me. She told me I had good veins. People say that a lot. I hardly felt the needle's plunge into the folded space just above the crook of my inner right arm. I complimented the nurse, told her she was an excellent phlebotomist. She smiled and weighed me. We joked that my clothes and boots amounted to about 4 pounds to be taken off 160. The nurse took my blood pressure. I asked her if it mattered that I was left-handed. She said no. I sacrificed my right arm. She wrapped a sleeve around it, held in place by Velcro. She inflated the sleeve to a point that bordered the uncomfortable and just at that point, held it, and began the slow deflation back to comfort and relief: 115 over 90. I wondered if the caffeine heightened the diastolic first reading. She said it was fine. In the form about my history I said my father had died at fifty-three from a bad heart—so I was told.

I say "so I was told" due to the notorious unreliability of information by word of mouth about my immediate family. Acrimonious divorces, migration, and early deaths might be to blame for the unknowable family epidemiology. My parents married young, emigrated from Guyana to England, and divorced early while in England as their five young children lived with grandparents in Guyana. I should write that twice for clarity. The whole experiment of bettering themselves by striking out into the unknown together ended in hostility. They quibbled over photographs and my dad got most of them as memorials because she got us, the real thing. The result of my past is a lot of hearsay, conjecture, and plain, willful ignorance—no longer in a position to care for the other party given the bad history between them. My genealogy resembled a time bomb. Not the flowering of unknown gifts into creative biography but the detonation of a grenade. The possibility that I might have cancer and that it would become the measure of my life.

My maternal grandmother died of bone cancer. Another mine buried in my field of genes. The cancer started in her hand. She resisted surgery partly out of vanity and partly practicality. My grandfather was long dead. A new handsome gentleman courted my grandmother. Apparently, he was so well groomed that you could smell his cologne before you spotted him, and not one starched stitch on him was out of place in the most casual of settings. He had Mister, always Mister, before his name. The house full of grandchildren always reconfigured into a child-free zone when he appeared and my grandmother in her starched and perfumed fineries met him at the door. We piled on the covered back stairs and played with matchsticks for people (chewing gum on the tops of the matches for women with big hair) and bottle tops for vehicles, and we partied with those matchsticks and took them to drive-in film shows and street drag races without saying so much as a syllable or bumping into each other's cars and people, or scraping against the stairs and railings.

My grandmother worked with her hands all day. Mostly housework, and she talked with her hands, gestured a lot, and she had a lot to say, so her hands were occupied all day. This made her hands indispensable. (Not that we should think of our hands as dispensable, say like the smallest outer toe or the smallest finger.) Not indispensable as tools, though she proved that, more as expressions of her. She could not do without even one little finger. Meanwhile the cancer marched on and up her arm. She held out against surgery for as long as she could. And when she accepted losing the hand, too late, after the amputation she continued to decline from the metastasized disease, with further surgeries to remove more of her arm. She was dead at forty-six. Her handsome suitor migrated to Canada a while before the cancer took hold of her and knocked her for six (as local parlance phrased it, a term lifted from cricket, the national sport of most former British colonies).

The doctor says my enlarged prostate concerns him. *Concern* in another setting might be casually deployed to mean that a thing is on one's mind though not central to one's thinking. As used by the doctor I know it packs much more power. In fact, *concern* takes on the air of a lab setting, something scrubbed of emotional resonance as a deliberate qualification for its use in a patient-and-doctor exchange. He has my full attention. He says only further tests can really tell him what is going on. He adds that I should not worry ahead of the results of those tests and that when they come back and he has a chance to look at them we will speak again. As a precaution, he schedules me to see a surgeon. He says I should not be alarmed, he has to make the appointment early because openings are hard to come by, and my date can just as easily be canceled if it proves unnecessary. The date with the surgeon is in two weeks. The doctor shakes my hand goodbye. I wonder if his light touch—soft and glancing—has anything to do with my compromised longevity. His heavier grip reserved for persons with more time on their hands.

2

I DO NOT WANT TO ALARM YOU

Debbie and I are in the kitchen and abutting breakfast room with our three children when I broach the subject of my cancer. Christopher, aged twenty-two, our eldest, is searching Debbie's partially completed puzzle, spread on the breakfast table, for a corner piece that only he seems able to find, every time, hidden among the mass. Nicholas, aged nineteen, the second, as I like to think of him to avoid the middle-child stigma, is at the stove concocting his famous three-egg omelet into which he sprinkles an array of powders, onion, garlic, salt, black pepper. Debbie is seated on the sofa that is next to the breakfast table. I am microwaving a cup of coffee that I reheat periodically throughout the morning and top up with almond milk and fresh coffee. Liliana, aged thirteen (the baby girl of the household, mollycoddled by us as a result of our shock at the ultrasound that revealed she was a she and not the expected dominant family requisite male), is seated at the center island eating her bowl of ramen noodles.

Guys, I do not want to alarm you but I do have a health issue.

They turn from their respective tasks, Nicholas pushes the pan off the flame, Christopher looks at me and keeps a puzzle piece in his hand, Liliana places her spoon in the bowl and clasps her hands and glances at her mother, who looks up at me and rests her phone in her lap.

I saw a doctor and I have an enlarged prostate and an elevated

PSA from a blood sample. It is most likely cancer, though I have to take more tests to confirm that.

The three of them do a double take of wanting me to repeat what I just said even though I said it and they heard it and want to disbelieve their ears. I pause and busy my hands with setting the microwave to one minute.

Does it hurt? Nicholas wants to know. I shake my head, no pain, just a weird feeling of pressure.

Can you die from it? my daughter asks. Again, that dismissive headshake and I reassure her that what I have is treatable.

Just wanted to give you guys a heads-up, since the coming weeks will be busy for me.

Christopher half smiles and shoots me his thumbs-up of understanding, and goes back to his puzzle. Nicholas looks at me for a moment and I nod and he pulls his omelet over the flame. I smile at Debbie and she smiles back. Liliana forks curlicues of her ramen to her face. I retrieve my coffee from the microwave the moment it beeps.

The next week I have an MRI (I googled it), a.k.a. the magnetic resonance imaging machine. It resembles a capsule for sending me into the future, or for sealing me in a deep century-long sleep. The clinical all-white room, meant to reassure me, makes me feel like a huge germ in a germ-free zone. That the whole of me, not just my unruly prostate, is in question seems apposite as my dark skin tone pops out, spotlighted, in the contrasting white space. I want the machine to be accurate in the way it assesses me, to make transparent a covert disease in my body, a disease about to stage a coup.

Debbie insists on accompanying me. (I am not sure she should bother.) I do not want to trouble her and embarrass her and me by having a witness in the room. The fact of our marriage does not diminish this feeling of inadequacy at all. In secret I am glad to have her by my side. She waits outside for me. I undress and put my clothes into a locker and keep on my underpants but don a hospital gown (I am told to wear it with the opening at the front so that I can keep it closed and stay warmer).

The radiologist asks me to recline on the gurney. He hooks me up to a drip and feeds the dye into it. The dye enables the magnetic waves to highlight the bloodstream and the dye travels and draws this map of my blood system. He tightens a sheet around my body so that I feel as if I am encased in a condom with only my head peeping out. He plugs my ears with two sponge plugs. I've never had someone insert plugs into my ears before. What a trust exercise. How intimate. His touch is light and businesslike, gently probing as he settles the sponge pieces into place. He is a friendly guy. From Vietnam. We chat briefly about the legacy of America coming to a foreign land and the good fortune for those of us able to reap the benefits rather than the penalties of a colonial or imperial encounter. He feeds me on the gurney into the wide, round mouth of the MRI contraption.

As instructed by him, I hold my breath at the right time for a few seconds as the machine resonates—quite loudly, hence the earplugs. What exactly is the noise? Think of a jackhammer that the road workers lean into bodily to break up a road. Short bursts, as if discharging armor-piercing rounds. Is that just my impression, seeing red in every situation pertaining to my condition? I will myself to breathe deep past my sternum and visualize the tall neck of a vase into which I pour air rather than water to flower the stems of my ribs, or some such reasoning, just to defray the rising sense of panic and urgency about what must happen to me in the coming weeks to save me from my malady.

Given my prostate-specific antigen (PSA) reading—which is one hundred times higher than what it should be—I wonder if I will experience all my waking hours with increased concentration and razor-sharp clarity, if the ordinary, the quotidian, the routine of my day, will become supercharged by my awareness of the suddenly limited number of days on a measurable calendar. My research on prostate cancer highlights the possibility that time may not be on my side or time could be mine only if I act quickly.

*   *   *

Well, reality, supercharge me. Show me your bluest skies, make light cut into a room as if onto a stage in Vegas. The demonstration snaking past the quad below my office window ricochets off the surrounding buildings. The quad teems with so much life, its antagonism registered with me as vibrancy, necessity, a vital course charted by the pulse of the given. The bullhorn asks: What do we want? The marchers reply something indecipherable. The bullhorn asks: When do we want it? The marchers reply with a resounding Now. I want to find out more.

Ordinarily, I would have headed outside for a better view. Not today. I feel tired and flat. I care but not enough to change the course of my lethargy. I remain in my seat—not even bothering to stand, as is my usual practice, at my computer mounted on a platform, mounted in turn on my desk. The ergonomics of longevity seemingly out of my reach now. I languish in disease mode. My head, chock-full of morbid detail, needs additional room in my body, already rented out to my disease, to accommodate everything. I am in the middle of my life. This cannot be the sum of it. I have to fight this thing.

Flomax relaxes the sphincter muscles and eases the flow of urine. The weak trickle regains some of its backbone though in no measure anything resembling the fire hose of my ESPN days. I take one pill at night and go to sleep and it helps me make it through the night without having to fumble in the dark between the bed and bathroom. Flomax is my new best friend, an enabler in the truest sense of the term; that is, someone who helps a person to grow into a better human. The chemistry of it is of some interest to me. I am intrigued by the way the drug targets my contracted and depressed sphincter, surrounded and oppressed by my prostate, and induces the muscles to bow before the pressure of my urine.

I wish that Flomax had a similar force against the cancer that self-proliferates and enlarges my prostate, and hampers my urinary tract. Could there be a Flomax of the depressed spirit, able to open the spigots of optimism and induce in me a positive viewpoint that might banish those cells and shrink my prostate? I want to believe in the power of the mind over the matter of its house, the body. My body is in full rebellion against me. My mind cannot run fast enough to catch and curtail the body's wild sprint toward the cliff of oblivion.

I wonder if art is up to the task of healing. If autosuggestion helps in any perceptible fashion, or if a positive outlook is tantamount to my mind fiddling while the Rome of my body burns. For I burn with cancer. Is my mind, with its penchant for recall in the middle of a crisis as a coping mechanism, simply whistling Monty Python's "Always Look on the Bright Side of Life" while faced with the devastation of life? For my life is threatened with a summary end. I wonder if my speculation about the many things that could go wrong with me is a symptom of my propensity for camp exaggeration in the face of a fine-tuned assault on my being.

Since my late teens, when I lived in London, I had rejected the idea of the medical model, thinking that doctors and hospitals would not work for me. Back then I supplemented it with something that was all to do with me—my natural leanings toward positive thought as an antidote to dark despair—with my childhood in Guyana surrounded by homeopathic remedies for illnesses and then in the UK taking my lucky good health as a sanctuary from scientific medicine.

So that today, I believe intuitively in, well, yes, intuition; that is, in the capacity of the mind in coalition with the spirit to turn destiny or what purports to be inevitability topsy-turvy. There must be some help that I can muster on behalf of the medical model that I embraced in order to ride with this condition. I say *ride* after Parliament's 1975 "Star Child" (A-side) and "Supergroovalisticprosifunkstication" (B-side) "let me ride," injunction to the quarrelsome spirit to chill, to fall into harmony with an easier way of working with a bigger force, not by direct opposition to it but by flowing with it. There is not a shred in me of acceptance of my disease as somehow too far gone. I keep to the front of my mind that if I can maintain this positive thinking then I can slow down this thing and help the drugs and other medical methods perform their ministry. Together, my mind in partnership with medicine can overcome, chant down, Bob Marley fashion, the Babylon of my disease.

The ghostly ministrations of intangible forces such as positive thinking are things in the world, invisible but felt presences that can be co-opted on my side, if I dedicate my mental powers to them. At the cellular level, Flomax (tamsulosin), an alpha blocker, stops the hormone norepinephrine from reaching alpha receptors at the uptake point of cells, thereby robbing them of the necessary chemical messaging that tells muscles to contract. Flomax operates on my behalf by latching onto muscles in the bladder, neck, and prostate gland and lulling them to sleep. At the level of the idea, I see a force, or feel it, I should say. I think that my frame of mind might rein in the diagnosis and turn it around in ways difficult to measure, yet part and parcel of the changes brought about by medicine.

A second doctor conducts a biopsy of my prostate. It's an outpatient procedure. Debbie accompanies me. She never leaves my side. We wait in a small room where I am told to undress and wear a hospital gown with the opening at the back. I ask if I can keep on my socks. The nurse looks at the green leaves on the pair, and by the way she nods and smiles I tell her the herb of those leaves does not figure recreationally or otherwise in my life these days. With my back to the nurse, I lie on my left side and face Debbie. The nurse shows me the probe, about a foot long and as fat as a truncheon, covered in a condom. She explains that the doctor will insert the probe into my anus and push it up my rectum and out of that probe needles will shoot through the walls of my rectum and into the afflicted areas of my prostate and extract cancer material for analysis. The perforations in the rectum wall, she tells me, are minuscule and they self-heal quickly, though I may see traces of blood in my stool for a day or so afterward.

Debbie laughs at the ghastly rocket of the probe. I nod in astonishment at the size of the thing. I can feel my sphincter shrink as if I have waded into the North Sea off the coast of Aberdeen. (That one time was my last time and my then lover made me do it.) The doctor comes in with a colleague. He introduces himself and points at the monitor that he says will guide the biopsy. There is a camera on the steel probe. He warns me that the process of going through the wall of the rectum, though painless, feels weird, as if someone snaps a rubber band against my skin. Debbie takes my hand and the nurse uses most of a tube of lubricating jelly to cover the probe. (That has grown with my alarm to resemble, now, a baseball bat.) I stop seeing what happens next. That probe is huge. I feel stuffed beyond capacity. The doctor asks me to breathe deeply and to keep breathing no matter what I feel and that I should remember it will be over fast. He says he needs up to twelve samples from my prostate. He speaks with a slow baritone. Great, Barry White is my torturer. He says that he has an image of my prostate from the previous test so he knows exactly where he needs to go to obtain the samples. I want to snap at him to get on with it. His slow delivery adds to my ballooning alarm about what is about to happen to the interior of my posterior.

Let the games begin. And they do. A silent movie runs. Moving images composed of touch. The probe fills up my rectum and the twang from a rubber band is more like a needle puncturing the roof of my mouth. One dozen of those pops. I count down. I raise my eyebrows. Guess my eyes must have looked as if they were about to pop out of their sockets. Debbie has turned pale with a look of being trapped at the uppermost point of a roller coaster on the verge of a precipitous descent. The doctor is accurate about the strange pain. Not of damage to the skin, more of an interior wreckage that is too deep to identity, that unfolds and most certainly stays central in my mind's register of discomfort. Breathe. Try not to crush Debbie's hand. Let cancer have its way with me—backward, forward, and upside down. I abandon my body and retreat mentally to my childhood memory of a game where I drive, in complete silence, two matchstick lovers to their drive-in movie date in their bottle top cars along the road of those wooden railings on the back stairs.

A few days later I see a third doctor and he tells me in the company of my wife that another test is necessary to be certain that my bones and other areas near the prostate are not affected by the cancer cells. He says the biopsy results confirm cancer spread all over the prostate and perhaps elsewhere too, going by the MRI. He assures me that my enlarged prostate gland and hugely elevated PSA reading, though causes of concern, were not in themselves sufficient diagnostic tools to form the basis of a treatment plan. The cancer is present in large amounts but more of a sense of its locations (plural, his word) is needed before attacking it (his word, attack). He said I needed to have a few tests. A computerized tomography (CT) scan, a bone scan, and more than likely a final scan aimed specifically at a search in the body for antigens generated by cancer cells on the surface of the prostate; that's at least three more tests, which qualifies as a battery of them.

In one test I react as if there is an awful texture and taste that I repeatedly swallow to try and rid my mouth of and it makes me feel that I am on the verge of throwing up. In one hour I consume the two pints of that emetic-like substance. In another test the doctor wants me to receive a nuclear injection that will glow around the areas of the bone trained to absorb the dye if those bones were damaged by disease. I brace myself for the unpleasant as a means to procure the resplendent: that medicine with a bad taste, this other medicine with a bad feel, both working in the only way they know how, by being medicine; that is, not nice in order to do some good.

I always shave for these appointments and dress my best as if about to face a classroom or my doom. For the next test I am not allowed to eat or drink. This time I savor a small coffee—not my usual two giant cups—and eat a light meal, a banana and a slice of brown bread topped with goat's cheese and avocado, a tasty power food. The nuclear medicine, methylene diphosphonate (MDP) renews this avocado taste in my mouth. The hospital makes it (the MDP, not the avocado) to order with a shelf life of mere hours to do its work before it breaks down. I lie on my back. The radiopharmaceutical fluid is injected through a drip set up in my arm. A small dose, no more than a couple of tablespoons of liquid (26.4 millicuries, or mCi, to be exact) feels cold running into my right arm, a weird kind of cold not on the skin but worming its way under the skin and into my flesh. The cold feeling disappears as my warm blood floods the meds.

I tell myself to relax and breathe deeply and slowly. I summon two visual aids: the first is Blackheath Hill in South London at six a.m. with a light fog and a highlighted fox glancing back at me periodically as it trots across the hill, a stone's throw from me on my paper route; the second, Marie Curie in her radioactive lab of perilous discovery. The radiation photography begins.

About halfway into it I feel a wave of nausea. I don't just mean that I feel what is akin to an urge to vomit wash over me. I really mean a wave that sweeps me off my feet and bowls me around in deep sand and pebbles. (This tumble-in-a-washing-machine experience happened to me when I tried to bodysurf with my kids. Reader, it was horribly embarrassing.) And the nauseated sensation grows rather than lessens. I call out to the technician, Hello, I feel . . . and as he rushes in and pushes a tall bin next to my gurney, I turn my head just in time to expel coffee, toast, and grime from my guts. The effort of throwing the operation of my body into reverse makes me break out in a cold sweat. I apologize as I retch (try speaking and heaving at the same time) and he says not to worry, it happens to a lot of people. He hands me tissues. I wipe away slime and grimace at the awful feeling that flares and subsides almost immediately after I retch up avocado and stuff. I soon feel better. He says the nuclear cocktail fed into my veins sometimes causes the body to think that it has ingested a poison by mistake and the only thing to do is expel it. That the act of retching fools the body into believing that it has succeeded in saving itself from an attack via its gut. Yes, well, you could have fooled me, dear technician. That vomiting was for real.

By way of contrast the medicine lights up the lymphatic pathways around bone as though shining a light into a dark room to reveal the furnishings in it, monochromatic bone with a soft, fuzzy look, angular as bones are but almost porous in appearance and so, in my mind of associations, close to looking at a fine bone china teacup that is almost translucent, that is in the shape of a fragile body. On the monitor the dark patches swirl around. Apparently the medicine links to tissue that has traces of the prostate-specific antigen. The nuclear binding is chemically designed to seek out PSA exclusively. The medicine captured on the magnetic resonance imaging monitor resembles iron filings dancing to the push and pull of an invisible force. Somewhere in there, wrapped up with all that frenetic activity, is the disease, which is called out by the radiopharmaceutical to see if any of it has latched on to my bones. I cannot tell. The technician will not say. I ask him if when I get angry I'm going to burst out of my clothing and turn into a green, muscle-bound giant. He laughs and says there are no side effects except the nausea, which should clear up soon. He wishes me well and sends me on my not-so-mirthful way.

I think the nights are longer and the days shorter for me. I sleep and the last thought is of my body; specifically, my crotch. A weight registers around the area, a heavy feeling of trouble brewing. I beam a positive electron stream at the location below my bladder and in the space behind my penis and in front of my rectum. That beam contains an outdoor concert at Blackbushe in the Hampshire English countryside, in 1978, the summer before the tragedy at Jonestown, Guyana. I attended the concert with my friend Geoff Hardy. He turned me into a Dylan fan and Dylan was performing with Joan Armatrading (and, I want to add, Van Morrison—of *Astral Weeks*—Bob Marley, and, I believe,

Tom Robinson, among others). I should ask Geoff, whose memory retains an encyclopedia of these things, but I will not ask him, because, in this instance, I do not want confirmation that might contradict my ideal.

I approached the portable toilets in the dark, and some way off from the actual portable cabins men formed a loose line as they urinated in the general direction of those toilets. As the night wore on, the line of men emptying bladders widened even farther away from those portable toilets until people just took a few steps toward the location of the bathrooms and unburdened themselves by aiming at the general vicinity of the portable potties. The women, more evolved, queued respectably for an age. The bolder ones wanted to use the men's loos but found them too disgusting.

What a map to stave off my insomnia! In this case olfactory but no less real as maps go, a psychogeography as far as the attention that it commands in me is concerned. Just one of Calvino's numerous invisible cities (cities constructed out of one sense or another and tacked on to experiences of the actual places that I lived in, Georgetown, London, Miami, Los Angeles) that accounts for my life up to now. Places I return to periodically and know intimately as if I have never left them. Their sensory map now made visible in the service of my malady. Cancer is a city with a rampant population that seeks to expand its parameters into a sprawling body. I hope my return to a past moment of unencumbered joy, conjured and brought to bear on a troublesome present, might reduce the present-tense toll on me.

I am in an odd place moodwise. Not good company and feeling drained after socializing (with my awful secret). I've cut back on social life in order to gather my thoughts and feelings and face up to the shock of my diagnosis. Would you believe this is my first hospital/doctor drama? Haven't even broken a bone up to now. I view the medical establishment with some skepticism after my stint in it as a psychiatric nurse in South London in the early eighties. The way it captures the body and infantilizes the spirit. Its insistence on knowing what is good for the patient, who must submit to the regime or miss out on the benefits from the encounter.

*　　*　　*

The surgeon says he needs eyes and this next MRI, a prostate-specific membrane antigen (PSMA) test provides that sight, lights up the pathways of the spread of the disease, so that when he goes in he knows exactly where he has to head. Only problem is the test is not approved by the Food and Drug Administration (FDA), so my insurance will not cover it and it costs three grand. I agree to pay.

My frame of mind (I am the one, not Debbie, who is strapped in a car at the zenith of a roller coaster) never enters my thinking until I find myself lying awake in the dark listening to the cat snore and measuring the breaths of my wife by touch as our spoon-sleep posture allows.

I have to Ngũgĩ wa Thiong'o my mind; that is, decolonize the mental frame of my cancer, which has colonized my body. Ngũgĩ models his analysis on the mental chains that survive the physical dismantling of colonization. The postcolony is really the colony by other means, the same situation with different faces operating the old structures of oppression. The Marley invocation to "emancipate yourself from mental slavery" is a spiritual rendition of Ngũgĩ's philosophic and political mission conducted on this psychological front (with material ramifications).

I modify Ngũgĩ by working within the structure he admonishes as the thing that compromises the thinker. For Ngũgĩ it is not possible to operate freely with the tools responsible for oppression in the first place. Lucky for Ngũgĩ that he can think in Gikuyu; that is, outside the frame of English, before moving into English to break it down. My cancer thinks (if I may personify the disease) inside me, and I have to think within the frame of the disease. I grapple with cancer as if the disease itself carries the emblems of my cure as much as my demise. My fight is not a binary of one thing against another but of two things conjoined.

In one sense I need more Marley than Ngũgĩ. I must chant down the disease, smooth those spikes of its register in me. To sleep at night I need to be at peace with my disease, not peace as in surrender. The kind of peace, uneasy for sure, where opposing armies live cheek by jowl and know that both parties have to share the same space even if their views about the use of that space may vary.

The song of my cure resides in my sense that chant, movement, deep breathing, some drum and a little bass go a long way toward making me strong. With strength I can react in less negative ways with the drugs. I say *drugs* after I start to take a pill to block the production of testosterone considered a food by my cancer. The tablet, bicalutamide, is bitter and much smaller than the Flomax. I am warned that it may result in hot flashes, to which my wife responds, "Welcome to my world." I ask if it means that I might grow breasts. My wife guffaws, shocked at the suggestion, and the doctor nods and admits that some breast enhancement may result from the medication.

Bicalutamide, 50 mg once daily, is the latest recruit into my army, the one that I have to raise to combat the cancer. Its action of stopping testosterone means that my body will soon be depleted of that male stock. As a carpet-bombing military strategy, that is the equivalent of collateral damage to me as the drugs attack the cancer. There is always this trade-off with medicine. To get better there has to be a transaction with a personal cost attached to it. Die of cancer or live as a testosterone-empty male.

I teach that gender is fluid and we must in our state of gender binary revise our outlook to take on board the flotation of gender, its fluidity as a condition of our modernity. My students are at ease with the use of plural pronouns for singular fluid bodies. I have to adjust. Now if I feel tender in my breasts or come over all hot and bothered I have a visceral reminder of a cultural state of affairs for many. A by-product of the drug treatment for my illness, unintended and beneficial, is that I begin to belong to the consciousness of this new societal norm.

Rastafarians want us not to under-stand a thing, rather to over-stand it; that is, to truly comprehend a thing by overcoming our ignorance about it. To understand it would be to capitulate to its overpowering colonization of our consciousness, literally, to accept our subjection to its strictures. To over-stand is to rise above the subject and see its true dimensions and so free the mental process of the chains of the thing. The mind wishes to get to know, or over-stand, in order to be free of those straitjacketing mechanisms. The Rasta vibe in me with the help of chant and drum and bass (though no puffing on the smokestack of a spliff's herbal transportation) fancies itself attuned to liberation.

The tune of liberation from my disease, on this personal and metaphysical plane, is a combination of these rhythms from my cultural and philosophical life. Goffman's *Asylums* and Foucault's *Madness and Civilization* helped me frame some of what I am going through in terms of my life as a reader. The act of reading illuminated what I thought, provided form for thoughts that were otherwise scattered and rhapsodic. I read Goffman while I trained as a psychiatric nurse and Foucault at university. I glean from the former the way the place takes over everyone, doctors, nurses, administrations, porters, and patients alike. The institution becomes an organism. People pool their nervous system into its workings in nefarious ways. Our modernity amounts to a madness in light of this institutional transformation of individuals. So that I feel bad and mad: bad that I question my medical experience, and mad for thinking that I may be wrong to be critical at a time of dire need.

Liberation is too strong, though I feel indebted to my consciousness for housing Goffman's world. I am both the subject of a disease and its incipient host, the person talked about and the person generating that talk, so that the drama of being taken in by something and becoming that thing is now two things folded into the one body and mind captured by the disease. Put another way, I am institutionalized by my disease, which forces me to behave with it as if hostile to my plight and impelled to conquer it.

This is hard for me to reconcile with the politics of illness as the shape taken by our contemporary moment, that the times are mad for taking this shape and in so doing electing to be ill as part of being modern. Foucault obliquely addresses my cancer by situating me in the entrails of a modernity designed to procure cancers of various sorts. That I have cancer signals that I am in modern times, and how I react pulls me into the rules that govern a body afflicted by disease in these times.

In order to modify the term *liberation* as an operating system in my life of disease, let me say that what I am going through and how I decide to cope with it is my way of assisting the work of the drugs: to help the chemistry with a body and soul philosophical practice. Together, pharmacy and philosophy might be able to defeat the spread of the disease and even banish it from its stronghold in my prostate. In the absence of any conventional religion, I see that I need a spiritual frame that is usually the remit of religion. My secular spiritualism insists on having access to the same depth charge of meaning as that supplied by the best of religion; let's say, the Psalms.

Though my body is overrun with disease, my spiritual cup runneth over with the help of music, politics, culture, education, arts. Poetry with its many colors may well be encoded with various registers of this overcoming of the disease. The poetry in me of chanting, music, boom box, and meter of my walk and move and groove, when taken together conspire to lift me from depression instilled by disease. A poetry of the senses insists on all five senses, and a sixth sense, come into play in over-standing my disease and making moves against it embedded in my prostate.

What are the sights, touches, sounds, tastes, and smells of my liberation? Where around me might I lay eyes on this useful approach to add to my cure? Is it in the sight of the arrival of morning? Could it be in the pleasure of trees? My daughter walking up to the car to meet me after her school day? My sons at their desks looking up from gaming to talk to me about something? My wife at my side grilling the doctor about the specifics of a drug regimen? A painting or sculpture or elegant building? I think I may (as a condition of being awake and even while asleep) extract from all these visual stimuli emblems of my over-standing.

The same can be said for the other senses. They too help me to garner aspects of truth to add to the curative approach to my disease. Not to mention that sixth sense. Some see it as aligned with superstition. As somehow the hunch or feeling that you get that makes you change your conscious course. Or a practice to counter obvious totems of ill will—the poor black cat that gets a bad rap, the dropping of utensils that to my Guyanese elders signals the arrival of a stranger (a fork for a woman, a knife for a man, and spoons I do not remember, perhaps for a child), the seeing of a likely outcome based on an instantaneous eureka moment of insight supplied by this intuited knowledge. All of them define this sixth sense, ethereal, that shadows the chemical and physical other five.

With that in mind I turn up to the hospital for an injection (Lupron Depot) that delivers a three-month dose of testosterone blocker into my buttocks. I am told it is like a couple of flu shots to the arm—not one but two. I read up on it and the witnesses say that it can lead to all kinds of ill affects. The site gets very sore a day or two afterward. The mind becomes a little skittish. There may be a dull headache following you all day that you cannot do anything about except devise ways not to think about it. And of course the ever-present feminization of the body, with augmented breast tissue and hot flashes.

I arrive for the morning appointment, having moved around a few work meetings, equipped with all this knowledge and still afraid. The nurse is chatty and takes her time to point out the bullet marks of possible and probable side effects that run to four pages. I ask her how much pain I should expect from having syrup pumped into my butt muscle. She says it is more of a liquid than a syrup. I ask her if the one-month dose is less of an amount than the three-month dose. She says it is not; the mix is the same volume though the dosage is different. I watch her mix a powder and liquid in a syringe fed by tubes with two compartments to it. The white powder turns slightly gray once it comes into contact with the liquid that is meant to reconstitute the medicine.

Which side, she asks me. I pick my right buttock, on the assumption that I am left handed and favor my left step when I walk and may well favor the left buttock when I sit (though I have to think about this for a moment since I assume that I sit square on both and I do not cross my legs when I sit). I open my trousers and lower the right side and she asks me to lean on the gurney and contract that right buttock. She sanitizes the area with vigorous rubs of a cool menthol wipe. I take her slight aggression as a declaration of her business approach. While in the vicinity of an erogenous zone the last thing a nurse wants to convey to a patient is the slightest intimation of intimacy. Those vigorous rubs declare a sort of nonchalance, a degree of utility, like drying a plate before putting it away.

She asks me to relax my right buttock and take a deep breath and prepare for a little pinch. I shift my weight to my left leg and let that right buttock fall. I inhale and sure enough the pinch follows, more a stab and puncture of a bicycle tire by a nail, dear nursey-o, than a little pinch. She applies a plaster, which she says is to protect my clothes in case of a spot of blood at the site of the injection. I tuck my shirt into my pants and zip up. She wishes me well and we part with smiles.

I want my pushback at my cancer to bring multiplicity of form to that splurge of content that is my cancer as it threatens to break out of its confines to my prostate and invade the rest of my body. My cancer has a form of its own that it deploys against my body. That it spreads with its deformed outgrowths by invading healthy cells and subjecting them to its deformity. I know that it feeds on the very nutrients meant to keep me healthy and functioning and that it hides from the troops in my body that look for sick expressions to surround and drown.

I do not know what to do with what I know. I do not know how I am going to write a poem or chant and direct those forces with any certainty against such a methodical spread of disease in me. Even with meds on my side and with the promise of a surgery to help me, and further radiation therapy, I wonder if my self-help of chanting and the arts can even make a ding against such a virulent thing. The doubt is not despair. My outlook consists mostly of uplift, more positive than negative, more realist than pessimist, and therefore hardwired to see a lit path where none might appear to the darkened outlook.

Poetry as a force whose composition promotes an under-, no, make that over-standing of my illness, and contributes to my cure, still seems like a stretch. I have my doubts about an art that resides in, yes, doubt, in order to generate inquiry. I have to sort out the lucrative and foundational doubt of my art from my doubting of art's ability to have a curative effect on me. The two forms of doubt—one agitated, doubting Thomas, the other celebrating doubt, Descartes—look much the same. They differ in how fertile each proves to be for me. All my writing years, from my early twenties, I relished doubt as an impetus for artistic inquiry. I began with questions spurred on by doubt that resulted not so much in answers as in modes of inquiry.

The second kind of doubt feels like an invitation to despair. To doubt the efficacy of my art's metaphysical properties, wholly trusted up to now, as poetry-, drama-, and fiction-generating procedures, seems to me a sign of my weakness faced with the implications of cancer. Literary forms might be the very things that I need if I am to face down, embrace even, my doubt. My capacity to prevail against the disease rests in techniques borrowed from art: slowness, meditation, repetition, controlled breathing, physical awareness, focused thought, rhythm, sound, silence, movement, the weight of the line, sentence, paragraph, the clarity of the image, memory, and imagination.

I want doubt in my life as an aid, not as an insurmountable hurdle. It is natural to have days of doom and gloom without surrender to the medical model as the only sure way to battle the disease. Perhaps, there is a way forward in which I do not view everything nonmedical as fluff, as too subjective and as not open to test and confirmation, measurement and its coterminous deployment. My intuition tells me that I have to trust the very sense of being unable to verify what good positive thinking might do for me and just keep doing it, just keep on visualizing the shrinking to naught of that prostate, the trap and retreat of those cancer cells, the chanting down of the walls of my disease and the improvement of my lot.

Never mind the fine tremor in my hands, the feeling of cool in my body and my need to wear a tee under my shirt and jacket on bright, warm days, the back burner of a mild headache, the attention to my bladder, the odd relocation of my attention to my body just to that area below my pubic hair, the thoughts about the two meds that I have to take and how they are working on my behalf with that lethal (I hope to the cancer) injection, a surfeit of lethargy when it comes to exercise, and not a little fear, which surges involuntarily every couple of hours. That my calendar may be truncated and each mundane hour that I waste contributes to a countdown to zero time left for me, and my view of it as somehow routine, amounts to a criminal waste of a limited resource.

I cannot live each hour as if it were my last. I do not have the energy or the necessary indulgent spirit. I need to string together those moments of a complete lack of self-awareness, of being on automatic pilot, not hearing my heart or breath, and not even present in my body. The only constant is my inability to hold on to animosity. There is no room left in me for it. In my condition I could have tea with Mussolini. (Except that I am afraid that it would be my last cuppa.) I feel so vulnerable in this frame of mind. Close to inexplicable tears that I put down to the total annihilation of testosterone in me. In the suit of my black skin that peels under the gaze of racist eyes. That cannot stomach intimate touch. That shuns attention of all kind. That I love. I refuse to feed my doubt of it. I cannot leave it behind me, as I forge ahead in search of a cure.

My skin, my flesh and bones, my nerve suit of consciousness, we are all going down together on the *Titanic* of my being. Let the music play on. Giant gong hit with sledgehammer. Going down as one. Dolphin pod swan-diving through sea currents. Down as my art in life. A life without art is not worth living, not without the worth of art in a life. So chant. Dance. Breathe. Conjure the bear, Baloo, in *The Jungle Book* (Disney's version), who sings his evanescent song, "The Bare Necessities," to school Mowgli into the bear's ways of survival in the jungle. Focus on living that *thang*, that Rastafarian *livity* that makes life a multifaceted approach of enrichment. I lean heavily on Rasta speak, from Marley to Tapper Zukie, to the terminology derived from my teens in London listening to reggae at dancehalls in South London and buying records pressed in London or imported from Jamaica, of artists singing politics and culture guided by Rasta ideology. The music provided a compass to navigate and make sense of the city jungle. Calvino's *Invisible Cities* would cast a different light later on as a reality that I passed through in my youth, a map of the heart and mind whose coordinates were otherwise an abiding threat and palpably lonely.

To be fair, other types of music figured just as heavily. My English teacher befriended a few of my peers and me, and we listened to Bob Dylan, Joni Mitchell, and other sixties and seventies luminaries like Santana, Joplin, and Hendrix. My mother, to her credit, played LPs of Motown soul that we listened to as we did our chores parceled out by her. She danced and sang along to Marvin Gaye, Al Green, Gladys Knight, Diana Ross, and many more, as she vacuumed. The week I began my paper route with my older brother we started buying James Brown, Herbie Hancock, the Crusaders, and other funk acolytes. In addition I encountered Fela Kuti. I picked up on blues, step forward Robert Johnson, Lady Day, Ma Rainey, Muddy Waters, and more. I heard Coltrane and Miles and felt my nerves and mind scrambled.

I coupled my love of music with an ear tuned to the music of poetry. I scribbled in my spare time and memorized poems as

well, in part thanks to Geoff Hardy, that English teacher extraor-
dinaire who read aloud chunks of the romantic poets, "Fern Hill"
by Thomas, "Ode to the West Wind" by Shelley, Keats's *Odes*,
Coleridge's "Kubla Khan," Blake's *Songs*. I mimicked the style of
those poets as a way to find a style and content of my own. There
remains for me now as it did at the time a thrill in the recall of a
poem in its entirety; a mental walk-through renews showers of
diction, syntax, rhythm, and feeling, given by poems that lend
themselves to recall, composed as many are as mnemonics, as
shelves for the library of nerves of memory.

I admit that I danced too. Caught up in the social sexual drug
of the disco era of clubbing though never as a wallflower, never
there just to lean against a wall and peruse the dance floor, but a
wild occupant of it, gyrating, spinning, bumping, and getting all
the way down until covered in sweat and drinking pints of water
to keep on grooving until the lights came up in the house. My
older brother, as a result, took up dance for a living. I found out
the limits of my dancing ability next to him on the dance floor.
I felt I was fighting the music and always playing catch up to it,
whereas Greg, he controlled the groove and moved with economy and urgency.

I go back there to help me move through and with this current
emergency. Back to those energetic days summoned by the mere
whiff of cut grass, an olfactory trigger for a panoply of memories.
And deep too, a dive into inner resources submerged and intuited
as there and waiting for me to call on them to spring up to my
assistance. And so there is a rhythm to my resistance to disease,
a groove that my recovery may draw from by mimicking, by going through its paces for measures of my cure. Vials of the stuff
that I see as buried in my senses and my artistic practice that I
summon want to help me now in my hour of need. Not just the
numinous—though credited as such—more than that, the lumi-
nous as well, and a word I do not like, ludic. That which shines
and emits a pulse, those invitations sent out to the self to incline
toward solace.

3

IS THIS WHAT DYING LOOKS LIKE?

I have no defense against the experience of seeing my thirteen-year-old daughter burst into tears. As she cries so I am made immobile, catatonic with confusion that my condition drives her to such distress. She and I are in the car going to her school on one of the last days before the city stopped all social gatherings. We are a bit late and she has to make a stop at the pharmacy. She cannot settle on the brand of tampons and pads that she needs. I have my eye on the clock. I hurry her along. I am agitated even before this detour. I wake in the night, run to the bathroom or lie awake and wait for sleep to wander back to me. I eat, dress, and interact with Debbie and the pets on a reserve tank of civics, with most of my mind in the realm of the disease newly revealed in me.

In this frame of mind I tell my daughter to hurry up. She tells me to stop rushing her. I tell her she is wasting time and not taking school seriously. She tells me that this exchange is the precise reason she wishes that I had not brought the family to LA to join me. She starts to cry as I drive. I feel a rush of steam between my ears. I am like one of those *Looney Tunes* cartoons from the seventies where the maddened animal character literally becomes a steam train of rage and flies about wrecking stuff. I tell her that she is selfish. She cries and blurts out that my anger is abuse and a mark of damage and poor parenting. Her very words! By now I am seeing red, and that last contribution from her is a red rag waved in front of me. The traffic is terrible on Pico Boulevard,

too many cars and too many red lights, and hardly any movement. I tell her that she is spoiled rotten. She cries harder. She says
that she wishes she did not have me for a father and that any other
adult would do for a father except me. By now her face is red and
her nose is streaming as much as her eyes. The car is full of our
static. I glance at her and freeze. I do not have to pull over since we
are hardly moving. I say to her that I am sorry that she is right and
I take back everything that I said. I tell her that I am under pressure. I apologize profusely and offer her my prized handkerchief
from my jacket top pocket (I cannot get at the one in my trouser
back pocket). She takes it and blows copious amounts of snot into
it and folds it and dries the spigots of her eyes. She says she is sorry
too. That she feels pressure and sadness because of my cancer.
That she does not want me to die, that she hardly knows me well
and loves me and wants her father, me, and no one else to be her
father. Now I am the one in tears and with no handkerchief I
sleeve my eyes clear. Thank goodness for LA's grinding traffic or
stops and starts and low-mileage cruises that require little of the
driver except the will to defray boredom. I ask her forgiveness.
She says that there is nothing to forgive. I reassure her that the
cancer will not take me from her, not without a fight. That I have
a lot of good medicine on my side and so much love from her and
her brothers and her mother, and with my army of love ranged
against cancer, I will be unbeatable. We hug across the gearbox
console. I tell her I love her very much and she tells me she loves
me too. I drive around the block of her school for her red face to
clear and for her to stop hiccupping with upset. I beg her to forget
everything bad that sprang out of my mouth. That I am a fool at
the mercy of my diagnosis. That I lack the necessary control to be
a proper father to her. She says she wants me to be her dad, none
other, and that she loves me and she will be fine in a minute or
two. She offers me my soaked handkerchief. I tell her to keep it
in case she needs it again. She says that she is fine. We have never
been closer and with such intensity—thanks to my cancer. We
are late for the start of her school day. I tell her if she feels bad just

call me or text and I will leave work and pick up her in under ten minutes. She says she will be fine, really. That I shouldn't worry. That she feels better. She asks me how I am doing. I tell her I feel better too. We part with a brief lock of eyes and hurried mutual I-love-yous.

Thank you, cancer. I called you a fucker for turning up uninvited and ruining what was supposed to be the party of my life. Now I thank you. You turn up the intensity in my routine domesticity.

There is a dream—isn't there always?—of me walking into a bar or restaurant or assembly room of some sort with a counter and staff, and crowded with customers. I see all this through the brick wall and oak door—as dreams tend to allow the dreamer to do. Two featureless people are ahead of me. A man and a woman, going by the gender-specific clothes each wears: a gray suit for him and a pencil skirt and frilly blouse for her. First, the man enters the crowded space and someone behind the counter rings a bell and announces, Man with prostate in the house, and everyone whoops, applauds, and hollers approval. The same happens for the woman ahead of me. She walks in and again the bell rings and another voices shouts, Woman with ovaries in the house, followed by the same noises of approval. I enter and no one looks up, no bell announces my arrival, nothing. I wait for an age to get served or find a table or whatever the fuck reason made me go public with my cancer in the first place.

I wake up still stuck in that bastard dream though all alone this time. I reach down to my crotch area as if to console my anatomy shamed in public (in a climate of prostatism or ovarianism as the prejudice might be known were it to exist in the real), only to find nothing there, all of my block and tackle gone, an empty region, just a pelvis covered in skin. I wake up with a start and a frown. Man with or without a cancerous prostate, I wish to stay out of the limelight. The only recognition I want is from life, is life, its continuity in me.

It's not the first time a bar features in my life. Way back in the late seventies, '79 or '80, my friend Geoff and I were about to enter a bar and he stopped and asked me, which one of us should be the first to enter the pub, the fag or the wog? My frame of mind that evening did not allow for a hierarchy of our oppression in that slave-memory-allergic city of my birth. I said both and we squeezed into the door and heads turned as they do in these small turnstile-like settings and we got to the bar and ordered a couple of pints and the pub settled back into its indifference. No one questioned that these two specimens of the male gender possessed prostates. What mattered more was the fact that one was black and the other was gay (my friend was headlights full-on camp).

Fact is, I have to lose my prostate and soon or keep it housed in me and risk its wildfire spread throughout my body. So toll those bells for me. Man sans prostate it has to be. Necessarily missing a part to continue my part in life. I catch myself just in time. Pull back on those reins before I gallop ahead of myself. Whoa, there, buddy. What an opera queen! Listening to too much Sylvester. More Liberace, I see the glittery cape trailing behind me as I rest my forearm on my forehead and lament my situation. It's me as Laurence Olivier playing Othello (when it should be Paul Robeson) in that black-and-white footage of big gestures and rolling eyes on a blackened face.

Fuck that browbeating shit. Let me not whine, dear Lord. Take me down in a lasso and hog-tie me rather than let me lose my shit. I need every ounce of my energy to cope with this disease. Some room in my body and mind that I kept under lock and key all these years must now be broken open to release whatever it was I was saving up for a rainy day. I forget what is in that room. I know that there is such a place in me and that I kept it, saved it up, for a time just like this one that now presents itself as an ultimatum, drink this hemlock and lie down, place your head on this block, lower your neck for this noose, bare that chest for that bullet, and so on, as the cape comes back on and the stage lights flood in unison, and the darkness that I look out on from my stage might be the calendar that has run out of days for me. Cancer wants a fight. I am ready for a fight.

There is a shadow calendar that does not look outward at any clock for confirmation of its location in the day or night. It beats with a pulse and it moves with the flow of blood and the rhythm of a body on a stroll or run. This calendar's measure, if lineated, might be spread across the entire space of a blank page with lines of varying length broken according to breath and the ability of the tongue to wrap around those clauses. Rather than flowing from the mind to the mechanics of the body to be broadcast to the world, that calendar informs and shapes thinking; that is, it travels from the body to the mind, where it finds linguistic expression.

Could it be geared toward cure? Are its coordinates amenable to alteration dictated by a mind in search of obliquity, the intangible, and numinous, as ways to marshal resistance to virulent and authoritarian disease? I ask because my daughter on the way to school tuned in her phone to my wife's Bluetooth system in the car that I borrowed for the day. Up blared this tune with a bold bass and drum rhythm and a repeated phrase that my daughter bounced to in her seat, pulling on her seat belt and rocking the car. I found it infectious and joined in with a modified old-man bounce of my own. For a couple of traffic lights we were propelled by this song and swept up in a current of delight. I was lost to myself, invisible to my disease, transported, as it were, to a plane of unselfconsciousness, akin to body without ego. Joy returned to my humble diseased machine.

The fact that I incline to such waves of ebullience, that I am susceptible to the contagion of joyous transport of the self away from itself and into a shared mode of exuberance, belies my usual front of cool and calm. Meaning, that I wish to be in that place and space more often and by all means at my disposal, including my daughter's natural effusive charm. I learn from her how to be uninhibited, how to make myself freely available to strategies for my cure that are otherwise seen as off the grid or inaccessible if not intangible and invisible. Those threads of meaning that shadow my calendar as if deliberately invoked by the material location of my days on a grid, that serve as counterpoints to all calendars by their very immateriality, their ethereal nature.

How to swerve clear of a binary between seen and unseen, material and immaterial, physical and spiritual, and sustain its dialectical relations?I see this shadow world indebted to a plurality of sources. For example, on the creative front of poetry I depend on this shadow world's intuited, phrasal, and clausal procedures that result in the poem. An intelligence that feels its way forward and relies on one step to generate the next. There is linear propulsion at work, velocity, and circular and deepening schemes as well, forward moves in terms of time passing and details accumulating, and a depth charge of exploration, as emotion deepens in complexity thanks to the passage of time marked by accruing detail.

Force exerted by this creative outlook and inward gaze might be directed toward ill parts of the body in need of repair and restoration or transformation. If the body is full of regions of forgetting, neglect, and trauma, it may well equally be a repository for restorative powers and open to their deployment in sick areas of being. In league with meds I may be able to double down on my oppression and topple it from the inside. Not just something administered to my body from the outside into it as meds do; rather, an approach that emerges from the body itself, as if the body knows best what ails it and prescribes what it needs to cure its ailments.

My voice rises from within me aided by breath (ribs and diaphragm), throat, tongue, and palate, and so on. The physics of my voice depends on an underlying awareness of intent to make a sound, perhaps from a thought, not quite conscious or willful. I feel the birth of sound in my body as it masses and rises, and I send it out into the world. In a similar way I may direct this curative thinking and sound to other parts of me in need of their particular magnetic resonance, their vibration of cure. Of course my voice (as a coalition of thought and sound) is not alone. Other forces conspire with it and join its train of insurgency against disease.

They include the arc of positive thinking that emits positive vibrations. The yoga of movement that releases locked-up and knotted energies trapped in pockets of the body so that the body feels elated and lighter without those negative energies and taxing thoughts. And the catharsis of creative composition, of making something whose end is not known but whose procedure pays dividends to the person engaged with it. I place my trust in the shadow history of knowing, which is not knowing, or unknowingness, as properties for this realignment of the spirit, whose recalibration cures my sickness.

I remind myself to beware of willful forgetting, a kind of amnesia that amounts to a neglect of the spiritual, of memory as a contract and bond with the past needed in the present to shape a more purposeful future. Forgetting has its charms when it comes to the fresh feel to a familiar encounter, its sensuous delights; and forgetting has its benefits, say, in the face of a surfeit of trauma that traps the sufferer in a cycle of despair. Forgetting as a prerequisite for a traumatized community to continue onward and for it to become unstuck sounds plausible, but the better tool of remembering is its portal to dig deeper to recover something curative and familiar. The maxim that we forget so that we can remember at a deeper level places forgetting at the center of any act of memory, there to help shape how we remember.

The difference resides in Keats's notion of *negative capability*, that place of uncertainty and insecurity where poems languish and grow. Keats wants us to stay with insecurity rather than run back to certainty and miss out on poetry. Imagination thrives in that uncertain mindset. Poetry abounds. All the poet has to do is trust in discombobulating feelings rather than run from trickster emotions back to familiar ground. I say *all*, as if it is all or nothing, and knowing that is a lot to ask of a mind invested in certainty. Ludic coordinates threaten imbalance, even breakdown. An invitation to stay in that space for the procurement of poetry might be asking for trouble.

Keats tells us that we can grow from the exposure to uncertainty, as poets and people. Could there be room for cure in this tremulous place of uncertainty? Is going there an act of opening the self even more to unwanted damage, more bombardment of the nervous system with poison? For Keats it results in a negation of self and identification with the subject of the poem so that the poem enacts that assumed subjectivity. Alan Watts answers the injunction with a wise quotient written into the insecure, in his *The Wisdom of Insecurity*. The obverse, security, is the illusion. Insecurity is the normal condition for all affairs, material and otherwise. We dupe ourselves into believing that the trappings of materialism somehow underwrite the spiritual, actually lead to satisfaction. Watts argues that we cannot get any satisfaction—without conceding ground to the Rolling Stones' clarion call for sex and more sex—without taking the risk of walking away from the self. The frustration is existential for Watts, an ego invested in too much devotion to the materialist quest as a substitute for spiritual vacuum.

Watts and Keats fold into my arsenal of tools for me to tackle my trade and standoff with cancer. The rhythm of recall of these early readings that helped me find a place in my body and in the space where I lived, that provided solace, might be the lesson in itself. Not a vehicle that conveys something but the structure of the thing. My feelings in my body know what I mean when I say the word *rhythm*. My body remembers rhythm as tied up with feelings of transportation, of goodness. That rhythm of transport and transformation carries with it such riches that surely they might help me with my quest for cure. If I am true to Watts I know I must be careful not to strive too much after a thing that defies being pinned down. I know that the condition may be entirely psychological, a mental plane of existence, a state of mind, rather than a property to be captured and deployed in my favor.

So I chant, sing, dance, breathe purposefully, move with a method to my madness, voice with direction, all in the hope of mustering an atmosphere conducive to cure. I seek the numinous without setting out on a quest (a quest would be to lose even before I begin my journey). I conjure the spiritual, a wave rather than a straight line. It wobbles like prodded Jell-O that soaks up the velocity of the prod without collapsing. It trembles like leaves that give shape to the wind by their frolicking. It hums as that same breeze squeezes between blades of grass. Cobweb strung overnight beaded with morning dew where light plays and the web vibrates like an instrument. There it is once more in a stick plunged and held in a clear pool so that the stick bends and waves underwater, bends with water, wavers with light. The blast of energy from all these things felt and seen turns toward my disease and drives it from my body.

I cast aside doubt. Usually, doubt powers my art. I generate poetry, fiction, plays, and essays as a direct result of doubt playing on my mind. Doubt makes me begin again on another poem or story rather than settle for what already exists in a library stuffed to capacity and beyond. Doubt invites me to dare desecrate the unblemished beauty of a blank page whose startled look invites the gaze and diverts attention from less challenging undertakings. Thanks to doubt I have the ability to start all over again from a new angle, renewed each time by fertile doubt to tease out a new question or sensory haunting or memory.

The creative doubt into which I plunge fosters the kind of insecurity that is necessary for literary production. But the same doubt and insecurity, when turned against my belief in a cure for my cancer, wreak havoc on my mind. I pivot between inviting those two conditions into my life for their benefits without succumbing to their negative effects. Doubt turned against me by my disease is a disaster for my prognosis. I begin to feel insecure, in the sense of being unhinged by my cancer. As a result, the floodgates of gloom open. The bad feeling makes me wonder if there is any point to all the meds and marshaling of a personal existential prescription for my return to health. With doubt working against me, I stumble and founder in the face of the disease. I see my calendar as half doors, top and bottom halves that close on me if I duck under the top half or climb over the bottom half. Doors that leave me in the dark, excluded from the march of time and the quantum leaps of thought and feeling, and from the spiral of imagery that progresses to newer and more profound depths of insight. Doubt on the side of my disease, as my enemy, once my friend, may be the most damaging force of all.

I can't account for the switch of doubt from friend to enemy. Nietzsche's saying that what does not kill you makes you strong may have something to do with the change, that somehow the property and quality of most benefit to my creative life could be the force for accelerating my descent into my victim status in the face of my disease. Doubt powers faith. I have no faith in the conventional sense, so the reason for keeping doubt anchored in that binary relation to my psyche appears to be lost to me.

Despair is one of many faces of doubt, just one of its many masks. Despair feeds my sickness, helps it along the marathon road as the disease metastasizes. I aim to stop that spread with a firewall of meds and positive vibes and ultimately drive it back and banish it from my body. Despair breaks down that firewall and doubt is the parent of despair. The same doubt that powered me to shepherd a poem to a point of many questions and leave it poised as unfinished business for the reader to complete and augment, that doubt sides with my cancer.

A reader of my body, I no longer feel right about my body. As the saying goes for the reader of the text, the reader is always right, but not this reader, my dear reader. Instead my reading of my disease is as untrustworthy as the obligatory unreliable narrator of fiction. Excoriating self-doubt is an agenda item where the writer is absent from the discussion. The self that remains is so mired in doubt that it forgets the uses of doubt that brought it to this point in its life. It's as if doubt makes the self forget that in an earlier time the self worked in harmony with doubt. Cure may rest in acceptance of the limits of the power of the sick body to summon wellness. *Cure* may be the wrong term altogether for a condition of permanence, of dying anyway, and this diagnosis may just be a question of a specified path, well lit and announced in advance, and available to me as my disease, whether I'm ready for it or not. I am ready. I am not. Depends on the day that my disease catches me.

Catch me on a rainy day with the water inveigling paths down my shirt collar, water coming at me at a slant, and my outlook matches the sky leaden with water. I move slower. I think like a spoon moving through thick porridge. I keep my eyes planted at my feet. My shoulders slump. As if I were a smoldering campfire doused by a bucket. There is only the memory of fire. There I am cooling fast with no room to think outside my condition. The part of me that cherishes water on my skin loses out to the part of me that feels cramped by the bleak and cold and wet.

Catch me on a day full of sun and I shine with it. I bounce along. I look up at the birds and the trees. I sniff the air for more than traffic fumes. Every thought in me is a sensory record of delight. And from that arises the notion that nothing can stop me in this life except its corollary, death. And death always looks light-years away on a sunny day. If I could whistle, you would hear me coming up the path before you see me. A bird whose wings though missing, nevertheless soars in song. A body made lighter by the bright and the blue.

And if the day is a bit of both, then I am your in-between person, by turns cheery and somber, head down eyes up, ready to hop over a puddle or shatter my reflection if my hop drops short. Prepared to remain in that place of having embarked and never able to arrive, always on the journey and so always on the move. Flux that includes stillness; thought with room for contemplation. What luxuries amid this clamor of our days. How kind of disease to remind me of what counts in this short sprint of a life. Thank you, for now, for nothing. The season of my affect is the reason for my days.

For now I must gather all my reverberating strings of being and pool them into one emboldened self of understanding, fight, and cure. Cure may be trying to put the genie back in the bottle. Perhaps I need another conclusion to my diagnosis, not one that erases it as if cancer never existed, but some new state of being with the disease under my control and no longer in control of me, present in me without imminent danger to me, my companion of sorts, one who holds both halves of the door ajar for me to catch up as it walks over the threshold and into oblivion.

The image that goes with this is of a jazz figure resembling Miles playing with his back to the audience in part disdain for their insistence that they dictate his output rather than learn from his innovations of sound and to hear the members of his band and signal swift and subtle changes to them. There is a funky rhythm section to the jazz horns and keys straying into strange auditory territory. And I am rolling across the floor to those ministrations, I mean on my feet and on the move, arms swinging this way and that, head bobbing and my body trying to separate ribs and spine according to the push and pull of muscles in my back and torso.

If there is color for all this frenzy then the palette must be rainbow, rainbow, rainbow, as Bishop chants at the end of her poem "The Fish." For it signals continuous renewal. The spirit lifts to levels only color can map with any accuracy. For the rest of my days that I wake in the disease I'll be forced to breathe it in and out, and see inside it too and look out at the world from my insider's location. This condition of living with the disease, and inside it as well, provides perspectives on the disease and on the routine of my world, as if looking out of windows in a large house and those windows permit iterations of landscapes of the disease. So I had better find something recuperative in what I see out there and in what I feel about my life inside cancer. Both. Or else I perish in a living death of being trapped on the inside looking out and seeing my reflection as I look through it to the scene outside.

My gaze at the outward world launches from a blaze of nerve endings. I land on objects that send back signals of their names and in those names are the sounds of moods: happy, sad, calm, and more. I do this looking-out thing to separate my disease from what I see, as if sight could ever be independent of the mood generated by the reality of my sickness.

The inward gaze that begins my day operates with my eyes shut and my ears blocked against the outside world. A dreamscape. Next, my nerves dig deeper into my body to defy the dimensions of my five-feet, ten-inch, one-hundred-and-fifty-eight-pound frame. Those nerves open a psychic space of awareness. My mood floats in that space in the company of my disease. I am Gloucester sans eyes, blind, and in possession of a powerful inward gaze, able to "see it feelingly." The inward gaze is a tune-up for the outside world. When I open my eyes my muscle memory and nerve-based intuition charge everything that I see.

I start to walk around my neighborhood with alacrity. (Alacrity sounds like a character out of a Dickens novel but I am thinking of Dickens's nighttime walks around London.) No detail misses my eye and my feet take on eyes in the way each picks a place to land. The map of the place becomes layered like a wedding cake, one layer for each walk, one memory for each sense each time I walk, and never the same walk twice, never once if the Zen maxim is to be believed, a walk made by each sense on its own terms and so never able to create a single take of the journey, more a plural happening bundled from each sense. My cancer with eyes, ears, nose, tongue tunes to that walk those layers made for my cancer.

Is this what dying looks like? Am I on the last rites of my days as a way to face the end of my time on earth? Hell, no. What has kicked in for me is my poetry. It grows nerves out of every second that I live this crisis. My poetry senses want to rescue me from catatonic shock and stasis. Poetry insists on charging the everyday by bequeathing attention to it. The everyday wants to bat away focus by playing possum with boredom as its principal trait. Poetry does not fall for the trick and so zeroes in on the most humdrum detail in recognition of its live wire charge. And my cancer appears to copy my actions as it continues its shadow play of me.

Take that urban cockerel that announces the dawn every day without fail. City ordinances clearly state that no such fowl should inhabit the city limits. No one told the owner, or the owner doesn't care. No one told that cockerel who sees around concrete and brick buildings and through glass that something outside matches an interior clock and in obedience to the two forces, one inside, the other out, that cockerel crows his lungs and heart out. And on a good day I want to run out the front door and stand in the street with my arms outstretched, and join in with that cockerel and crow as well: to announce the new day, to lay to rest the old, in celebration of my breath, pulse, inward gaze, and outlook. Cock-a-doodle-do!

*   *   *

My office is sick after the building flooded and a lot of my books turned to pulp (I see it as ecological literary criticism). The plaster had to be cut away to remove the insulation and banish all mold. The city is sick with the COVID-19 virus. The globe is shutting down with countries and with commerce. How to turn that global pattern around and at what cost? Imagine the planet as this ailing body. Forget triage, if only because triage admits a trajectory of dying that must be turned around. What is left? What remains for that body to do to save itself from extinction? This is where wellness, collective wellness performed on behalf of all parts of the body, comes into its own.

I am a neighborhood, a city, a state, a region, and a country, and ultimately the globe. The big systems all pass through me in miniature, all of me mimic all of it. As a river flows with fish and fresh water meets salt to become a sea and ocean, so my blood flows around my body from capillaries to veins to arteries and into and out of the great pump, muscle, nerve bundle, and thought-drum of my heart. It is this connected, interlinked sense of my life that makes me invest in my body as the world and everybody as me, and every other living thing, including that feisty cockerel.

Just as I posit my body for the city, state, country, globe, so my office flood and COVID-19 join forces with my cancer to battle against me. The fall of water from the upper floors to my third-floor office, a reverse flood in miniature. The large sweep of COVID-19 infecting cities, countries, continents, and the globe. Fear of the cyclone of COVID-19 empties the streets of the city and shutters commerce. The dead pile up. That fear grips me as my cancer already rooted in me. All I have to do is breathe in COVID-19 to inhale another manifestation of my cancer, a pincer attack on my life from outside and from within.

Flooded office and worsening COVID-19 crisis conspire with my disease to ruin my days. It's early March and the hare turned up with an increased level of madness. I start to have a string of bad days with my disease. Outdanced by cancer, my toes stepped on by it, in a system that does not see me and sees only the disease at a certain stage of help or hopeless. Am I finding it hard to come to terms with my body as viewed in the latter camp, not open to cure but in need of accepting my lot as doomed? The bell rings for me—not a toll but a ding-dong of the overly dramatic, and a call for me to pull back on the reins of that six-horse-drawn wagon that gallops out of control. Giddyup, despair. Ride me. I am wild. Break me. I may throw you. Hold on for dear life.

What happened? No energy. I feel cold. Old. No longer bold. My body zooms into a swarm of heat that makes me peel off the sweater that I pulled on to keep warm. I sweat. My armpits itch. My back too. I avoid chemicals on my skin and make sure the deodorant is natural as natural can be; that is, no Es and no parabens. I olive oil hands and limbs and head too, to obliterate those dry patches that trouble my skin and scalp. No hangnails that tell the story of my dry skin, that make my nails look exactly my age against the presentation of my sixty as fifty, which I value, vaingloriously.

Be humble, I hear Kendrick Lamar intone. Sit down. Humility

works if it stands up for social responsibility, if it does not mean surrender to a certain vibe of authority that insists on keeping me in the audience so that it can remain onstage and hog the limelight. Humility is a white flag to my disease whose virulence depends on my passivity. Not today. I may feel tired but my mind remembers what it means to be energetic. If I act full of energy maybe my body will follow my example and jump up from its slouch and take its place onstage. No more the poor me. No more dress me with a sign on my back that says kick me up the butt.

I am that person Maya Angelou sings about who insists against all odds on surfacing above oppression. Who comes up for Orwellian air in a time of stifling despair. Who may be in Sontag's America but not ensconced in its reptilian values. So as I rise I take with me the best of me for the rest of us that is part of me. Solve that riddle on behalf of wonder and in celebration of puzzlement. The up in me tells the down in me to ease up and let go of my flow. How did we put it in Airy Hall, East Coast Demerara, Guyana? *'Low me leh me bubble like a surf!* Step back so that I can breathe this COVID-19 air, sure, but air unburdened of LA's usual traffic. Give me elbow room. Count me down but do not count me out. I have a knee on the canvas, granted, and cancer stands menacingly over me, alongside COVID-19, but can't you see that I am about to push back up to my feet? Look again, more closely this time. I hesitate to draw deep on this reduced exhaust air for its trace of sweetness brought nine miles inland from the sea with the gulls gathered in the parking lot at the mini mall.

All of the above to stave off the bitter feeling that my disease settled for me to claim my body. All that freshness surfaces in me as well as that bitterness, and I find confirmation for two opposite registers in the world around me. Crows on the lookout for empty nests with juicy eggs chased off by mockingbirds. A lone hawk adrift, wings fixed like a jet's, riding currents overhead. I feel lethargic as the sky emptied of airplanes. I look outside and the flight of parrots across my field of vision staggers in slow motion as if out of bandwidth. A car passes and as I stare the wheels spin in reverse. A person in layers of clothing, ready for all seasons as the homeless must be to survive the cold nights, pushes a cart brimful with things (could be tins and plastic returns) and the slow crawl switches from passing in front of me to circling in my head. I swallow and taste bile. I blink dust away that feels like razor blades. A heat wave, another drug-induced hot flash, engine of mine robbed of testosterone, sweeps me off my feet. An instant film of sweat makes me peel off my shirt.

The physics of my disease tightens into the metaphysics of thinking about it at all times so that it becomes a condition for my consciousness. Writer in America. Teacher in America. Black in America. Parent, husband, friend in America. Under COVID-19 and with cancer in America. What started out as physical becomes a state of mind, no longer reliant on the body. My cancer grows wings. I know I am in Fanon territory, where racism injures the psyche of those who live under its pressure. How is my cancer forged in the crucible of my race? If the former is real and the latter is a construct? A body-forged manacle for a disease in a mind-forged manacle of a body stigmatized by race—two versions of Blake's hell on industrial earth inhabit one space. It converts Fanon's intangibles that afflict Black bodies and minds into the currency of despair. Fanon with a stake in every malady of the body whose dimensions extend to the mental plane and operate so far from its origins as a physical disease that I might almost forget that I have an ailment, given how rapt with cancer I have become in my outlook.

Just as my state of mind is dependent on my cancer, so my cancer depends on my state of mind. The gravity of my cancer relies on my ability to control how much it influences my thoughts and feelings. If I capitulate to cancer, then it claims me as its own and takes my life. I am to rise above the pool of the disease in which I am immersed, propel myself out of that pool and float in defiance of gravity, over that water, and look down on the scene as a way to regain perspective on my disease and retain control over my mind. My shadow ripples across the face of that pool and I am out of reach of the element of my cancer. I cannot countenance how much real estate my mind must devote to my disease. I am frustrated with thinking all the time inside the disease. I search for ways to look at my illness as if located outside it. I search for a way to be on the inside of my disease while looking out and, simultaneously, on the outside of the disease while looking in at it.

4

FRED, DO NOT BE AFRAID

I beg your pardon, I hear my disease answer in reply to my many charges leveled against it—of trespass, hijack, squatting, invasion, vandalism, anxiety, psychosis, psoriasis (of the mind), catatonia (of the spirit), a Gordian knot (of my reason), poisoning, pollution, warping—I did not grow in you uninvited by the way you lived and the life that you were given to begin with. I started in you with time and from time. I opened my eyes thanks to you finding the combination to unlock my presence in you by the way you lived your life. I had no intention to riot against you, my host, upon whom I depended for sustenance and a quiet life—which is all I ever wanted. I did not intend to finish you and me in the process. As long as you lived on, so would I. As long as you left me undisturbed, I would keep quiet and dormant in you until the end of your days.

You see me as spikes, barbed wire, and broken bottles, all cutting edges in you, and you forget that you set me going, turned me on and cut me loose in your body. I did not expect it. All your talk, reading, and tree-hugging company, and demonstrations for good, signaled to me that I would not have a hectic life that charged to a rapid end for my host and for me, but that I would be in a quiet place, unseen and ignored and quite content to amble to an octogenarian's crawl and walker decked with tennis balls for a snail's mobility, staggering brakes and watch-paint-dry stoppage. I could see it when you meditated or did your yoga or ran or lifted weights or ate greens, lots of them, with poker-faced enjoyment. I stopped thinking of a day when I would be free to run to my end and in the process, bring about yours preternaturally early.

That would have been that had you kept your days free of poisons. I mean situations of stress in which you stared down a blank page and filled it and scrapped it only to fill it again and kept at it into the small hours and from dawn to midnight. For what? The glory of your name at the front of a book. Or some sense of what your days might be if strung out across the page or in broken lines patterned on the page. That was you poking my cage with a stick. I ignored you for as long as I could take your teasing. You kept on facing the ineffable. You persisted in your provocation of nothing for the something it might surrender if you put it under the duress of your concentration.

As you persisted your body fired all manner of tensions around it. I could not dodge or retreat to some safe place. I depended on the shelter you provided. I was written into your biology—by your father and maybe your grandmother as well—even if the writing had to be provoked into meaning or invoked by you for it to mean something to your life. Your insistence on a writing life in the middle of a life to be lived added to the duress I experienced in you. Your choices lit me up. I stirred, looked up from my prostate bed and rolled up my sleeves, and here we are in a fight started by you and to be finished by me.

I say amen. I say now that I am awake in you let me do what I am made for in bodies that store me. Do not fight me. You delay the inevitable when you fight me. Your resistance adds to my ferocity. The time you gain fighting me is taken up with the fight and loses meaning outside that fight. You do not win. You gain respite. So why fight? Why line up your days for battle rather than for living what is left of your life? Embrace me. I come in peace. There, I said my piece. Though I know how that sounds. That you should recline. That I should have my way with you.

I belong to a family of diseases and we rule your so-called modern living. My patience with you has just about run out as you cry in your proverbial beard over your ailment, a condition brought on yourself by your bad habit of writing yourself into worry, anxiety, depression, debt, and now me, waiting at your door to collect you. I needed patience to put up with you. I needed to bide my time in you just to live as long as you but with me in my dormant state. This way, with me awake and virulent with my life, I get to live with quality rather than simply survive in you.

I know you understand that it was either of us, and that I won this one against you, whereas with your colleagues or friends the result might be the opposite—their defeat of me. It is the roll of the dice. There is a way you can help us both. Stop your ruminations about your condition as a conjectural truth and embrace me as the most likely outcome at this late stage of things. Do that and your time eases for you. To begin with, you can put a stop to those calls to get the doctors to take notice of you. You do not have to keep pumping those drugs into your body that slow you down. They only give you hot flashes, cold sweats, constipation, headache, dizzy spells, and breathlessness now that you cannot exercise with vigor. And sudden itches and dry mouth that turns your food bland. Fighting me is a fool's errand. Fighting me serves merely to slow the inevitable and eat up what little time is left to us both in your shared house of a body.

All I ask of your body—on the decline anyway—is to capitulate to my program of accelerated and strategic degeneration. Take drugs for pain if you like. Take drugs to escape thinking about me. Just do not see me as the enemy that you have to battle against in order to live longer. There lies delusion, frustration, and hopelessness for you, my friend. That is where you lose what little time you have left. You should be living each moment not thinking about your next strategy to defeat me. You should be partying like it's 1999. That is the way to stretch your time without watering it down or squandering it. That is the way to deepen the time left to you and make it meaningful. Do not be time's fool by battling with me.

You are not the first to think that you can win by delaying my claim on you. That somehow all the meds, expert consultations, and talk with your feel-good books can result in an alteration of your time that remains, and in your relationship with me. I do not go away. I retreat to a quiet and inaccessible place in your body. I continue my work undetected. I stake my claim one way or another. As you continue to breathe you take me in. As you eat, drink, and sleep I am fed by your sustenance. I belong in you as much as you belong to me. Do not fool yourself that I can be killed inside you and you walk away from me and resume your life where you left it when you started your fight with me.

I think you will be at peace with your world and everyone in it if you embrace me. Take me into your life, and your days gain meaning. They are limited without me on your calendar. You subtract from them by fighting with me. Together we can face what time is left to you and prepare for the end of your body and mind as you know it and work out what follows your death—that is, our death, since I go where you go. If you sink into misery over me, that is no fun for me. If you accelerate your end by your hand, that fails both of us.

You should vacation with me. I prefer a beach to a city. Hey, work through that bucket list of yours. Stop putting everything on hold just to devote yourself to fighting me, as if you can win and get back the time spent battling me. You cannot win against time lost or the fact that your time must run out. I grant permission for you to use me as your excuse for living each second as if each one meant something to you, as if each carried equity of some kind that enriches your awareness. Use me since you cannot refuse me. I am here to stay; once awake I cannot be cajoled into going back to sleep. I will not be evicted from your body by surgery, chemo, hormones, or yogic chanting. Why waste your time on those things when you can have me?

I nearly added the word *baby* to that last missive of mine. I withheld it to spare you ribaldry in the midst of your anxiety over me. All I want to do is convert your red-light view of my invasion of your body to a green-light embrace of your condition. See me as currency credited to your account without you having to do a thing. Spend me. I mean, take us out on the town. Not this town that has shut down, thanks to COVID-19, but its onomatopoeic cousin, the tongue that you carry around. I refer to your imagination. I ask that you enlist it on our behalf to help us have some fun. Together we can beat time. Something I know you find hard to believe and something that I can prove to you if you let me. Lend me your ear.

Fred, do not be afraid. The island of your mind really is full of noises. I am a part of that cacophony. All bitter. Every bit of it a source of worry. See the fear of what I bring as worse than the thing that I am in your life. Treat your fear of me. Spend your hours trying to reduce its outsize growth in your mind and forget about your prostate and whether the wildly elevated PSA readings indicate that I have traveled up your lymph nodes to staple my progeny up each rung on the ladder of your spine. Fear keeps your eyes on me. And your energy ranged against me. While fear itself escapes scot-free from your prescriptive attention.

What is up with that? If you carry yourself differently because you are scared of living, you are no longer alive. You have become the fear that you are afraid of, thinking that I am to blame for how you feel. Live in fear and you die in life. Run around scared and you may as well stay in bed and rot. You might locate me and target me in your prostate, but with fear there is no location that is not what you represent. With fear you are its hijack victim: your heart, your mind, and your soul. Now you sleepwalk as fear. Now you are not the Fred who is sick of his cancer and wishes to get rid of it, of me. You have become fear. Now fear pilots your mind, body, and spirit.

I make this distinction between the cancer, which is my name (that I would change by deposition if I could be bothered with the bureaucracy of your modern life), and your fear, which I see as manufactured by your view of me. It is important for you to see the difference between your fear and your cancer, me. Fear me, for sure. If you allow your fear to outgrow your focus on me, you become the thing that you desire the least and it guides your every strategy. Well, that just irks me. I am the one you should be worried about. I should be foremost on your mind. Not your routine of yoga and meditation and light weights and sit-ups and breathing and riding that ridiculous stationary bike of yours.

5.

YOU ARE MY MORTAL ENEMY

Hey, fuck face, we are not on first-name terms. So stop the Fred this and Fred that. You call my name in vain if you think I would fall for the bait and switch of you saying that my fear has nothing to do with you and that it is independent and unworthy of association with you. Fear is your emissary. Fear and lots of other negative forces in me right now all work on your behalf. To hide behind it is your cowardice, and cowardice is one of your many names. To think that I would devote my mind to battling my fear as something separate from your presence in me is high-and-mighty wishful thinking by you in your grandiosity.

Why you think that I would view my enlarged prostate covered with your growth as some companion that I need to bring meaning to my life escapes me. I do not need you in my life to see meaning in my life. My days are numbered. Duh, I know that. Your tax of what is already a scarcity in me gets up my nose? I do not see why my inevitable end should be made any more urgent and imminent by some declaration of yours and raid of my body so that the last part of my life is rife with strife fighting to wrestle control away from you.

I see fear as wrapped up in your presence in me. Not fear for myself but for my family, who must deal with my trouble as well as the challenges thrown at them by life in a coronavirus-sick society. You are right to say that fear accompanies doubt and the two generate anxiety in my writing and act as prerequisites for my writing life. You are right to see fear as multifaceted, and as a force that influences all aspects of me. You are wrong to think that I do not see a ruse on your part to distract me from the real fight at hand, and that is a multidirectional approach on my part to your multiple moves on me. My flexible thinking tells me that I should see your talk about fear as something that is separate from your desire to allow fear to run rampant in me. That you achieve this illusion by having me focus exclusively on you as somehow a local entity in my prostate. Against this view is the fact that you may have spread to my lymph nodes and one of your disguises is that you wage war on my psyche by taking the shape of all my fears about you and about my end.

I do make a distinction. Not between fear and my cancer. Those are one and the same thing in multiple disguises. I begin to distinguish the many faces of fear presented by cancer from the fear in my writing that encourages me to be brave and continue to write. Similarly, I begin to understand that the fear of my dreams keeps me dreaming big in order to face down failure. Not to be perfect, since I grant that perfection is not possible in a compromised body. I embrace Beckett's dictum of repeated attempts at art as diminishing results for failure, that somehow the next time is a more spectacular run at failure and as a consequence a bigger haul for art as a success. In other words my temporal body makes failure concomitant with any artistic enterprise. My sole option is to remember the last failure so that I can reduce its presence in my next attempt at art.

Cancer, your success depends on my surrender to my fears, the ones sent by you to scout my body, mind, heart, soul, and spirit. You name those parts of me as if you cared about what parts compose my being. All you care about is your success in running us both over the cliff and ending life early. Your thrill is in an early death. That is your reward. It is nihilism. And I do not embrace it. I prefer to fight you to the end rather than accept you as my end. I want to fail in my fight against you rather than surrender to the fact of you in my life as a condition for my continued life brought to an early end by you.

Your gift to me is that I assign added value to a life already made valuable by my art and family and friends. With you in my life I know that I have to put up a fight for all those things that I hold dear. Not to fight you would be mad of me. A white flag held to fear and to you. I would rather succumb to Dylan Thomas's rage than accept your offer of a song and dance. What kind of dance would that be? With me standing on your feet as you waltz. With your sole voice singing and filling my head and heart with lead. No thanks. The fight is on in a war declared by you on my body. You have my attention. Your fear, which you send around me and ahead of your march in my body, that too has my attention. I can multitask.

I can write in columns and read down each one and then across them for their many meanings. Can you? Are you able to mount your attack of me across multiple fronts, and by that I mean not just as fear, and some loathing on my part of the feeling that comes with fear, but by dodging all the meds and positive thinking that direct my strategy against you? I doubt it. I believe in my victory and that belief fuels my fight against your presence in me. I separate the doubt that I need to participate in art from the doubt that you bring that I might not be cured of you. I understand both shapes taken by doubt. I invite one into my life and I block the other from my mind. I do both. And then some.

I would rather face you and spend the rest of my time engaged in that battle than accept you as my inevitable end and finish my days in a state of surrender. That would make my days unworthy of my presence in them. That would sell my art to the highest bidder, you, my abhorrent cancer. That route engenders madness. Give me cunning, resistance, and invention any day. Against cancer; for life. Against, fear of cancer. For, doubt in my art. Against, lying down in the face of overwhelming odds presented by cancer. For, a last and valiant stand. That is my song. There is my dance. I do not need a conductor or orchestra. The music is wired to my nerves and written in my blood.

If you doubt me, cancer, look at the road ahead for the two of us. What do you see? Every troop I can muster on my side rallied against you. Every particle of my being primed for a fight to the end. All of me on my side and not one cell in my body lulled by your discordant music into accepting its lot as somehow doomed. The road for you is full of traps, attacks, and my music blasted at you night and day. I dream in this sound that I send out against you. My music is in all the colors of a rainbow and in all the light sent through a prism to make colors so far not defined on a spectrum and quite possibly unseen by your defenses.

That is the nature of my fight and my resistance of you. We can converse all you like, friend. Friend, I do not think so. You are my mortal enemy. I combat you for the remaining time of my life to be unblemished by you, not curtailed by you. I see the limit of my body and think beyond it to a launch of my spirit to some other manifestation not perceived by this body. That the temple for my being is my body doesn't mean that I can't reside outside that temple in some fashion that I can't comprehend from inside the temple. It means that I struggle to pin it down because of the limited view of my location in my body.

I have to conclude that if I can think the noun *spirit*, then there must be some truth to it even if I can't explain the idea of the spirit to any degree of satisfaction. I believe. In love. In my ability to see the error of my ways and to adjust accordingly. To concede that to pit myself against the disease is to accept a binary of my relationship to it rather than the multiplicity of relations based on modes of comprehension, of the disease as a biological fact with physiological and psychological ramifications for me. Not a battle, or a win-or-lose situation, more long-term control of the virulence of the disease and my ability to live with it, not die from it. A rejection too of the binary of a dialogue between the disease and me, when in reality a lot of systems inside and outside me are ranged against the disease. I mean with you, cancer, insofar as you affect my days. As you seek to draw me into a warlike view of my relationship to disease—that I should surrender to you—and not the symbiotic and all-systems-on-board view of my movement with the disease as a way to reduce its control of me.

To escape all those given binaries—it's dialectical, to say the least—it is important for me to acknowledge the temptation of embracing those views in the belief that I can triumph against cancer on terms dictated by the disease. I know this cannot be the case. I understand that my body is henceforth afflicted by disease. In my medical history and in the threat that if it does not claim me wholesale it certainly may never leave my side. That disease inflects all my actions with fear and loathing. Makes everything I do in favor of or against the interest of my cancer. There is a flow of understanding and harmony in my actions that seeks to live with the fact of cancer. I do not wish to be consumed by a war with something that wins anyway, that will die with me and that is limited by the limits of my body. Cancer cannot surf away from my body the way COVID-19 is able to fly around the globe and alight wherever it pleases. Inasmuch as cancer depends on my well-being for its amplitude, I embody the parameters of its influence. When I die, cancer dies too. As long as I thrive, cancer runs amok in me. Unless treatments succeed, in which case, the cancer withers away.

This means I must accept the rhythm of cancer in my life and keep company with something that I wish to limit in my company: walk a path potholed with disease that influences my navigation along that path. I see those potholes. I drive around them or walk around them and face oncoming traffic directly in my path that also navigates around holes in its path. We race at each other and know when to veer out of the way to avoid a collision. This is my request for eyes in the back of my head to supplement my sight, for intuition and hunch to come to my aid and keep me afloat and on the move, to fight for me on one of the many fronts that I face as I embrace the disease.

Perhaps there is an element of a dance to the relationship. Rather than the disease carrying me on its feet, a diminutive version of me, childlike, ferried around by a parent in charge of the choreography, I invoke a dance in which the tune directs the two of us. That tune is composed in my breath, my walk, talk, and thought. That music plays on the xylophone of my ribs and spine. It rings in my inner ear just out of my register of it as a sound. One of those frequencies my teenage children can hear and my wife and I cannot. It drives my blood around my body. I feel it dappled on the pebbly bones in my wrist and ankle. It rotates my fulcrum at shoulder, elbow, knees, finger joints, head, and neck. There it is once more in my double take of a flash of hummingbird across the backyard.

I should call out the names of those accomplices without whose aid I would not be in a position to match up with my disease. My army of invisible helpers: the intuitive and the invisible force fields around my body that insinuate their mischievous ways into my eyes and every other sense, that inform too a sixth sense. I name them not to shame them or blame them for my failings. I call their names as a mantra to smooth those spikes in my mind and on my spine. And they play for me. Gather their orchestras for me. Tune up and strike out for me. And fill my life with their music.

The numinous defies regulation. All categories work against its discovery. It enters life where there is no obvious opening or even a subtle aperture. The temporary room offered by a bud when it blooms into a rose. Yet this thing with so many names and faces soaks into my skin. It sits on the corner of the eyes. It is there when I sense something just out of sight and I turn my head to catch a glimpse of the unnamable. There it is again in a thought that I started and could not finish, because that thought switched from reason to emotion and back again. And so it opens a gap and invites me to fill that gap if I dare.

With a hop, skip, and jump into the gap I launch a bridging imagined thought, the thing most likely to follow from where I stand and take me to where I wish to be (that could be an image, phrase, short poem, paragraph, story, essay, run of dialogue, or combination of these, variations). The thing that surprises more than anything, that may not be practical. There is no automatic beauty to it, though there may be much elegance to how it looks and sounds and chimes on the heart, nerves, and lungs. There might be puzzlement at the end of reading, hearing, seeing, or feeling that bridging thought. So what? There is contradiction, of course; how can there not be contradiction after Whitman gave it style.

His sprawl. His grandiose, multitudinous, amoeba-like claims for his imagination. His arms-wide embrace of everything in the world because all those things reside in him. Whitman's thirst for life as an imperative for living. His multiple perspective, generated by his splintered sense of self. How he is receptive to difference on the basis that somewhere in him there is a compartment ready and willing to receive the thing that he does not know and wishes to become acquainted with. The many-roomed mansion of the curious heart with its endless capacity to accommodate new and strange things. That heart expands as it meets new stimuli and proves to be endlessly accommodating of the world.

And next to Whitman's sprawl, I keep Phillis Wheatley's compression of her history of her capture and sale (sail too) into a life of enslavement. "On Being Brought from Africa to America" (1773) enacts in eight lines what has taken two and a half centuries to comprehend.

ON BEING BROUGHT FROM AFRICA TO AMERICA

'Twas mercy brought me from my Pagan land,
Taught my benighted soul to understand
That there's a God, that there's a Saviour too:
Once I redemption neither sought nor knew.
Some view our sable race with scornful eye,
"Their colour is a diabolic die."
Remember, Christians, Negros, black as Cain,
May be refin'd, and join th' angelic train.

Her words travel from her cancerous time to my cancer. I join my carriage to Wheatley's propulsive engine for the help with history that she offers me. She invites me to employ her poetry's resources for my ends. To see Wheatley caparisoned in the cancer of her age, the system of enslaving Black bodies, and watch her mount a counteroffensive of compressed creative practice, sent ahead to my time, for me to continue to battle on her behalf, emboldens me in my calamity.

I want her artistic cunning in my life as I face my diagnosis and embrace treatment of it. Cancer wins if I die from it. If I die from something else, cancer loses. Cancer wins if I keep waking up early with worry about its progress. If I sleep through the night, cancer loses. There is a room reserved in me for the cancer and I wish to keep it there under lock and key. I do not want it to have the freedom of the house, to roam and vandalize things. I might even wish to spring-clean that room and evict cancer from it, throw cancer—since cancer floats—out the window and into the moat below. I take a baton offered to me through time by Wheatley. Where her poem ends, I imagine beginnings: the likely trajectory of her life before her capture, to celebrate her strengths and define the sustenance that I draw from her work.

The accordion of her words compresses a dictionary of feeling and supposition in just eight lines. My conjecture expands that instrument to the point of its fullest extension for help with my cure.

6

TO FALL, FALLING, AND NEVER LAND

Today I catch the spread of light across the east paving the way for a ripe sun to climb this ladder of clear blue. Though it is out there and far, far away (the second far doubles the distance and stretches the heart's elastic inclusiveness to the max), I manage to draw it into my body through my eyes, ears, mouth, nose, and the pores of my skin until that sun rises in me. The day starts in me and it is a good day. I incline my ear to the body for the slightest ping of any symptoms to do with the cancer, and I hear nothing, feel nothing, and think only of this sunrise extension of me, this shining thing. How to hold that feeling for the rest of my days? Yes, in part, to Pope's eternal sunshine of the spotless mind as a condition for conscious life from now to when I am laid low by time (not, I hope, by cancer). Not as forgetting to start over fresh, as if anyone can wipe the slate of memory clean, more as a pivot between the two as a way forward, inviting selective forgetting for the hopeful sun to germinate that space and repair whatever damage lingers in that spot. With cancer as my focal point, as the damage in me that needs to be repaired. With repair as an endless process, of flux, each new stimulus drawn from my sense of history and from autobiography.

My disease depends on fixity. Cancer wants me to sit and be still and let it run rampant in me. Imagine me reclined. See the cancer pick up speed in exact proportion to my passivity. The more static I become, the more momentum cancer gains. This is not stillness as contemplation. This is inert and passive surrender that operates on physical and mental planes. In a conversation between Derek Walcott and Seamus Heaney at a writers' conference in 2012, Derek made the case for the writer who needs solitude, stillness, and quiet to help bring about a readiness in the poet for poems to arrive or emerge. He called for a stillness and quietude of the mind as much as the body and its surroundings. As Derek made his case I saw Seamus lean forward a little. The moment Derek ended his convincing argument for this ideal environment that brings about poetry, that constructs an ideal place and opens up a coveted space for the reception of poetry, Heaney lifted a hand with a pointed index finger and blurted out, "Ah, but we dwell in clamor."

Of course, both conditions obtain for poetry. The clamor of the world, that is outside and inside, needs to be quelled sometimes for poetry to breathe and be and cannot be evaded so much as brought on board by poetry. We need both, and. The *and* part of the equation is that which cannot be described adequately, which the mind and heart sense intuitively as present alongside clamor and contemplative stillness. *And* suggests something unending, that is always being made and remade, something that can be grasped partially, and so the poet must try for it. Such a stance is not conclusive. It invites perpetual rehearsal (Wilson Harris's term). The unfinished business of poetry. Poetry's endless flux. The tilt of the poet as a permanent reach and gesture, slightly off balance always, and always that necessary feel of being about to fall in order to recover only to feel that tilt once more.

To fall, falling and never land. Fly with no end to that flight. No windmill of arms, no flare of legs. A crawl, as if to take on board the velocity of flight. Hip dip, shoulder duck, head bob and weave, foot stomp, as hands carve the air. Move yourself. Hear this dub beat out of 1970-something. Dark room, ganja smoke–filled vibes stacked with bass boxes from floor to ceiling. Mr. Operator, please do not stop the rhythm. Not unless you want a riot from the crowd strapped to that sound and linked to the ground.

The 45 with a doughnut hole on the turntable. Spin it. Inhale. How long did it take to get to this place? Our generation wanted more, always more, which amounted to wanting nothing to do with a system that wanted nothing from them, except their Black sweat and blood. Rock on. Against racism. Against sexism. Against homophobia. Against poverty, police brutality, the prison system, nuclear weapons, and any other schism that happened to rear its mean, little, institutionalized head.

Echo chamber of the sound system mimics the pump of blood around the walls of the heart where blood picks up speed for its current around the body. Blood beat. Linton Kwesi Johnson (LKJ), step forward. Dub, bass, and rhythm guitar twang, measure this salt-and-pepper tongue-lashing of the system. Skin drawn over the drum of a skeleton that moves to the beat. Is there cure in this? How can there not be some salve for the soul in this monument of skin peppered with a history of the transatlantic slave trade, so that the bow in the sea and sway of the ship gel with the rhythm of the pulse? Atlantic in my blood even if I did not bathe in salt water. King Tubby, Tapper Zukie, and LKJ's scatta-matta.

Help me with this mantra for my cure of my cancer. That may or may not be the best cure for my disease. If what I have may find a path through me to end both of us. Turn left and you bump into my writing hand. Turn right and you meet my echo above my head and underfoot. Hum breath. Fill those pockets under my arms. Lift me off my feet. I hum in breath and tongue to drive back the thing in me that is a part of me only insofar as I let it become me. No amount of wise words will suffice for this journey. What is the technique behind the niche that I must take to another level?

It is the beat. Drum. Bass. Reverberations. Delay. Stir a bit of rhythm in the pot. Pepper it. Echo. Move with the Operator, that mixology for a palette strung by ear and heart. Birth of the B-side generation. Version excursion. Show me my cure. I am ready, or not, as the case may be for me. Studio bells toll. Not for me. For my disease. Herald its end in me. Not my ending thanks to it.

What is my thumbprint if I hold this raw ragamuffin pulse to my ear? I was there back then in the mid- to late seventies and into the militant eighties in London, and I carry the snow water of all of it in the breadbasket of my brain stem. I hop on the bus heading for a destination not on any map. How time flies without my clocking it. What is that Marx Brothers maxim—time flies like an arrow; fruit flies like a banana? Before I know where I am, or who, for that matter, I catch sight of gray hair on my head as I brush past a hallway mirror, gray that sprouted seemingly overnight.

Digital dub takes the baton from reels of tape. Composed in my youth by that sound, in my twilight years I decompose to it. How did Derek Walcott phrase it in his calypso riff "Spoiler's Return"? "Tell desperados when you reach the hill / I decompose but I composing still." Or so I thought until the arrival on my radar of this disease. Sit me between walls of speakers and allow the bass to drive disease from me. See how my clothes tremble. That is the work of air displaced by the speakers that shimmers the flesh beneath my cotton socks. Bass, shake my fillings, still the tremor in my hands and the twitch of my feet.

My world, inundated by a vast wash of morning light, stirs, so that a steady wave begins in the east from an opened sky, last night's aperture birthing a sun. Stand up in this vaulted sky and mind you do not bump your head on the ceiling. That recedes, recedes to hands that pull, draw in, and gather the wide span and haul of a net cast by a strong arm to catch us all in it. We are a silver catch that net releases onto a beach where we jump and flick light off our scales. We are afloat as dust in a sunbeam that falls slant across the room. (By *we*, I mean my disease and my engagement with it.) In that lime-green flock of parakeets swerving over the skinny palms of Mid-City LA. They pull a veritable market of noise in their wake.

I convert the currency of my recognition of my cancer from negative to positive, from a thing that worries me to something noteworthy and in need of a solution. I address the disease and it addresses me. I call and it responds, or I respond to its call on and in me. If the disease is my enemy, it is my friend too; if it wishes to destroy me, it seeks to help me to live a better life. My cancer reminds me of that stained-glass panel in Durham Cathedral that says TROUBLED BUT NOT DISTRESSED. While troubled by my cancer, provoked by its machinations in my body, I refuse to be distressed by it, become its victim.

The cathedral is my body. I invited cancer into it. The disease worships as it sees fit. I conduct a ceremony to quell and steer that behavior toward terms that preserve rather than destroy the cathedral. It scares me that we share the same space. As sun and moon share sky, so my cancer shares my body with me. It is not a question of proportion. There is no balance to be struck with cancer, no bargaining with this devil. Any amount of cancer is too much for my body. My conversation with my cancer is to persuade it to desert the space that it occupies, since it has compromised the entire organism. There is no switch of roles in which each may take a turn to lead and follow.

* * *

The novel coronavirus shutters the city. Civic and work life grind to a standstill. Traffic becomes sparse and the shelves of the supermarkets empty like a shebeen raided by police. Birdsong replaces the usual traffic hum of the city. Light falls unimpeded by what the city sends up into the atmosphere so that the air itself feels lighter, though I may be giddy from the exigencies of the emergency. This adds a new clause to the things that I have to worry about. My doctor's office is not handling calls and my emails to him remain unanswered. I see this halt in the affairs of state as a reflection of the disease being granted carte blanche. While the disease earns a green light for its progress in me, I receive a red one in my quest for a cure. Cancer gallops around my body while I sit on my hands and wait for help to deal with it. I am among the compromised bodies in a stricken city that cannot afford to host another malady.

The last straw may be my despair, my propensity to ruminate on my last days as full of pain and an early end to my life. It saps my energy. I move about the house like a sloth. I don't want to wash and shave. Despair that proves to be an art form for some people vandalizes my imagination. I cannot write, cannot think outside cancer and its bad outcomes. Despair takes over my life. I prefer a pinch of the bleak for this house of my body, rather than painting my house black, from pillar to post, and closing the blackout curtains.

I want to spin bleakness out of its concentric vortex and into the widening ripples of light, of hope and purpose for consciousness. Spin it into the light of my childhood in Airy Hall, a village about forty miles outside Guyana's capital, Georgetown. Back then and in that place we skipped stones to see who could make the most skips before the stone sank out of sight. We loaded the smoothest, flattest stone we could sort that lay near the lake, and gripped it near the edge of our palm close to thumb, index, and middle fingers and tensed our shoulder and leaned low and fired that stone at the flat face of water. Those skips happened fast and you had to focus to get the correct count. We whooped and flicked our index fingers against our pressed middle finger and thumb. We slapped our thighs or high-fived with the champion stone flicker, searched for more flat stones and tried another round to beat that high score.

As the stone skipped, ripples sprang up and widened and grew less and less on the surface of the lake until they sank back into the water. The lake absorbed our energies. Those stones stopped skipping on the surface and dived out of sight to the bottom of the lake and added to the lake bed whatever life was taken from the lakeshore. If we thought back then that the stones would just as well pile up on the bottom of the lake as languish on the shore, that our skipping of them meant nothing but an interruption of such kept and adhered-to positions, we might have missed out on a laugh and the exhilaration of a shared phenomenon: the best stone sorted from the pile, the close study as that stone's life blazed a trail across the lake, and the moment when it vanished from us after opening this unbridgeable gap of skips between it and us. The warmth in our activated shoulders radiated to our animated spirits. Our eyes met in confirmation of this life and as we tried once more to outdo our last best effort.

*   *   *

Things start to go wrong when around mid-March I can't seem to put a foot right. I become jittery, infused with the tremors of the drugs' side effects. Not fear. Just feeling off, thanks to my biorhythms, or horoscope, or some juju of pins stuck in my effigy by my enemy, make that plural, enemies, on three continents if my paranoia serves me justly, and if I fall in with this run of things going wrong, or slightly off kilter in a tilt of the field of sorts for me, so that my aim and gestures miss their target by a centimeter, and so I may as well have not taken aim in the first place, which leads to mounting bad feeling in me and short temper in my dealings with others in the house, who seem to move in slow motion and do not hear me when I speak, and if they hear they misunderstand, and that just adds to my frustration with them, and my feeling that I am disconnected from everyone all the time, and in need of more than language to help me correct my course, which has veered too far off the path for me to even think that I can resume the journey, or take it up where I left off, as if my life is a lost and found of aspects of my fortune waiting for me to collect them, parked as they are in some legitimate space, or place, for just an eventuality as this one, of me waking on the wrong side of the bed or getting out of it and leaving the best of me asleep and so my day starts without me in it, and I move out of sync with everything around me and all that grows in me is this frustration that I cannot defuse or reduce or escape.

This is where a cuss or two might be cathartic for me and reset my day and recalibrate my discord. I think this surge of bad feeling feeds my cancer, adds to its delight in me. The more I act out of anger or frustration, the more of that ill persona I assume. Whoever I might be is sidelined. I can feel the bunched muscles in my shoulders at the base of my neck, both sides aching now and knotted, pulling my shoulders up around my ears, and hunching my back. I lean into my misconception of everything and increase the likelihood of more mishaps coming my way by my obvious show that I am primed to receive such negative messages. I want to take on Caliban's aspect of using language for one thing alone, though with a gift for more than cursing, as his dream speech proves.

With Caliban's crude tongue, given its vituperative might, I too can cast spells, the way he spits insults in a stream of frogspawn akin to a witches' brew. I reserve his poetry for another occasion. For now I launch his tongue to drive back the bile of the air, the furniture and people as they all conspire to add to my knotted shoulders and hunched back. All such poisons internalized by me and made so private that they aren't even dependent on the external factors of air, people, and furniture clipping my knees as I sweep past. To set them off in me, they just need me.

I conjure the Caliban of my imagination rather than the creature from Shakespeare's *Tempest*. A Caliban of the mind, part invention, part resurrection, to drive back the bogies of my mind. A creature modeled, in part, after Aimé Césaire's rendition of the colonized being. Césaire's image is of beast of nature vested in ecology. His monster's persona operates as a necessary corrective to our mechanized ways. So I greet it, rather than shun it, or act as if I'm afraid. I say, Come here, wild thing. Come to me. I need you on my side to feel I am doing my best to resist cancer. An untamed beast like you inside me registers my condition of rugged resistance.

Where are you now, ghouls? I am close to being prepared to engage in combat with you. Cancer's troops: You flew in the air around my head and climbed in my spinal column. If I live long enough you will lose interest in me or you will all be dead. If I do not grant you room in my heart and head, you might wither away like the capitalist state as decreed by Marx (Karl). How long must I wait? I am not that patient. Able to remain focused and grow a beard as I wait for an outcome that I know must arrive at some point. All I have to do is wait and learn how to practice waiting as a craft and an art. That place where the sensibility is stationed for a long time and is vigilant. To wait with interest, with waiting as an activity in itself.

Hot flash again. Unheralded, unwelcomed, and out of my control. I cringe as it opens my pores and holds this flamethrower close to my skin. I grit my teeth and wait. This too will pass. There is no pattern to how it claims my body. Just the claim launched at irregular intervals of no algorithm except the fact that it recurs and wakes me when it happens at least three times in the night and hourly in the day. As my cancer proliferates and sends me yet another iteration of itself as a mean ghost and shape-shifter, I summon the creatures of my culture and education.

In addition to Caliban, I call on the being who birthed him, his mother, Sycorax. Her spells bring that coveted nothingness waiting for us at death, that no-place where we send our thoughts when those thoughts grow tired of their ties to history and biography. We send them in spells of our own, songs we identify with and dances we see our bodies performing even if we have two left feet. It's a place not found on any map, where poetry pools its moments from history and myth and politics and sex and gender. Where each spirit bides its time, having walked away from the skin, and parted company with the sex of history and politics. To dance and parade in this communal and no-gravity carnival space of nothingness. Of being disembodied, a spiritual reliquary.

*   *   *

The second time my daughter cried over my pitiable cancer condition I remember thinking that this should not be happening again because of me. I was supposed to be in control of all this. Yet it did. We were driving back from the end of her school day, just before the imposition of citywide COVID-19 restrictions. I met her and she was in a funk. She said she had a terrible day. That she heard such and such a friend say something about such and such a person and that she laughed and word got back to the person about whom the remark was made and that person was pissed and others were pissed on her behalf and she, my daughter, was in big doo-doo (her word).

Soon her phone rang. And it was the very person against whom the cruel thing had been said by someone else in the presence of my daughter. My daughter had the call on speakerphone, as befits her generation for whom the most private exchanges transpire in public places. The girl's tone was that of a headmistress. My daughter was conciliatory, apologetic, and confessed to all manner of sins against others going back to kindergarten. The girl intensified her tone of upset, anger, and superiority against my daughter, and said that my daughter had done *a bad thing and a cruel thing* and that my daughter should think before she laughed at anyone in the future and that there would be consequences for my daughter's laughter. I made repeated slashing-of-my-throat gestures to my daughter to get her off the phone and away from a conversation that sounded like false piety at my daughter's expense. My daughter ignored me and when she did hang up after more exculpatory remonstrance, she burst into tears. She said that it was all her fault. I said it was the fault of the person who made the cruel remark in the first place and where was she in the whole conversation, why was she not the one under the microscope (more like turning on a spit)? And why apologize so much for something that might be a natural reaction? And why volunteer new information about yourself that has nothing to do with the current controversy? My daughter renewed her tears. She said my sickness, my cancer, had made her edgy and vulnerable and unable to think. That my being ill was the most worrying thing to her and that she could not function properly. I said to her that her reaction was perfectly normal if the remark was funny and that the person who made the remark was the one who should be catching umbrage, not her, my daughter. I said that the person who told the girl about the incident, about what was said and by whom and who laughed at it, that person was not a kind person for making that report to the girl. Why was the girl not mad with the person who told her about it or the person who said it in the first place? My daughter cried harder and repeated that my illness had made her react uncharacteristically (her word). It was back to my cancer and me. We were the real stars in this middle school drama. Well, hello, cancer, another fine mess . . . But wait, I said to my daughter, as she cried. My cancer has nothing to do with it. My cancer is not the one who made the remark or the one who, in a normal reaction, laughed. My cancer did not run to the girl and tell her chapter and verse about the incident. Keep my cancer out of it. That is my business. Our family business, no less. I was mad. Did not see red, exactly, but definitely heated up at the prospect that my cancer could be the fall guy in my daughter's school melodrama. I had to defend my cancer. I could not sit idly by and watch my cancer's good name being maligned. I said that what made my daughter say too much and give too much airtime to that manipulative bitch (my word) was my daughter's guilt that she was wrong to laugh at the remark rather than have the wherewithal to say to the cruel tongue of the utterer that to say such a thing was unkind (the remark concerned the girl's overweight). My daughter said through her tears that I didn't know how hard it was for her to live with her father dying of cancer. That I was too wrapped up in it to see her pain over it. That she was a child who had to process my bad news and I should remember that. I relented right away. I apologized for being hard with her. I said, of course the cancer is a beast to contend with for all of us in the house, not just for me and doubly so for a young mind, a daughter afraid that she might lose her father. I said that I was mad for her, not at her. Mad that the girl could call and extract such a confession from my daughter for doing nothing except react to something that was probably funny (though admittedly unkind). I added that the remark was made away from the girl, and the person who reported it to her was not a good person but mischievous. I told my daughter to put the whole thing behind her—it was a ruse. I apologized for causing her so much worry. I assured her that the cancer would not win, not if I had anything to do with it. I offered her my handkerchief from the top pocket of my jacket. She snorted into it and by the time we reached home she had regained her composure. She offered my hanky back. It was not as soiled as the last one from the previous incident. I told her to keep it for next time. We exchanged I-love-yous and went into the house, where the whole thing was recapped for her mother.

My wife said, It is fine to worry about your father's cancer. It is a worry. But do not use it to cover what you do if you feel embarrassed about your actions. That is not cool. What you did by laughing at a remark may have been unthinking but it is not a capital offense. You may have been embarrassed and so laughed when you really wanted to stop the speaker in her tracks and tell her what she was saying was not kind. That is a matter of reflection miles after the event. The point is, while your father's cancer is upsetting it's not the reason why you are so upset by that girl's blaming of you for laughing. The girl was attacking the wrong person. The speaker of the remark and the person who reported it to her are the ones at fault. Not you. I listened and nodded emphatically as my wife hit those salient points. All the while my daughter shook her head. Her conviction was clear. We hugged. It was over. I said I was not going to die from cancer. My daughter said she believed that too. I told her I loved her. She said the same. My wife chipped in with her declaration of love and with hugs. We had a group hug. It was love, love, love, and no room for anything malicious. Mr. C. had not won the day, this time. Had failed to wriggle his way into the middle of our family affairs. Though present in my family, he was not a prime mover in it, though a prime mover in me. Cancer, you should know that I have a drawer full of handkerchiefs and I can drive, listen to my daughter crying, and hear her complaints, all at the same time, without getting into an accident.

The next day I run with my daughter around the block in her practice to reduce her school track time. She runs for about one hundred yards, stops, walks for the next hundred and runs again. We do this for several laps of the block, heading counterclockwise around the houses so that we pass our house about four times. This adds up to a mile. During the walk phase I ask her how she feels about my illness. I say that I understand the strain that she's under thinking about me, whether I'll be around for her high school graduation, as well as worrying about her school grades. She is a straight-A student who worries about every project and test. She says that she thinks a lot about my having cancer. I tell her to remember that I'm in good hands with UCLA's treatment plan for me, and that I want to beat this thing and believe that I can and the best thing she can do to help me in my fight is continue to thrive in her schoolwork. I tell her she's doing so much that makes me proud—her excellent grades and her healthy handling of her peers, to name two. I don't say that I mean by that that she's open to exploitation of her feelings by the more Machiavellian of her peers. I just tell her to watch out for those types. I have to explain Machiavelli to her. I say he was a bastard manipulator who didn't have a good bone in his body and who did everything to fuck up others and shore up his position. We move on. To fears that can blow things up out of all proportion to the situation; to cancer as that fearful thing for being unknown. I boast a bit when I say that cancer couldn't have happened to a stronger person in our house. I exercise, don't smoke, hardly drink, write in ways that promote imaginative strategies for problem solving and have more to lose as a father and husband, and more to defend. I tell her that her mother and brothers and her provide a huge boost to me in my fight with cancer. She is sweaty so we hold hands for a few steps and she resumes her run with me keeping pace beside her and watching out for the death trap of the sloped and cracked sidewalks.

A week later my surgeon calls to say that the tests all point to a need for him to operate on me and remove the cancer, as a matter of some urgency. I want to press him on how urgent a matter. Instead I ask him how this will work with COVID-19 restrictions. He tells me that he will make the case for my surgery as an emergency rather than routine or elective. I take him to mean that my cancer is virulent and not decorative in me. A heat flash takes over my body. I break into a cold sweat and do all I can to say goodbye and I look forward to his next call about a date for the surgery. I hang up and the phone shakes in my hands.

Where is Anansi when I need him? In one story that fits my situation, Anansi plays a trick on his family even as he feeds them and shows he cares about them. I heard the story from my grandmother in the countryside of Guyana, where I spent my childhood. I could not have been more than six or seven years old. It stayed with me through the years because I pitched my absent father in the role of Anansi. As I grew up in London and in my adult years there and in the States, there were many instances when I felt I needed Anansi's guile in order to survive a situation. It was hardly a matter of life or death. It turned out on reflection to be more a matter of pride and to deflect a degree of shame. I exhume the Anansi story with my father tagged to it for the simple reason that the story served with each telling, one piece at a time, nudge by nudge, to wake up the cancer biding its time in the waiting room of my body.

The Anansi story went something like this. On a day full of birdsong and brash orchestration of morning light, Anansi left home in search of breakfast for his family of five. He could see the bunk beds in two rooms where his oldest boy and youngest boy slept and where his second-born daughter and third born dreamed the flavored dreams of the young with no inclination to ever grow old. In the third room he left his wife, an act of scooting away from the spoon of his embrace of her, more a folding of his many limbs around her already folded many limbs to form a relaxed coxcomb or the crown of a peacock at rest. He scrambled toward the heavily fortified banana plantation.

He wiped the cobwebs from his eyes, real cobwebs since he

really was a spider. The next minutes needed his full concentration and all hands of his spider sense on deck. There were dogs and barbed wire and an electric fence to negotiate before he reached the heavily ripe banana trees, and to renegotiate on his way out of there. There was the temptation of bearing so much fruit and not sampling any of it—against his better nature of selfishness, of always serving himself first and leaving crumbs for others who depended on him—so that the fight against that urge took up the lion's share of his spider sixth sense while he battled the plantation's defenses with the remainder. His fight never amounted to a battle in the strict sense of that term. It was much more a game of wits. His limbs though numerous were flimsy. His body though wily lacked any ability to absorb a direct blow from an assailant. But his wits, well, had there been in existence a device to measure them, that reading would have been off the charts.

Anansi sniffed the fruit and held the bunch close to his face with his head inclined toward it as he scrambled out of reach of the leap and snapping jaws of the three Dobermans. He treated the barbed wire as if it were a multidimensional and multidirectional limbo dance, an almost dislocation of his limbs to stretch and sidle, crouch and tiptoe through a maze of wire, the escape route discernible only by his spider sense. As for the electric fence, he heard the hum and closed his eyes to vault it. Anansi leapt with the stolen fruit cradled against his chin for that exhilarating smell. His technique matched the Fosbury flop of an Olympic high jumper. He curled his back over the barrier at such close proximity to the live wire that the fine hairs on his bottom sprung upright as they almost grazed that electric field.

I pause here to illustrate one instance in which Anansi saved my life. Back in my teens I rode an open-backed bus that allowed passengers to board and alight from the bus without having to wait on a door to open or close. In the winters of London this resulted in people sitting as far away from that rear entry as possible by heading to the front of the bus or climbing the stairs to the top deck. On warm nights it was common to hold on to the bar on the landing of that exit and bask in the breeze as the bus sailed from one stop to the next. I would arrive at the exit early and hold on and close my eyes and measure by the force of the wind how the bus slowed as it approached the bus stop halfway down Blackheath Hill in South London.

On one such evening I made ready to disembark. I opened my eyes in time to hop off the platform just as the bus lined up for the bus stop, about ten yards from it, at a speed of about ten miles an hour. The drop to the road required a slight lean back on the heels and a slight bend to my legs, as rapid steps were needed to halt the forward momentum of landing on the move. All I had to do was glance down and hop off and complete the short run and brake to a casual walk away. That night my vibrations were not aligned with the city's waves of movement and stasis, red light and green with a flash of amber in between, horns and engines and the odd shout of a greeting, call, or curse. I moved out of sync.

I landed on Blackheath Hill's steep gradient with too much of my weight on the front of my leading left foot and I stumbled and toppled forward. This fall at ten miles an hour would mean landing flat on the face. Such a fall can be nasty even for an agile teenager. Something in me felt the jolt of my foot on the road and the pitch forward of my torso. And something in me kicked into action at that very moment. It happened in slow motion outside the time governing the moment. I heard my grandmother talking to a group of us children about Anansi's switch in times of crisis from his human form to his spider incarnation, that he transformed faster than the blink of an eye. I heard her talk not as a strung-out sentence ruled by her breathing but outside linear time as an instantaneous, complete comprehension that flooded my reaction to the sensation of falling. I became Anansi. I altered, from a teenager falling after disembarking too early from a moving bus, to a fully fledged spider with eight legs that kept it stable no matter what the momentum or angle of the drop from one surface to the next. I landed as a person and rolled like a spider and bounced back onto my feet and walked away with barely a shake of my head.

Anansi scrambled away from the dogs barking on the other side of the electric fence and away from the plantation. He sniffed the hand of bananas and glanced at it. The yellow and green skin, the curved shapes joined at the head to form a bunch, the way those bodies tapered off to pointed loose ends of individual fruit. Anansi's mouth watered. Which leg or two or three to steady the banana and which to tug at the top of the fruit to loosen first one strand of skin then another and another until the fruit stood bare chested or lower still, naked to the navel, a bit more than half of it exposed, the torn strips craned backward and elastic in their patterned fall. More saliva flooded his mouth. He had to swallow. He laughed out loud and picked up the pace of his scamper and swung back to his home and his family.

Anansify my life. Unleash those shape-shifting gifts. If wit, trickery, mind and body morphing are called for, so be it. I am that spider from my childhood. The spider whose story survived the Middle Passage and three hundred years of plantation slavery in the New World to a second-floor verandah in Guyana where a grandmother tells a gaggle of her grandchildren about an Anansi that befits her countryside life.

Un-Anansi my cancer. Let me match the dexterity of my foe with this West African myth and legend and telltale tall tale, made taller still by evenings lit by a gas lamp on a sheltered porch. Though tripped by that cancer, that I may fall and land in a many-limbed and limber roll of recovery. And resume my stride, my rock and roll, twist and turn and shout, whistle and chant, through the best that is the rest of my days.

Anansi ducks to avoid the top half and walks through the bottom half of two half doors at the back of the house. He walks into his kitchen to find his four children and his partner, their mother, waiting at the breakfast table for him. They look at him and smile and keep that smile as they move their collective gaze to the bundle that he cradles in his left hand. Can they smell fruit as they remember that smell to be or as a result of the roomed-in and still air? Their mouths water. Anansi smiles and sits at the one chair empty for him, the one nearest the back door.

At that moment Anansi computes the error that he failed to see during his quest for a meal for his family. Even as he shifts the hand of bananas and he parts company with it, his shoulders drop and all his limbs lower to his side. He slumps in his seat. His youngest boy takes one from the bunch and passes it to the youngest daughter second. She takes one and passes the remainder to the next in line in terms of age, the second daughter, older than the first by exactly the wink of an eye that it takes a child to break free of its gestation in an egg. She takes her share of one banana and she hands the last two to the eldest, who passes the last banana to his mother.

At each juncture each child follows the action of the last and the next in line and counts down the hand from five to four to three to two and to one and none left for their father. None left for the person who made it all possible and who should have known better than to return with this dilemma. He is Anansi. The greatest trickster of all. The father purported to persuade a dog to offer up a last juicy bone, a squirrel to sacrifice its last saved nut, a mosquito to withhold its primed proboscis from the warmth of a limb. Anansi the spider.

Seated at the head of the table with an empty plate and his family, plates full, ready to eat, Anansi looks forlorn. His wife says, Take half of mine, dear. Anansi holds up one limb as if to halt his partner. She stops and looks at him with knitted brows in her attempt to work out just what new trick her husband may be up to now. Into that gap jumps the youngest. He looks at his father and takes a knife and cuts off a third of his banana and places it on his father's empty plate. The other children do not pause. (Anansi suppresses a glint in his eye. He pushes it to the corner of his eye and narrows his eyes a little to hide that glint.) They cut a third as well and pile it on Anansi's plate. His partner does the same.

Anansi's limbs shift from their folded and resigned pose to something of a spider about to pounce on a prey. His mouth turned down for that look of disappointment involuntarily springs up into a broad smile. His eyes water and his partner and children take it as his gratitude at their sacrifice on his behalf welling up inside of him.

Anansi adds up his one-third shares. For each member of his family's two-thirds portion, he has one whole banana and an extra third. He dives into his meal. His wife and eldest son exchange a glance, shake their heads, and start to eat. Anansi's wife looks at him, long and hard. She wants him to give back each of those pieces to his children, if not all of it then at least take that extra third and cut it into four and distribute it among the children. Anansi wants nothing to do with parity or the extraction of a life lesson for his children from a teaching moment. He raises his eyebrows, shrugs his shoulders, and eats.

Anansi, as a collective, amounts to the sum of his partner and their four offspring. His trick never ends. He plays it on himself and on his world. I extract from his story those nutrients my mind stands to benefit from the most. The family sups at a table laid on my body for me to look at in all the ways available to Anansi, his multiple limbs, his sixth sense, and his trickster mentality. I gain from that body, memory, and imagined affinity with a folktale and with my father and my mother (two spiders in my heredity). My body morphs into a communal body, never alone and always assisted by many helping hands. I travel through time and across continents for these benefits. I descend (after a tiptoe skip of a flat stone on the skin of water) like that stone, to the bottom of a lake, river, or sea for a similar lesson from history, from the land, sea, and air.

7

HELP ME, ANANSI

My surgeon calls me three days after his last call. This time I do not hear the phone. I play back his message three times: once for me, once for my wife, and a third time for my hard ears. He says he has a date of April 1 for him to operate on me but the novel coronavirus has halted everything. He says the equipment, a bed, ventilator, the staff, are all on reserve for the expected surge in demand for hospital rooms by those with COVID-19. My cancer is aggressive, he says, and he hopes to convince the hospital to grant me that date for my operation.

Things are bound to change in the three weeks before that operation, he says. COVID-19, which has locked down the city and freshened the air with the absence of cars, and turned up the volume of birds in exact ratio to the decline in traffic, dictates everyone's calendar. The doctor's message ends by saying that we should talk again in a week or so. I grip the phone and stand quite still for a long time. I conjure the peace and calm of light falling more freely in air less polluted, light that shines more brightly in that freshened air, so that leaves catch a breeze, and the skirt of a tree stitched out of those leaves is thrown up to reveal the white underside of leaves, or a run of that same light over water that becomes pleated with it. The image of washed air is from this moment, now; the idea of the skirt of trees is from back then, as a child. I roll the feelings linked to the two images into one entity with double the power, to help me now.

I stop seeing the operation as an emergency. I practice views of the operation as a thing I might postpone and schedule at my convenience. Rather than walk into a sick environment and subject my body to a debilitating operation and make myself vulnerable to catching a wildfire disease, I should place everything on hold. Forget the operation for the time being and spare myself the gamble of walking into a hospital where everyone is cheek by jowl with the incurable virus. Stay home as ordered by Los Angeles's mayor, and by the state governor, enjoy my confinement to my house, and persevere with the work of understanding my cancer and seeking out homeopathic ways to tackle it. The Caliban in me is quiet, no curses. I listen for what Anansi has to say.

Anansi includes his partner and their children. Mrs. Anansi showed reserve in her gaze directed at Anansi, and in her quiet. She could have challenged him and spoiled the meal with friction and the correction and diminution of the family's breadwinner that morning. She reminds me of Debbie. Debbie watched me over twenty-five years. She could have said a lot to me and taken us down a path of conflict and arguably my cowardly flight away from her truth telling. To keep me engaged with her and to bring me around to seeing the error of my ways she said a little and stared at me a lot. In her look I heard her protest. I took my time but I came around to a self-scrutiny that highlighted my faults and showed a path for repair and renewal. Debbie sat at the same table as me. She knew there would be other meals to sit through and more opportunities for me to act in a more selfless manner.

I cut the cord of our eldest son. I buried it under a tree at our house in Miami. Debbie labored for a day and a half, and we walked up and down stairs to accelerate the labor and bring about the birth of our son. We walked the child early in the morning to avoid the steaming sun of South Florida. We searched for a rhythm of life that honored the growth of our child. If there were a meal to divide I would eat last, after the baby and after Debbie, if called upon to do it. There was never such a demand made by our situation or one that Debbie would allow to come about. In that sense she prepared the environment for the meal long before my arrival at the table. She set that table for all of us. She called the children to take their seats, and she left a place for me as though she heard my arrival long before I announced myself.

As I ducked through those half doors—I mean by walking under the top half through the open bottom half door—I could see that I was not just Anansi, his understudy, but that all our children and Debbie combined operated as me, with me as their emissary and all of us combined as a way into this world, a way forward in it. Debbie's look sent volumes across so many tables to me for me to mull over and dream my way around. She waited for me to find my way back to her and our children. She made the table ready with our children and reserved my place on it. She must have seen me coming before she heard me bluster into the room.

Anansi condensed to a partner and four offspring is, in fact, a multitude. Imagine lifting a stone in a yard and a huge spider jumps out at you and on the ground one hundred baby spiders scatter from the light aimed at them as if that light poured from a garden hose. Two big spiders, Anansi and his partner. One hundred offspring. It's for them that Anansi goes foraging to the nearest plantation. Anansi is an adult, over six feet tall. He is a man in a spider body. The miracle is that he succeeds in escaping those Dobermans and the electric fence and barbed wire. Each limb carries an entire branch full of bananas. He throws them over the fence and leaps just in time to dodge the jaws of those Dobermans. You should see Anansi run with his body laden with bananas enough to feed one hundred baby spiders and his partner. It is to that table that Anansi returns and so his mathematics of recall of a part of his meal from each of his offspring and partner results in a feast for Anansi.

We splinter into our children. They grow into their own abilities independent of us. I know nothing of the hand that lifts the stone that we huddled under. One moment we sheltered under that stone, the next, light flooded our hiding place and we scattered to find another safe space. Since Anansi must leave to go about his trickery, it is to this community that Anansi returns laden with the fruit of his labor, fruit Anansi has to share in confirmation of his stature as master trickster and to affirm his unity with his progeny and partner, all splinters in this light refracted through a glass prism.

Anansi tricks his way across time, from my grandmother's time to mine. Her story about him takes on new shape in my life. He eats at his table in her story. But at my table set for him on my terms he sacrifices his bigger share that he won by a trick on his family for the fast that feeds him at a deeper level of satisfaction of seeing them eat after each gives up a portion of food to him, which he gallantly refuses to accept. He turns against his own trickster nature in his story as told by me in my time, and so proves his shape-shifting is not confined to his era or even to his body; instead, it is a function of telling his story then and now and again without end.

His eldest notices what has happened and puts it down to his father's mastery of the spider's sixth sense and trickster nature. His partner smiles at his change of heart, knowing all along that the gift of transformation was not confined to the physical plane but had a spiritual dimension to it as demonstrated by her husband in front of his children. She says she is full halfway through her meal and she covers her plate with a napkin and sets the remainder of her plate to one side of the kitchen counter. The children eat up and leave the room and she follows them. Anansi listens to make sure no one is near and that all the children and their mother are occupied and he sidles over to the covered plate and devours the banana, peel and all. Peel as well in the belief that all the goodness in the banana lies just on the inside of the skin. On that reasoning he eats the cast-off skins of all the children and his partner. He is full.

I am Anansi, both spider and man, able to change my shape and alter my mind. The cancer is a test of my wit as a trickster. Can I overcome the cancer or will it beat me? I see my quest as a hunt for a meal for my family. The banana plantation guarded by Dobermans and with a barbed wire and electric fence waits for me. My grandmother watches over me to see if I stick to the details of her story. My father parades as Anansi in the story that she tells. The entire scene unfolds in my body. Not just my grandmother's story but my update of it as well. Both Anansi stories, past and present, unfold simultaneously in me. I am a student hearing and seeing the two stories. I play all the parts in the two stories as they play out at the same time. I usurp the parts of my father and my mother. I extract valuable lessons from both. This is my challenge: I carry a disease, and in the shared space of my body I must make room to deploy a cure that preserves my life. Help me, Anansi. I carried you for five decades not knowing why I kept you in me. Now I ask that you carry me. Together we tell the story of Anansi, one for that past time and another for this time that I find myself in with the fight of my life. Trickster that I have become, two spiders in one, past and present incarnations in me, I feel ready to take on cancer.

Lewis Hyde sees this trickster as a universal figure and as a progenitor of worlds. He privileges story with more than knowing the world and gives it primacy as the world we know.* Hyde's Anansi is that conscious mind in the world. All things that we know about the world originate in the play of the story of the trickster figure, his twists and turns, his current nonbinary incarnations, his bend of gender and slice of it into a multiplicity. The presence of the trickster globally makes the local and the global aspects of the same thing seen in multiple ways. My grandmother's Anansi story that urges us to share and be grateful for what we are given is told on many platforms across the globe to the same global end, that the story organizes certain principles about growing up in the world in a way that makes those principles memorable and easy to transfer from storyteller to listener.

---

* Lewis Hyde, *Trickster Makes This World: Mischief, Myth, and Art* (New York: Farrar, Straus and Giroux, 1998).

And for the listener to become the teller of the tale to another
group of listeners in a chain that runs through time and across
cultures to cover the globe.

*   *   *

One side effect not seen as yet, though I keep a sharp eye out for
any traces of its beginnings, is that I may grow breasts. My wife
and daughter find this enormously funny, in an alarming kind of
way. I do too. I find it irksome and outright unsightly, at least on
my body. It is not the idea of breasts that appalls me, I quite like
the appendages in women—they are erogenous to me. What irks
me is that the drugs aimed at a specific intervention can be just
as proficient in bringing about an undesired action in my body. I
do not want breasts, thank you very much, I want a cure for this
cancer of mine that threatens my life and curtails my days and
nights, and crowds my thinking. The breast side effect, or threat
of it at the moment, adds to the number of things that I have to
worry about on top of the cancer that rages in me.

Will I need a bra if this breast thing happens to me, or will I
let them hang loose and ignore the fact that I have added weight
on my chest? I wonder. I wish I did not wonder. I want nothing
more than to pole-vault over the cancer to a time when I am free
of it and have time on my hands to write what I want instead of
having to bring all my writing to bear on demands of the cancer.
I need a pen that lacerates. A sword for a pen, or a scalpel, something, anything to wield, that I can turn on the cancer and uproot it, extirpate it from my heart and mind and body and spirit.
Rather than this buzz of sentences meant to bombard the cancer
with what it cannot withstand: scrutiny. Though it may be one of
those illnesses with an ego that feeds on the attentions lavished
on it even if those actions are meant to root it out.

I see myself in a 36C. I pulled that number and letter out of
my dim knowledge of my wife and my daughter talking about

such things as we ambled along corridors of shopping centers. I think that if I can cup my breast in my hand and if my hand feels full of flesh then it must be in the vicinity of a 36C. At the risk of revealing a fantasy, that I like to cup breasts and estimate their measurement, let me say that I have not entertained these thoughts in this way before, not ever. That I would voluntarily take a drug that might make me grow breasts or stop the production of testosterone or shrink my prostate and my testes along with it, all are anathema to me. I do not want anything to do with any of those drugs and I take them for the larger goal of beating back the cancer.

If I was told that the cancer was present and I carry it around with me like a sixth finger with no threat to my well-being, I would live with cancer and do nothing about it. I will go one step further. If you told me it would grow in me at a slow pace over a quarter century before it killed me, as prostate cancer often does, I would take that over these drugs and the looming surgery and after that, perhaps chemotherapy. I can live with a venomous version of Anansi, brought into being by my cancer to outfox a friendly version of the same creative. I would find ways to encourage the friendly trickster, the playful one. For its sense of fun is not deadly to me. It's a creature that comes from a tradition of playing tricks in order to gain respect and a meal, a kind of court jester in the kingdom of my body. I would deploy this good Anansi against cancer's wicked version of it.

Since they are locked in a drama, I would write a play for the two Anansis. Not a play for a proscenium arch or in the round but one of those roving dramas in which the audience runs around a huge construction with a dispersed set of players, all versions of Anansi and all locked in forms of combative trickery that relate to one story or other as told by my grandmother, by the cancer, and by me, not to mention the perspectives of my wife and each of my children. This would place my Anansi play on several stages that move around with scenes that intersect and with an audience who must have the ability to look in many directions while keeping up with the different dramas that are the same drama, though splintered and multiple and layered.

I need my lateral and quantum thinking to help me with this multidimensional drama of the various Anansi characters. But I have an addendum to my breast-growing-saga worry. I said, falsely, that I would entertain the idea of breasts and even speculated about a bra. A size that fits my cupped hand or a number that sounded good. The truth is, I would not be one of those characters who discard a bra to be liberated. I refer my students to that sixties form of protest in our search for early examples of women who resisted male designs of clothing for women aimed at controlling female bodies along lines dreamed up by men for men. Instead, I would strap my chest to conceal those breasts. I can think of at least one musician who did this, Billy Tipton, and several women who volunteered in various wars and fought as men. My bandaged chest suppresses an opportunity, I know, to be unconstrained by norms. Along with the idea of letting such chemical augmentations flourish in view of all eyes and not give a damn, I worry that my energy will be absorbed by yet another infraction into my bank of energy, every ounce of which I need for my fight, dance, or whatever with the disease.

There was a time when my daughter was curious about my nipples. She was seven or eight and she noticed my bare chest when I walked around the house on a hot summer's day. She said my nipples were narrow and protruding (her word). She pressed on one to push it back into place and it sprang back up. She wondered if it was alive and worked independently of me. I told her that nipples came in all shapes and sizes and that mine varied depending on if I was cold or hot, at rest or exercising. This carried on for some months. She would see me and start a conversation or try to sink my nipple into my chest with her index finger and a lot of concentration on her part to land on her target.

At some point I said enough of the talk and touch and that she needed to take my word for it and examine her own and her mother's chest and leave my nipples alone. Was it inappropriate behavior that I sought to correct with a deflection? I think she made me aware of my body and of my allocation of a special status to nipples on bodies. My daughter was naturally curious about me for her age and was experimenting with knowledge and the limits of it socially as is fitting for a child. My response to her was the noteworthy thing and not her curiosity about me. I take the lesson all these years later as I face the possibility of growing breasts of my own to wonder if my nipples would grow in proportion to my breasts or remain the two sprigs that they have always been to me.

In a dream I dress as a man, leave the house, not walking but airborne, like one of those blue figures in a Chagall painting. I land and I undress in public, say, at a local pool or gym, only to discover that I have breasts. I wake with a start and reach up to cover my shy nipples and check on my status. I associate breasts, rather than the complete absence of testosterone in my body, with being a woman. I think I would have to find cover for them or hide them from all eyes and any notion that I was not a man. My cancer is in my worry. My cancer has shifted its shape to a worrisome thought. There is no evidence of cancer in the thought. What is cancerous is the way it occupies my mind. I think I am willing to pay the price of breasts to rid my body of the cancer, but the way I worry about having breasts tells me something different. Though I admire them a great deal, I do not want them on me.

Their status as "out there" as belonging to an "other," not me, may have something to do with my gratification of them. In fact, they are among a cluster of expressions that add to my ideal construct of my desire. In my mind's eye I need a number of body parts to be in sync to meet my stringent notion of a love object. Breasts are one important part of the equation. They would grow on me and remind me of my battle with cancer. They would not have the kind of love from me that I associate with their presence on a healthy subject. I would resent them daily and want them off me. I would see the cancer as having captured a part of my body, another part, given my retreat from its occupation of my prostate and its creep into my nearby lymph nodes.

Those promised and not forthcoming breasts of mine that are a source of fascination and horror to me, signal a body too easily amenable to change, and they signal my burgeoning Anansi shape-shifting sympathies. If I should turn into someone else— I mean transform in terms of one key gender marker, breasts—I might trick the cancer into thinking I was no longer present in my body, no longer the body in which the cancer started, a body now abandoned as a home for some other, more healthy place. Left behind in that way and tricked into thinking that the host has died, has fled, either or both, the cancer might wish to follow by dying to resurface as a new life, given its shape-shifting qualities, rather than perish in the abandoned shell of a body. I assume that breasts are akin to a cloaking device, a power that grants invisibility to male bodies, that once these breasts have grown in place they make the male bodies appear to be no more.

Breasts on my body, the threat of them, challenge my male gender outlook. I have nothing to defend about being male. It can just as easily perish if it means I change shape and trick the cancer into thinking it has nowhere to live because it no longer recognizes its host. The cancer brings about its own death in me, thinking me dead ahead of it. My male body appears to vanish, made invisible by my sudden sprouting of breasts, or so I posit in my search for Anansi trickster emblems to befuddle the cancer.

Which brings me to my fear of shrunken testes. In attacking my inflamed prostate and by blocking the production of testosterone, the two drugs, bicalutamide and tamoxifen, respectively, each taken once daily, along with the Lupron Depot, a three-month injection, have conspired to reduce my scrotum contents to the size of two marbles. And the sack itself has contracted to sit back and up against my body in the area behind the uppermost part of my penis as if in hiding from some malicious threat.

Bicalutamide works by fooling the cells that make testosterone into thinking that they do not need to work at all since the body is flooded with the stuff. The message sent by the drugs to the cells is that their work is done and the body is fine without their need to send more of the energizing chemical. The injection works against testosterone in the same way. The cells get the message and they lay down their tools and stop their production. The body soon runs low of testosterone, and organs that feed on it start to look the worse for wear. The good thing is that cancer cells relish testosterone. They too starve. Their growth halts without it, their spread stops. My testes shrink as well, starved and left to wither away like the capitalist state under surplus value gone rampant.

Flomax does better. It relaxes the muscles that control the urge to pee and allows the stream to widen for a better flow of urine. I found myself able to pee as before with this drug and with the bicalutamide even better off, as the prostate gave up its real estate around my urinary tract. Unfortunately, the side effects from the other three medications extended their efficacy to my testes, where they were not wanted but where they had to go to catch as much of the area as possible that might be afflicted by the spread of cancer cells. Between the four—Flomax, tamoxifen, bicalutamide, and the Lupron Depot injection—I have these four chemical incarnations of Anansi working their trickster magic for me.

I figure at some point soon I will not need the Flomax thanks to the success of the bicalutamide. My muscles, sphincter and others near it, can go back to their former efficiency with the bicalutamide reducing the size of the prostate and clearing the area near the urine-flow-controlling muscles of all obstructions. If only the drug could accelerate its shrinkage of the cancer cells, I mean bombard them or chip away at them until they disappear from my body.

My testes might come back after all this is over and done. They might swell to twice their size and hang somewhat as if absolved by some higher authority from the need to hide away. I look forward to it. I hold them a few times a day in the palm of my left hand to let them know that I have their back, that this is a temporary state of affairs, and that the fight to recover them to their former glory will be won by me with my cohort of pharmaceutical Anansis. They are cool to my palm, my testes, not cool to me, cool as they need to be under conditions imposed before my chemical bombardment of them. I do not need their populations anymore. I just need what they bring to the table of desire and lovemaking. I took my testes for granted. I called them block and tackle, as if they were bundled with my penis forevermore. They have distinguished themselves as independent emissaries and in need of my particular attention in my cancer state. They are not equipment for a job. They have a status as driving engines of my sexual economy.

If I were a knitter I would knit my testes a special outfit to demarcate them from the organs around them. It would resemble a bonnet fitted upside down and tied around the front and uppermost part of my penis with a bow, or perhaps a navy knot of some complexity and authority, rather than a savoy knot. Why not try for a sheet bend? Use two different-colored threads to make that bonnet. A poet might write them an ode to coax them back to life and instill in them a sense of their former glory. Something like, *Oh twin sacks of a sex sacrament, upon whose bed a horrible lime has fallen, hear me!* And so on. I would mount a monument in a village square for them. National occasions would have a special version of a salute for them, some gesture such as grabbing the crotch area as an affirmation of its pride of place in the national psyche, assuming nationalism is desirable in this instance and not a cancer in the first place.

I attach too much importance to my mutable body, as if all I know starts and ends with it. What do I do with the ineffable? I swore by the salt-over-the-shoulder, superstitious lifestyle of my grandmother in Airy Hall, of my childhood, that I would not turn my back on such things, that I came to know more than my body could contain, and that more of these intangible things thrived outside me and my ability to detect them, and that since

I could not see them or subject them to rational judgment, or scientific intelligence, I had to trust in their veracity. That a sixth sense occurs independent of my ability to register it and that just because I can't quantify it doesn't mean that there aren't conclusions that I can draw from that lack of hard evidence on my part, other than that if I ignore something of such importance to my Guyanese childhood, my life would be the poorer for it. This outsider existence continues unabated despite my body's decline and death, just as it was ongoing before my birth.

Somewhere in that phenomenon there reside aspects of my physical life in metaphysical modes of being that I feel and sense, and so must be true. It races ahead of me and falls behind me and mimics my shadow ahead, behind to my left or right or exactly under my feet. I see it out of the corners of my eyes as the thing that I glimpse and cannot define. I continue in the form of that numinous life when my body decays. My body belongs not to me but to my cancer. As the cancer rises in me I see that I must leave my body sooner rather than at some other deferred time. Cancer knocks at my door. I have to answer its call, not to accompany it right away as it demands. I can take my time to get ready for it. I might even play a trick or two with cancer to pass the time before I give myself over to it.

All my senses lead to this road where Anansi waits for me. While I may languish in perpetuity in the sensory and in reasonable deductions made from it, and while it may prove enough for a life, it is not enough for me. I see otherness as an asset in my fight with my cancer, my dance, my tandem bicycle ride, and my copilot in my flight. You see, I relish the first chance to be airborne and free of gravity and its demands on flesh and blood and sense and reason. I take it as a compliment that my heart may dictate a rhythm that when followed excels in tempo into other realms of being. Those modes are springboards for me, moments of departure, starting points rather than ends themselves.

That is why my body breaks down and brings about not an end but a transition. I cannot name where I am going. Not to name the unknown is not to discredit its veracity. I send this notion to the oceanic gates of my cancer, to let it know that there is no winner in its domination of my body, just a change of the guard, as I relinquish my hold on my life and the cancer takes over, and I expire in my bodily form for this other place that waits for my arrival. Do not call it heaven or an afterlife. There is no alternate place or end of life for another life. My body falls and I land in a place that accepts me in whatever shape I happen to be in after I depart my body. It is this Anansi aspect to my transformation that may evade the winner-takes-all game that cancer wants me to play with it. I refuse.

As a result of cancer, my body delights with its sensory engagement with the world, it speculates about this world as conjecture and fantasy. And the world obliges with a promise of no end to the time that can be spent with it. On one hand my flesh is fragile and temporal, on another there is the edifice of thought this flesh and bone and blood of my thinking builds that intimates an immortal life span. If only my body is not seen by me as the limit of life. If only the spirit can ascend to its rightful place of permanence as if still in a temporal body, though not confined to temporality. I wish this into my life as my doubt that this is all there is, this body, though my flesh and blood, imbued with spirit, tell me that though some magical everlasting life is enough for most, it just is not sufficient for me.

Cancer brings this home to me. Cancer says my exit from this life may be early and I must find a way to make it palatable somehow. Accept the end of days as the termination of my gaze. As if the value of this body happened just for me for this brief time, and all the lives before my own added up to a plunge into nothingness and only the legacy of our acts to be taken up by those who follow us. And why not just this life? Why must there be an afterlife? What need is there for some haven after the sacredness and profanities and secular riches of this life? What manner of life after death could continue this consciousness tied to this vulnerable body? The certainty that it is lights-out, kaput, when we die, that clear conclusion evades me. I cannot settle on it definitively. And not because I lack the proof of a life after death; I don't care for proof. I turn away from certainty as a natural response of my thinking in part due to my creative practice of cultivating uncertainty to bring about poetry.

Meditation settles my mind. Who says that my body must surrender to the facts of its hungers? While I value my body for what it provides and I see it as holding in common the fact of my consciousness, I do not see that consciousness as the function of a certain number of chemicals and electrical impulses. That seems reductive. While chemicals and electricity drive my consciousness, they do not limit it. Consciousness alters as the body alters and when the body ends consciousness finds another shelter or expression for it. Or so I dupe myself into believing in what is a loose version of spiritual secularism.

I admit that I may be deluded and my reasoning along these lines keeps company with the magical thinking of religious types. It may be my inability to accept the limited value of my body in the face of its limitless capacity for thinking that keeps me on the side of the mystical. If I dismiss this spiritual realm on the basis that it cannot reasonably be known, would that dismissal not be an act of limitation by me? Just when I need to be accepting of mystery I shirk it in preference of the limited scope of science and my senses and language.

I call on Minnie Riperton's five-octave coloratura soprano versatility for my cancer analysis. Anansi gave shape to my thinking around my cancer. My body's changes encapsulated my need for versatility and depth to my thinking and feeling in the face of my cancer. Her worship of the sensory attachment to her lover in her hit track "Lovin' You," instructs me about my need to serve my body as the principle harbinger of my mind and not become divorced from the mutual dependence of the two. Riperton tapers off her praise of her lover with a rarely attained falsetto note to signal her abandonment of explaining herself in preference of the thing that drives her to sing about it. Her turn from charting her joy to her voicing of a note to denote her ecstasy switches from testimony to Rasta livity.

That condition of livity brings me to my wife, Debbie, as we scoot over in our bed to meet each other halfway to nestle, her back pushed into my front, my crotch pushed against her bottom, my arm draped over her to clasp her hands held at her chest, and settling with my breathing and hers working together like rowers in a long boat. And for this livity I thank the cathedral of my body. I pray for the morning to hold off a little while longer, keep me as still and close with Debbie for as long as I have flesh to feel and blood dancing around my body to keep me warm. Let my formation with my partner last through the night and beyond as we waltz in our sleep, our breathing joined and separate, catching up and falling behind, shallow and nasal in turn and then the settle of our breaths to hardly any rise and fall and their coupling in unison.

Until the crow of the Mid-City cockerel pulls us apart or the cats jump on us to wake us to feed them, or the dog barks to go out into the backyard. Or just this morning light shouldering through the curtains to crowbar the lids of our eyes open from our double-coffined sleep. Where we wish to remain undisturbed. Where whatever is good about flesh in unity resides. For the one body that is our two joined bodies, to stay planted that way in confirmation of the body's rule over our lives. For us to keep love warm as if we were both the eggs and the sitters who must keep them viable, sitting and benefiting from that warmth at the same time.

I call on my body for help to lift my spirits. *Here, body, here, come to me, I am waiting for you.* And the body trots up to me and nuzzles me and says that it is mine and at my disposal. The moment it arrives in the form of a burst of energy, I send my body away on the grounds that the help that it brings to my attention cannot cure me, may serve only to create an illusory sense of well-being. I take such loyalty as given and bank it until I see that my cancer sneaks in behind my body's ramparts and feels vindicated. My body has cancer. Cancer is my body. The shape of my body gives that cancer its shape. As I move, the cancer moves, harder than a shadow, with more purpose, steering me in any direction it wants to take. I have an enemy and that enemy is in me. Is me.

I do with it what I would do with any invasion: First I try to placate it with wishful thinking on my part, that the invader doesn't really mean its invasive action and that it might consider retreating and returning to where it came from. Second, I offer it peace entreaties—there is nothing to conquer here, and what little I possess I am ready to offer a fair share. Third, I consider raising a white flag of surrender: come and take what you want and leave when you grow bored, as you surely will in such bland territory. These tactics summarize my prescription for the cure of my cancer, the invader that has taken up residency in my body with fortifications that imply a long siege and a conquest without empathy or one that intends to win at all costs however Pyrrhic the victory, or earlier than that if I lay me down in those rancid pastures and die.

Each time I hear Paul Robeson sing "Ol' Man River," I think of a fight that cannot be won that offers an enriching though murdering experience. That as long as he sings I am fine and the moment he ends his song that unstoppable river resumes its flood of my knowledgeable body. The river is older than my body, and the mind of that river exists as a fragment in my consciousness. I feel that symbiosis as Robeson trills that song, more a boom than a trill and with a deeper resonance to it, as if I were submerged in the singing and the song was way below the surface of the Mississippi. Start over from the top, Mr. Robeson. With each singing I gain something new and take a little more from that wise old river. Bring me those currents to cleanse my body and rid me of that cancer, that sunken treasure that I do not care for that lies deep in my soul. That is where Robeson's voice delves. And for those innumerable benefits of his voice I give blood and a pound of my flesh. Cut carefully, one pound, not an ounce more.

I am neither shy of, nor locked in combat with, cancer. I embrace it like I would any partner who keeps me upright, balanced, and moving. At some point of my choosing I plan to part company with my cancer partner, that we may fall away from each other's embrace and take separate routes forward rather than stay shy and locked in what looks like a dance and really feels more like combat. Though my partner hides in me and hardly registers as present in me, now that the drugs have taken over, I feel things associated with the drugs that I view as surrogates for the cancer. Cancer Anansi who tricks me into thinking what I am feeling is all for the sake of the cure of my cancer. Anansi of the viral and venal. For your troubles, I offer one section of my body. Eat it as sacrament and drink the blood that I will lose in the process of your extraction of a part of me.

I have Guyana, the UK, and the US to draw from in my address of my cancer. I should draw from all three to launch my counter to the forces of the cancer. I have the globe as encapsulated by literature and history and politics. As I sleep I dream of cancer dreaming of me. From my vantage point I think that I cannot take a second away from my vigilance of my cancer, that any distraction on my part adds to the life expectancy of the cancer, which depletes my life expectancy. There is no dream life–waking life dichotomy, there is no seam between the two (though the two present as distinct entities), not as far as my cancer is concerned. My cancer never sleeps. My cancer has eyes in the back of its head. It sees with the compound eyes of a fly. And it looks backward and forward in time. I know from the string of my heredity that my cancer is a living history. I guess from the treatment program ahead of me, and the operation that looms on the horizon, that the cancer directs aspects of my future. Between past and future—in a present that announces its life and death moment by moment—the cancer shadows me.

I grant my cancer a consciousness that operates independently of its physical growth in my body. I struggle to separate my mind from the mind of the cancer in me. The two work in tandem. The two wear any number of disguises and they shape-shift too. One is the hare that races ahead in the fable, the other is the tortoise that keeps its eye on the long road ahead, rather than the rabbit-run of the moment. For my purposes, at some point in the race the two creatures swap places and roles switch between them, and the end of the race loops back to its beginning as I try to outwit the cancer and the cancer returns the favor with interest.

I see my body on the starting line of the race against my cancer. I move away from the starting line to buy some time. The cancer is not impatient. It has all the time in the world. The more time I take to begin to race against it, the greater its reward. My move to buy more time is something Anansi wants me to do, since for Anansi time is of the essence. Anansi cooks up all his plots in those moments when he is poised on a precipice or between two places or balanced on a fulcrum. The longer the race takes to start, the better his chance of coming up with an evasive strategy. I wish I knew what he was up to in my body. I think that I am Anansi until I reach these moments of indecision, when I know I need something to happen that I cannot predict or conjure, some surprise and lightning insight that makes a difference to the outcome. I am poised at that unknown. I have to trust in Anansi as both a character and a process.

At some juncture I realize that Anansi can't do this work alone. In the same way that I can't fight cancer on my own, so Anansi needs help in his spirit world if he is to defeat cancer. For cancer wages war in me on all planes (physical and mental), and Anansi fights for me in a place where he could use some company. I hardly have to ponder who to summon when up pops another fabled creature from my past.

8

WHAT BRER RABBIT DID

Brer Rabbit wants something or other and someone or other blocks him. Brer Rabbit's whole reason for being is to find a way to overcome the obstacle in his path to getting what he wants. Knowing what a character wants and putting up roadblocks along the path pursued by the character to realize that goal summarizes my task in the face of my cancer. The dictum captures Brer Rabbit's many adventures and my need to have him on my side. Quite often Brer Rabbit wants nothing more than to witness the confusion he causes to others. His goals are small compared with his sense of fun that he gets from the game that he plays with others. If I take Brer Rabbit's cue I might approach my cancer with a sense of humor and temper my earnest approach to the threat against my life.

What Brer Rabbit did—he was hopping along innocently minding his own business and he toppled into a nest of vipers—might be useful to me with my calamity. Brer Rabbit remained in a crouching position and hissed like his assailants. He was surrounded. He spoke with a lisp and hiss to disguise his rabbit accent. He said, "Do not strike me, my brothers and sisters, I am one of you though you do not see it. I have news for you to make you big and fat with fur just like me." They had not eaten in days. They said he looked like a rabbit and he certainly smelled like one and they were sure he would prove delicious to eat. He said he may look like a rabbit but that was just because he resembled the best meal he'd just eaten. He said he had news that would bring the same big meal to each of them. Listen. (As he spoke he kept turning this way and that to keep an eye on the ring of vipers.)

They could use him as bait to attract the many rabbits hiding from them. All they had to do to have rabbits galore for their feast was follow his instructions to the letter. First they needed to get him out of the hole they were hiding in. One of them reminded him that they were snoozing and that he had fallen into their home. He apologized. Of course, he said, he was on his way to join them and tripped due to his meal-shaped appearance. They did not seem convinced that he was one of them but the idea of a delicious captive who might bring them more captives just as succulent appealed to their empty bellies and greed.

Even in their doubt they wanted to be convinced. Even faced with a creature standing in the middle of them, covered in chewy fur, rather than prismatic scales, they still preferred the promise of a feast of plenty to the reality of a bite for each, if they shared. Though riddled with doubt, they were overpowered with greed, and so they told Brer Rabbit they agreed. He reassured them that going along with his plan was the wisest thing they would ever do.

Brer Rabbit organized them into a rope ladder and he climbed out of the hole. They headed in the direction of a mongoose lair. They pointed out to Brer Rabbit that there must be some mistake. This path took them to the mongooses. If they continued on it, those creatures would surely cook their geese. Brer Rabbit said the mongooses had moved their colony and that this path was now the safe one to take. The snakes did not believe Brer Rabbit. They said he was trying to trick them but they were not stupid. He had better lead them the other way, away from the known gang of mongooses or they themselves would eat him then and there. Brer Rabbit dropped his ears and slumped his shoulders. He said fine and he took the other path, the one that the snakes knew as the safe path.

The rest of the story is a meeting between a den of snakes and a troop of mongooses, and as everyone knows, when mongoose meets snake only mongoose walks away. This time Brer Rabbit as well. He hopped from the brawl as fast as his somewhat unsteady legs could without advertising his fear. He paid a price for each of his escapes from mortal danger and for each of his tricks that he played on others. The price of his experience increased the amount of risk that he needed to take the next time he found himself in a tight corner, or in a situation that had the makings of a juicy trickster event. His fall into the snake pit was deliberate. Brer Rabbit was bored at always winning. He put himself in a situation in which the odds were against him. He turned a blind eye to the hole and cast himself into it. He left the crisis feeling exhilarated though a little afraid as well, since exhilaration always kept company with fear.

Anansi versus Brer Rabbit. At some point Brer Rabbit had to meet his match. He had to come face-to-face with a challenge that was not a gamble he thought he could win. Not a dangerous place he could dive into with the inkling that he possessed the wits to extricate himself from it. To wander far from his briar patch in search of a creature to outwit and make his day something more than a quest for another meal. To come up on the spot with a turn of phrase, a pop-up and fizz-buckle brain brew in answer to an opponent. Even so, it never crossed his mind that any of those sticky situations might result in his demise. The only surprising element was in the order of the details of his encounter. That unknowable outcome came in the form of Anansi.

Anansi must have dreamed as well of such an encounter. To meet an adversary that justified his inordinate skill at trickery, his shape-shifting guile, his entry into contests he knew he would win always. He too relished the contest and never doubted the result, and reserved his surprise for how the feat would unfold for him. He secretly wanted to be stumped by a situation, to find himself in a corner and have no way out, just to see what that would be like even if it meant it was his last experience. The result of winning every time, no matter the odds or the opponent, meant that a part of Anansi's mind remained reclined in a hammock with a fedora lowered over his eyes, snoozing through it all.

Brer Rabbit and Anansi meet with the same mindset of un-quantifiable skills and inevitable success. It can be construed as the meeting of two like poles, an immediate repel of force fields, a bilious feeling in the gut and a spin of the head with the heart skipping several beats and having to catch up with itself with a drumroll. I play the part of Anansi, my cancer plays the part of Brer Rabbit.

I refer to the cancer as a person for the simple reason that it exhibits intention and will, and a consciousness and design, and awareness of time as a continuum, and of place and space to be explored or filled with its presence, and as a result of all of these may possess a dream life that operates independent of my con-sciousness and dreamscape. Cancer grows and feeds and breathes in me. Cancer splinters and multiplies, spreads and sprawls in modes of expansion akin to a human. I grant it personhood for these reasons and more. Cancer makes the most challenging foe that I will face in my life; everything else pales in comparison. If cancer wins in my duel to the death with it, I die, and in its victory over me the cancer dies as well. It is the only entity that wants victory for its own sake even if that means its own death. In this sense cancer is a person, in possession of blind conviction.

The contest between Anansi and Brer Rabbit is a screen put up by me to hide from you, dear reader, to hide the truth of my changing condition. That room in my head for the disease, the one that I keep under lock and key to keep things locked in as much as to keep my curious self out appears to have grown in size; though still chained, the four walls and alcove have expanded and the ceiling raised its height. The door looks bigger too and the lock now looks like an ill fit. I feel the contents of the room. There is a burden around the area of my bladder, a dull ache, and pressure. If you ask me to give the discomfort a number, I would say a two or three, but if you ask how much time I spend in worry about

that room, I would say eight out of ten. This gives the room cen-
trality in that mansion of mine of my interior.

In the last month and with the outbreak of COVID-19, my cancer becomes alert to the change in my surroundings and decides
the time is ripe to strike against me. With all nonessential surgery suspended to make room for people who have caught the
virus, my doctor promises to make the argument that my case
qualifies as essential. Even so, my April 1 date is pushed back to
the middle of the month, and a crucial test that the surgeon recommends strongly so that he can have eyes to see where to go
when he operates on me is now unavailable (COVID-19 restrictions have caused the test to be postponed). The surgeon plans to
go ahead using what imagery he has at his disposal from the tests
that I took previously. Interestingly, he tells me that were he to
operate now it would be in a semiblind state and that is why I really should have the PSMA in addition to the CT, MRI, and bone
scans. I don't want the additional test, because the university is
conducting an experiment, a study, with its patented machine
and procedure and seeks permission from the FDA to operate
it. The only snag is that I will have to pay the $3K for the test.
Being in no position to argue with the surgeon (after all, he is
the expert), I agree to pay for the extra test after he illustrates the
surgery as a blind undertaking for him without it.

An additional worry is that I have to walk into a hospital environment virulent with novel coronavirus. Having spent the last
three weeks splendidly socially distanced, I will be heading into
the belly of the beast for an essential surgery, assuming my surgery passes the test for essential hospital procedures. There's a
chance that I will catch COVID-19 and bring it home to my wee
darlings. With luck I might spend the two nights in the hospital
and dodge the bullet of the virus bouncing off the walls of the
place. The surgery is paramount for me. I want the operation's
promise that it can reduce or eliminate the cancer and increase
exponentially my odds of beating it. My future looks dismal

without the operation. As long as I draw breath let me fight this thing rather than roll over in life and surrender. I see my life as a song and dance, the humdrum and the routine, the repetitious and the fastidious all caught up on this web (and in the Web) of my days. I pictured it all taking me into decent old age.

Can you tell that I am preparing myself for the chance of my surgery happening soon? Daily, I walk the dog with my wife. Every other day, I ride the stationary bike for forty-five minutes. And do I sweat and pant! Every day I undertake some version of yoga that lasts about thirty minutes, sometimes forty-five minutes. I think of my body and of my mental state. I see the operation as a hurdle that I can clear. I listen to plenty of music— classical, jazz, blues, funk, rap—to set up those positive vibrations beyond my conscious ability to manipulate them. What is that Irish comic saying? "In your life may the splinters on the banister face the right way as you slide down." Maybe I should take the stairs, given my cancer blues. Or the elevator. Both Anansi and Brer Rabbit are on my side and consequently available to my cancer as well. The two live in me, so cancer has access to them. That means that they are not as powerful an aid to me, though it means I can match the cancer trick for shape-shifting trick. Also, I have an advantage as host and progenitor of the original tales. My life, with cancer as the squatter in me with squatter's rights, probably means those splinters on the banister face downward for me. May they face upward for cancer.

Some mornings I wake thinking I did not make it through the operation, that I died on the operating table and left my life in the middle of the muddle through my days (that should read *daze*). That part of my life that perishes in the operating room takes the cancer with it, and the two, my body and cancer, leave the studio-lit room of the operating theater for the dark room of the end of bodily consciousness. I rise, Maya Angelou fashion, from my fallen body and take on another form of being, so I fancy, rather than rush into a final darkness. I wake feeling sad that my sixty-year contract with this body has expired and that the cancer brought about my end and no means of extension to my life on earth could be found in time to save me. The operation turns out to be my funeral.

It takes an age with me limbering up my body with yoga and meditation to shake that feeling of defeat. I view my lack of energy on waking from this dream of my death as the cancer at work by extension from my physical body seeping into my state of mind. I see the worry not as a thing to be dodged or set aside but as deserving of my attention. I move in stretches that seek to free up stored energy in me, energy that I keep in reserve and now need to shake off an attack staged in my sleep by my cancer. My dream of my death is my worry about the forthcoming operation and about its likely success against my cancer. I stare it down to watch it wither under my gaze since it grows in the dark spaces in me, the shaded and locked parts of me, those regions that seem to evade my focus.

As the surgeon lays plans to wield his robotic scalpel to cut away at the cancer, so I deploy the light of my attention on that part of my cancerous body to shrink the disease, whether that disease is a mood, a sensation, or a vacuum pressure. As the surgeon works with massaging hospital rules and schedules to save me from the ravages of the cancer, so I am encouraged to work for myself to place me in the best position to benefit from surgery, to wake from it rather than capitulate to it. The surgeon's work entails robotic arms and deep imaging of where to cut and slice inside me. The cancer sits up in the surgeon's guiding light for those cuts. Some of me may be injured by those incisions made against the cancer. That is where my dream of my death waits for me to sleep and encounter it. That the best work of the surgeon may fail to save me from dying. That his intervention may bring about an earlier death than the one planned for me by the spread of my cancer.

Actually, it may be the anesthesiologist who kills me accidentally, whose drugs and gas send me into a coma and I descend so far away from myself that I become lost and my heart takes it that

I have left its harbor for good and so my heart stops beating for me, switches off its lighthouse-rhythm sweep of my conscious-ness, leaves me bereft. I know that the science of my surgically induced sleep mitigates against an accident of this kind. Outside the science, where Anansi and Brer Rabbit rule as supreme trick-ster beings, in their nether world, I wonder if I am at their dis-posal, and being put to sleep delivers me on a platter to them for them to divide between them the bounty of my mind and body. The anesthesiologist ferries me across the river to meet my fate, unknowingly delivers me to my infinite rehearsal conducted by Anansi and Brer Rabbit.

If not the surgeon or the anesthesiologist then the nurse who patches me and introduces a pernicious infection in my wounds that sends my body into sepsis shock. If not the nurse then COVID-19 running around the hospital looking for a new body to claim for its pandemic growth. COVID-19 waits in the hospital for each new arrival and for me. I see novel coronavirus as my cancer in one of its many guises in a game in which my cancer plays Anansi or Brer Rabbit or both interchangeably or simulta-neously depending on the challenge posed by me. I delight in the city slowed and quieted by the threat of COVID-19. How the city air smells clean robbed of exhaust fumes. I hear so many birds in Mid-City, mockingbirds, hummingbirds, wrens, finches, crows, seagulls (eight miles from the sea), their various calls made louder by the lessened traffic and imagined thinness of the fresh-ened pelt of city air. New leaves push through limbs, buds open regardless, and my allergies flair no matter the pandemic's devas-tation of all routine.

A friend says that this pandemic is a ripe time to dismantle all of capitalism as it grinds to a halt, take the evil bits of it apart and put it back together again with a green and communal eye. The list of things to be discarded by the reorganization of the current system, largely halted by COVID-19, becomes long and unwieldy once the many parts are laid bare by their enforced slowness and partial stoppage. Some parts just cannot work anymore as is. The experience of this time should soften up the public for a new system to be put in place rather than a restarting of the old one. Could this be true as well for my cancer and me? Am I on the brink of living out the last chapter of my life in a revolutionary new way? COVID-19 is capitalism's cancer, here to make capitalism stop and take notice and start again with heightened wisdom and hopefully a changed character. For example, we have two cars in the house and with social distancing in place we use just one car to make runs to the supermarket for supplies. What if, once the virus disappears, we keep the ethos of one car for all of our needs and even trade in both petrol guzzlers for an electric vehicle? Is there an equivalent trade that I can make to emerge safely out of this cancer?

What could I trade to secure my health? To know my valued holdings I need to identify the places and people and ideas that I have returned to in my consistent bid to make sense of the world and of my life. First, C. L. R. James's 1938 study of the Haitian revolution, titled *The Black Jacobins*. James shows how the first successful slave rebellion became the world's first antislavery and first postcolonial republic. The heroes of James's world plan war and economics along the lines of race as the demarcating factor. James's penchant for narrative makes a confusing episode from history read as if it were a linear story in a fictional enterprise. His personalities are imbued with astonishing leadership qualities such as Toussaint Louverture's wily dealings with the French and British. He appeared to enact Anansi. He knew that he had to employ military tactics and negotiation trickery to win his country's freedom. For C. L. R. James the first postcolony is a shining example of the way forward for the *longue durée* of the anticolonial and postcolonial struggles.

How does history help me in my epidemiology? James's 1938 study demonstrates how slavery as a profiteering enterprise cost more in human terms to keep it viable for a few beneficiaries. He certifies slavery's moral turpitude and inherent mortality as a system, how slavery's repression breeds rebellion and why slavery under those strains is destined to fail. C. L. R. James's biography of slavery has a hero, Toussaint Louverture, whose heroics, though costly in human terms (more than two hundred thousand deaths), result in the reward of unquantifiable freedom. In addition, the history of a successful rebellion would shine for other oppressed people to see and benefit from by knowing about it.

James's text begs the question, what if the encounter between Europe and Africa happened along lines of fair trade? History as we know it would be a work of fiction. There would have been mutual growth and development. Not the plunder and hurt of history in need of contemporary modes of redress. It is this James who walks with succession through the emergence of the James as literary storyteller invested in history as personality, and the James who sees history as a set of economic and cultural practices.

These changes embody the Anansi biography of multiplicity. They exceed revisionism or augmented ideals through time. That way a single body has of handling time requires shifts of persona. As his body shape-shifts, so James imagines a free space over a lifetime with his focus on Africa as his palimpsest. He dreams his way off his island nation of Trinidad and Tobago to connect with Africa. He becomes the young researcher who makes Africa a living place. In his book *Beyond a Boundary*, he brings into being a postcolonial geography and independent spirit. He seems to say that not all places continue from colonialism into a condition of the postcolonial, that some things may come about outside of that continuum. For instance, the sound of the cricket ball on the willow bat swung in the mind of the adult echoes as that ball sails beyond the boundary. If that struck ball ever lands it is for another generation to find it. What we have as James's legacy is the trajectory of that ball that he batted with his best swing for that sweetest of sounds that tells him right away "looks like this one gone for good."

With my cancer, I throw my arm up and that cricket ball sent sailing by James's scholarship lands in my open palm. I grip that ball. My reflex triggered by a sound. That sound traveled over time and across seas to reach me. It takes me back to the yard at the front of the house in Airy Hall. As kids we used the path from the front gate to the front porch as our cricket pitch. I do not remember what we used for a bat but I can still feel the pain of the ball that banged on my leg as I stroked at it and missed and it slammed into my shin and left a bruised bone. The better batters among us sent the ball sailing over the fence around the yard and the nearest fielder had to retrieve it and sometimes all of us had to look in the tall grass of the field to find that ball. The sound of the bat as it connected with the ball twinned with the smell of a bakery. Some note on a tuned instrument, one plucked string left to echo, one struck key left to brew in the air. The cries of us children at such a clean hit multiplied in the air and made us jump on the spot and slap our thighs and flick our index fingers against our clasped thumbs and middle fingers. If the ball sailed toward the sun you had to shade your eyes to trace it.

The bat-and-ball sound and children hollering are an instant stretched to become a constant maintained out of time. Always that stroke and crisp contact, crying out for joy. *Thwack*, drawn-out loud and long, that pulled on nerve strings, opened corners of lungs and mind. Made us believe back then as I do now in this extended replay that the highest obstacle merely presented the biggest challenge, rather than seeming insurmountable. Even if I grant my cancer a place on the team playing cricket in the yard all those years ago, and a seat next to me on the floor near my grandmother in her rocking chair on the front porch telling her Anansi story, even if the cancer soaked up, same as me, the sound of that bat driving that ball out of sight, and fielded patiently for a turn to wield that bat or bowl that ball, I would maintain an edge over the cancer.

Whereas the cancer witnessed everything alongside me, I played an active part in each of those emblems from my past. Whereas the cancer bided its time, I lived mine. All that I needed I heard in my grandmother's story. All I could ever be seemed delimited by the whack of that ball beyond the boundary of the yard's paling wood fence. Both story and game made me feel full of the goodness of life.

Bowl that ball, James. I have the bat in my hand and I am ready to swing for the boundary. Tell that story and fill my ears inclined your way. Even with cancer I am prepared to play, to listen, primed for this life.

My cancer says that it does not play cricket. Which is to say that it refuses to play by any rules outlined by me. Which is cancer's way of tearing up the rulebook of our relationship, as if rules were anathema to our relations. I reply that all of me up to this moment made the cancer possible and therefore everything about my past counts in my present, our (the cancer and me) present. In a roll call of my disease and me to see exactly who is on whose side—as if a line could be drawn in the sand between us when a circle is drawn around us and we move with it from one location to the next—things in our world answer to their names.

The cancer that occupies my body wants me to believe that it is indivisible from me. Each spell of cold sweat or hot flashes, of the several every hour, belongs to me. I cannot put it down to the side effects of the drugs, though that works as a partial explanation since I was free of these spells before I embarked on the drug regimen. I cannot blame the cancer for launching an independent campaign of terror on my flesh and blood and consciousness. Instead, each outbreak of hot flash as it surges through me and makes me tear off my cardigan if awake, and if in bed kick off the sheet and blanket, both cardigan and blanket that seemed necessary to keep me warm, as I felt inordinately cold all the time (again, the drugs, or the cancer or just me and my fear or a combination of all three), has to be embraced as my newly cancerous body in an altered history of my life. Life before cancer and life with cancer represent two life histories that I hope to enrich with a third expeditionary force in my biography known as my life postcancer.

If all works out with COVID-19 and me, that is, if the hospital accepts my operation as an urgent one and allows the doctor and his team to work on me. I can see all the medical professionals chipping in to help out with this emergency, each specialist diversifying to cover the demands on the system made by this novel coronavirus outbreak. April 1 came and went and I lost that date to COVID-19. Cancer won. Cancer wins each time I lose something or other. The next mid-April date might be canceled since the social or physical distancing and the spread of infections have together made all routine life in the city impossible to carry out. My operation is routine for my doctor and his team. They carry out several each workweek. COVID-19 puts all of that on hold for those of us who nurse life-threatening disasters and rely on medical interventions to save us. COVID-19, society's cancer, is mine too. The pandemic teams up with the cancer in my body to launch a pincer attack against me, killing masses of citizens along the way.

As if in answer to my worry about the long tentacles of cancer that seem to reach into every facet of my body and so every aspect of my life, the hospital emails me to confirm the mid-April date for my operation, and further to set a date four days before it for the expensive PSMA. That is the test that paints a detailed picture of the course set by my cancer cells that emerged from the membrane around my prostate, as opposed to the antigens that generally indicate the presence of prostate cancer. If the membrane-specific cells have migrated to those suction tubes of my lymphatic system, then a clear path will show from my prostate outward. It is to this picture that the surgeon refers when he says to operate without it would be to travel blind, to cut into me and see what he finds rather than have a map of what is there before he makes his cuts.

I pay toward my monthly insurance premium and have a copayment. Yet I have to foot the bill for a procedure that the surgeon deems necessary for him to do his work. This is broken medicine. That the richest capitalist nation in the world works by bleeding its citizens at every turn and every juncture of medicine and in their civic life makes that nation impoverished on many fronts; the ethical, first and foremost. I fear for the life of the citizen who is poor in this richest of nations. It makes sense that the poor and Black in the nation die earliest of all groups and the rich live long and healthy lives. Even death is sociological.

Of course I will pay for it (mine is not a case of Fo's *Can't Pay? Won't Pay!*) and I'll take home my free CD that I get after the procedure—a detailed picture of my lower interior. I am glad that the surgeon will have eyes so that he knows where to go when he cuts into me. I wish the whole enterprise free for everyone. I hate this monetary society. Though I reserve the bulk of my passion for my cure, there is always a modicum of it for targets that deserve my venom. My doctor is a magician and a mechanic. He works his magic of my possible cure and he fixes my broken body invaded with cancer by removing the invader, as far as that is possible. He may be a part of my Anansi and Brer Rabbit arsenal. Someone I bring on board to help me banish the cancer from my territory.

Alternatively, he may help the cancer by poking at it and waking it up to more virulent activity in me. He may find too much to cut into and so he may have to retreat and seal up my cut without doing anything about my cancer. My cancer may use the surgeon to legitimize its takeover of me by earning through surgery this medical and scientific blessing of its unimpeded progress in me. I will find out in mid-April how the rest of my days will be for me with this cancer in my life. More than a magician and a mechanic, my surgeon may well be a god, at least to my fortune with my dilemma. I am to walk into his cathedral a supplicant and with luck emerge from it the baptized convert. On a more secular note, he will cut me open, do what he can with the cancer that he encounters, and sew me up as cured of the disease or in need of further therapies to fight on against it.

The surgery should not kill me. I should not die on the operating table. I should lose consciousness and surface into my life with no memory of what the surgeon did to me to save my life. With

COVID-19 in the hospital I hope to dodge it. I hope the surgeon and his staff are well and the ward staff clean and clear of the virus, and the bed and all the implements that come into contact with me pristine and virus-free. That is my prayer. Hear, oh hear, as Shelley intones in "Ode to the West Wind," his secular and black magic invocation of the winds of political change, so I pray to all the forces I store in me to come to my medical assistance. If I cannot have Anansi and Brer Rabbit on my side, let us say that the two in me are canceled out by the same two in my cancer, then lend me any trick of apotheosis that is available to me.

COVID-19 assumes the role of an aid to my cancer. I must walk into spaces dominated by the pandemic in my quest to treat my cancer. I would be in my house were it not for my need to treat my disease. I run the risk of catching another deadly disease that's rampant in the city. COVID-19 is another iteration of cancer in my body. As the pandemic riots in the body of the city, so my cancer rages in me.

At my next appointment, I see a general practitioner who must verify my health for the operation. That means I walk into a hospital where the beds assigned for COVID-19 and the staff who care for them reside. Chances are that the virus is in the smile of that person who greets me at the door. There are too many ways for health professionals to pass the virus to me. The doctor who judges my health for the forthcoming surgery may have COVID-19. As he confers his approval on me he bequeaths COVID-19. The nurse who takes my pressure and pulse and tells me both are in good shape aspirates on me and her breath and her touch carry COVID-19. So the routine appointment appears to be my judge, jury, and executioner. I walk into the hospital with cancer that threatens to shorten my life and quite possibly leave with COVID-19 to speed up that shortened process.

This does not stop me from my exercise regimen as I prepare for the middle of the month—assuming I get there free of COVID-19 symptoms. Between the doctor visit and my appointment with the surgeon I have that chemical resonance test, the

PSMA. If COVID-19 misses me on the doctor's visit, it may get me on the second appointment. If not the second then on that third medical date, the one with the surgeon and overnight stay in the belly of the virus, many viruses, it must be said, since other post-op infections can catch me. What I mean to say is that my best ally, medicine, is about to take over; it remains my single biggest chance to stop the cancer in its tracks. I walk into its professional space that may be rife with disease knowing that this could be the blow against cancer that brings the cancer down.

Cancer needs a song: tambourine and cymbals and a choir, not to raise it from the dead but lay it to rest finally. This will have to be arranged by a songster. All I have to do is write the lyrics, the songbook, for surely cancer and I are in a production that is the scale of an opera. "You rocked me to sleep when you slept. Now I choose to stay awake. I shake with your laughter through years. I want to stop time in you and take your life that is my life as well. Here is to all the times that you moved without thinking about me. Here is to all your lovers and children. I stake my claim of your life. For my life is not worth living if you live on. My goal is to see us both dead. I live for this death of ours. Do not make me live a moment longer. For all your laughter, I feel pain. All your life is my despair. I am cancer and no good comes from me."

And for counterpoint, "I do not want you for a guest. There is hardly enough room in me for all the things I have become and all the things left for me to be. I wish I could take you for a walk around the neighborhood. Instead you hide in me and chew your way out. My body jumps and skips and twists to songs of health and wealth. Just as light stirs the world to rise and shine, so I wake and dance to the tap of that light on my heels, forehead, shoulders, back, and belly. The sugar and spice in me for life does not include you, Mr. C."

Reprised by, "Wait right there, I have to fetch my weapon. You bring rhythm, I bring your downfall. Let's swing until only one of us is left standing or both of us fall."

This is how it goes between my cancer and me. By turns

rhythm and blues, soul and funk, and jazz number. A trumpet or saxophone or trombone solo, all three take turns in me, with that guiding snare and bass drum. Cancer, we dance until one or the other falls or both. Let me be the one to see you off, even if I follow almost immediately after you. This is my body, not yours, you are an unwanted guest in it. You have overstayed your welcome. Now you wish to stage a takeover, which is really a takedown in which both of us fall and never rise again. For that outcome, never an option, I muster every fiber in me and within reach of my memory and imagination to fight against you, Mr. C., though we lean on each other in a club that carries on way after closing time with the band reduced to long solos in slow, slow time. A time out of sorts with the stopwatch of daily routine. A time not on any pulse. That slows the heart and settles the trembling Jell-O of the mind. And for this we dance on into the small hours in that slowly emptying wineglass of the club.

The hands of the clock in my body have stalled at midnight. That hour when the dark releases all its jewels of sport and joy. You see the night as thick. It presses your eyes. We walk through it, my cancer and me, as if wading into a sea. We inhale the riches of the night and our glasses refill automatically and we dance and never tire until we reach that point of no return. We lean against each other to stay upright. The wood floor accepts that our feet polish it to a shine of the lights of the house, wood polished smooth, sweat twisted into the grain and the grain worn. You know how certain tasks will wipe the fingers clean of their prints, well, that is how we dance through the night.

I tend to dismiss my cancer when I talk to people about it. I put Mr. C. in his place as a temporary distraction and a test I am destined to pass. I refuse to grant C. the kind of space and prominence that I have assigned to him in my head. I mean I do not talk about my cancer in those terms to my wife, and certainly not to my daughter. I think that if I deny cancer this recognition then I gain something, have some advantage over the cancer that it cannot do anything about to alter in its favor or fix on its terms. This psychological realm signals my unending and relentless dualism with my cancer. That I make no concession to it, having already conceded real estate to it in my body, been compromised by it and now its overt threat of my premature death.

I have not told Geoff, my best friend (other than my wife, that is), about my cancer diagnosis. He lives with his partner, Peter, in Shrewsbury in the UK, an ocean away, and an excuse for me to say to myself that I do not wish to burden him with my problems in an already problematic time with COVID-19 nesting all over the globe. Feeling overwhelmed, I feel he wouldn't be able to help me. Also, I don't want him to worry about me and add to my talk about cancer with what would be his regular queries and offers of advice. I struggle privately with thinking that says I can put cancer behind me as a single and private undertaking and save my friends the worry of the need for blow-by-blow accounts of my fight with it. I don't want to add to gossip about me, to hear people hear from my friend in an unspooling thread of talk about me that wouldn't happen otherwise. I feel bad every day about not telling my friend, and with each day that passes the feeling worsens and the hurdle grows taller and appears insurmountable. We are in touch almost daily, since he sends me pictures of his cycling trips with his husband, Peter. I always reply with a comment about his mobility despite restrictions, and the beauty of his location, and with some quip about my LA isolation with my family.

I have not told my mother. She is twenty years older than me and has congestive heart failure, some weight issues, shortness of breath, and arthritis of several joints. She is a miracle of life in that she has been at death's door for a decade now. Her plate is full. She has more than her share of worries to cope with without me adding to it with my bad news. Again, I believe I will clear this hurdle and so it does not merit my passing on the worry to my mother. That is the reasoning.

I feel I will not get any satisfaction from telling my mother my troubles. That it will only add to my problems since she is bound to alert my brothers, who will confer and resent me for not telling them earlier. She is parsimonious with her love and praise and so with her sympathy. I don't feel I'll hear anything useful from her to help me with my fight. I worry about my ability to deal with her sorrow at the news. So I continue with my WhatsApp messages every other day to her to find out how she is and she replies a couple of times a week, and our relationship of a respectful emotional distance full of pleasantries continues unfazed.

I have kept it a secret from my brothers too. I have six brothers, four from my father and two more from my stepfather. I am somewhat close to three of them. We talk when I have news or a birthday rolls around. We chat in a couple of exchanges periodically, on WhatsApp. Why would I divulge the challenge of my life to them given the flimsy footing of our relationships? I mean, it is courteous, but it is all walking on eggshells with us, no risk, no vulnerability, and so, no trust. It does not have the steady platform that a relationship needs to cope with the introduction of the heavy weight that my cancer brings with it. I do not want to be hurt by their response, which I can predict will be disappointing. I do not wish to fuel their talk around my disease without their need to talk to me.

In the past my brothers and I have talked among ourselves about the worst one among us at the exclusion of that pariah of the moment. We seemed obsessed with another brother's struggle. Or found it salutary. There but for the grace, et cetera. I know from our talk that we do not want that brother to fail, we just express amazement at his failing. It is this infatuation with someone's bad news that scares me off from breaking my news to my brothers. I do not want to be their topic of the day. Also, I can hear the advice from each of them, the platitudes, the inquisitiveness, the mounting feeling of "I wish I had kept my mouth shut" the more I go through this with them. The energy on my part needed to curate the responses of my brothers and mother would subtract from my days. I am better off hoarding my doubt at having withheld the news than my umbrage at having shared it. Gladys

Knight has a couplet in her song "Midnight Train to Georgia," in which she says, "I'd rather be in his world, than live without him in mine." Well, my sentiments are the exact opposite in relation to my family. Knowing what it costs to live in their world, I opt for solitude.

I am preoccupied with a riot of my emotions stirred by my cancer. Leave my family and best friend out of it. Preserve my strength for the battle ahead, the operation and recovery and then a protracted fight with continuing radiation and chemo. I'll need to harness every particle of resistance for my long road with cancer. Enough of those whom I did not tell about my cancer and how about why I even have to entertain that kind of talk in the first place. Who designated blood relations as privy to confidences? Who said that friends are true friends only if to them I can unburden my worse fears? My wife is my best friend. My kids around me are sharing in my news. We are under the same roof and in the same cadre of resistance to COVID-19. There is my confidence and they are my confidants, and those are my troops for my fight with cancer and COVID-19. My troops for anything else on the horizon.

The fact is that I am too much inclined toward privacy, too standoffish with others, too doubtful of the efficacy of the medicine of sharing. "Lean on Me" has not been my philosophy, though as sung by Bill Withers I feel more than hear the offer of support, the added strength conferred on the open and receptive listener, that help is already on hand just by feeling the truth of that song. Bill Withers died two days ago. I played his music all day as I did my chores, which consisted mostly of exercise bike, tidy of my home office, laundry, cleaning the boys' bathrooms, and some stretching on my yoga mat. I see from "Lean on Me" that COVID-19 is the time for that song, and according to the news it has seen a rebirth among people sharing it and drawing sustenance from it. I know the song has one condition before the listener is able to access the largesse of its loving world: the imperative to ask, to lodge the request for help. And how do I do that if I cannot bring myself to utter the words, not wanting to seem so vulnerable, and not wishing to bother others who appear busy with their lives?

I thought I knew why Maya Angelou's caged bird must sing. For freedom. For access to the world denied it that the song insists is the right of the singer. For Wallace Stevens's singer "beyond the genius of the sea." For the ability to tell "the dancer from the dance," that exquisitely indistinguishable pairing in Yeats's "Among School Children," though vulnerable to demarcation along the lines of the separation of art from life. I aspire to the quality of being in Bishop's "At the Fishhouses," of flowing and flown in keeping with the demands of our experience of historical time, with the two as constants (and formal constraints) sharing a point in time as if outside the demands of linear time. I sing outside the cage about other things to do with the love of song for the sake of singing. I sing to spread some good vibe worldwide to outstrip the bad, the unhelpful, and the downright evil. I want my life to be akin to a song with the plaintive note of Bill Withers. As if the simple at its simplest matches the profound at its most complex.

I see the worst aspects of myself in the way others treat me. A part of me thinks I deserve to be sidelined, unrecognized, with not enough of anything in my life. That cancer is my reward. For the harm done to others. For the grave secrets that I harbor about my life. As though I need to level with myself by a reckoning with everyone around me; that is, unconditional disclosure at all times to cure myself of my reserved disease. Just as reserve feeds my art's literary style, so it poisons my life. The cancer is my cure. What does not kill you, cures you, runs the mantra that I do not believe wholeheartedly, yet utter on a loop as I come to terms with possibly losing my fight to cancer, and as a consequence, in need of a belief in something if I am to survive that bleak prognosis.

Down I go, pulled by the gravity I deplore, the one that drags me down and plants a heavy foot on my neck. Do I stay there and capitulate, vanquished? I see myself on skis that take off on a ski jump, and this life is meant for me to put as much distance between the landing and me as I can, by leaning into the drive of that jump off the slide. Keep me in that lean forward to the last millimeter of my stretch as I fly and experience being flown, floating down to earth. Who would want to land with a bang or whimper? Keep me airborne. Open as much real estate between my takeoff and my landing as possible. Keep me outside distance measured by time. Give me that, and I beat the cancer.

For as long as I hear Linton Kwesi Johnson's beat down bubble down bass music character poetics filling my head cave and shaking my crowns. It is a beat, as LKJ says. Of the heart. He continues. And he takes the measure of that rhythm, the metrics of a tailor for the suit of a body that is for the ages. A suit that does not have a season. For I parade in it and with it along the catwalk as long as I have hips to gyrate, and as long as hip, knee, and ankle joints last. I float and I move to a beat. I breathe and I picture my past as if loaded into the tongue of a slingshot and catapulted forward ahead of me, paving the way for my progress. I'm airborne and do not wish to curtail my flight for anyone or anything. Now bring out your tape measure and tell me how far I floated in the ski jump of my life; how big that suit must be to cover me.

*   *   *

The third time my daughter cried I took her tears—upon first hearing them—as confirmation of the effect of my dismal condition. I note her tears to show how life takes up where it left off when it got interrupted. I note how interruptions linger and do not go away, even if they have to wait in a queue of other things to do with living. My daughter is the most aware person alive about how she feels as she feels it, not miles after the event like me, but moment by moment. I heard her crying through her bedroom door. Either she cried without restraint or else she cried to draw my attention; that is, so loud she could not be ignored except out of spite or malice. I knocked. Waited. Nothing. Just her loud tears. I walked in and there she was, head in hand, bawling her eyes out. I asked her what was wrong. I expected to hear about another episode of worry induced by my cancer. Instead, it was an online test that she took and could not solve a problem and earned a B, though there is no shame in it, not her usual grade.

I exhaled in relief that my cancer had nothing to do with her distress, and inhaled right away as the concerned parent ready to jump to her assistance. I belittled testing in a homeschool climate brought on suddenly by COVID-19 that left all the professionals scrambling to simulate the school day with a dispersed clientele. If the city could barely organize a few pickup spots for school meals, how can they hope to reproduce online the routine of populations that gathered under school roofs daily for instruction? I was about to add that I would write to her teacher to improve the grade on the grounds that the homeschool regimen was new to everyone, and bound to result in creases, that with time, would be ironed out.

Her dear mother intervened just in time to save me making a promise that I could not keep. She said that these things happen. You win some and lose some. That high school geometry for a middle school student needed hard work and sometimes with partial success, though a B was not to be scoffed at, and grades can always be improved. She said that my daughter should take this one on the chin and plow on with her studies. She hugged our daughter and sure enough the tears subsided and a wonderful calm descended in my daughter's room with me feeling quite useless and glad that Debbie was a part of the equation of this family.

My daughter crying is to me like having a root canal without suitable anesthetic. Her loud complaint and distress is a hand that dips into my spine and grabs a handful of nerves and pulls that spaghetti right out of me. When she cries I die. Just for today, my daughter's misery is bigger to me than my cancer.

I may tell my wife to stay home and let me do these upcoming visits alone. I can argue that by not accompanying me she reduces by half the chance of the virus getting into the house. I imagine stations of purification before I enter the house: peeling off my clothes in the backyard and hosing myself down before throwing everything into the washing machine and stepping into the house without touching anything and heading straight for the shower for another thorough wash.

I know she'll refuse to leave me alone for these appointments. We'll have to come up with a regimen of care, of not touching anything, including our faces and of washing our hands as much as possible, of standing in hallways or rooms away from everyone else, of taking up as little space as possible, and getting out of there as fast as we can. Everyone we meet will be viewed as contaminated. Everyone administering to my care could transmit COVID-19 along with curative expertise. I make a mental note to ask the doctor for the medication that blocks the growth of breasts.

I suspect they have begun to grow on me. I feel flabby around my midriff. Like I have a car tire strapped around my belly. I have put on a few pounds. I have not weighed myself. I can tell by the flesh that I grab in my hand when I reach around my middle and close my open hands there and it fills my hand with extra helpings of me. My chest looks different. I catch sight of it in the mirror as I shave my goatee and trim my hair. I have pecs but this is different, pecs with something extra added to them to give them both definition (which I want) and protuberance (which I definitely do not want). Debbie mentions a drug that helps fight cancer in women. It blocks estrogen, the production of my breast glands. It is yet another med (on what seems an exhaustive list) that I must request to add to the three that I take and the fourth one that is a three-monthly injection (due again soon, yikes, a long needle in the butt, or gluteus as preferred by my faint heart).

Though I think of Derek Walcott's take on exhaustion that pays dividends, I find the drugs regimen hard to stomach. In his book-length *Omeros*, there is a description of the sea in terms of literacy and history. The image of a tide that starts off Africa's shore and ends up in the Caribbean replays the forced migration of enslaved Africans. Walcott's image for it is "fountains exhaustion here." Typically, he coins a contradiction to encapsulate a traumatic condition. The fountain is where I glean my delight. As a verb I associate it with energy and productivity. To link it with the geyser of slavery's pain underscores Walcott's genius with the telling and memorable phrase. The fountain of history's hurts in the transatlantic slave trade repeats unendingly in that Walcott image, and in its repetition presents renewed opportunity for a treatment of injury. I say the lines and see the image and I am baptized by pain, and by the peeling away of those layers of pain for some relief offered by insight, and a coming to terms with the history that might otherwise prove indomitable.

Of course, in my coalition of real and imagined, a wave is a sideways fountain that wind ushers ashore. Both wave and fountain make that noise of a kettle brought to the boil. History has a similar sound in the way it plays on the nerves and on the heart and hurts my head. I need that palliative fountain, vertical and horizontal, its sound of the sea that's my cure. That settles my disturbed sense of myself, if cure could be a sound. As if the picture of that sea as painted by Walcott brought with it the sound of the sea and a smell of salt water. My daughter crying is in that sea of history. Her calm is that same scene without noise and movement.

I have to ask, with three imminent medical appointments, what do I know before I go? My drugs regimen attacks the cancer on three fronts. First, it blocks the cells from dividing and multiplying; second, it blocks the food that cancer likes to feed on to grow; and third, it convinces the cancer cells to commit suicide, by turning their outward drive to increase their numbers into a cessation of production and action, which is the equivalent of self-harm. The drugs have a number of side effects, some of them working in ways that resemble the behavior of cancer, and others that promote appetites that can lead to the growth of cancer. From cravings for food, to a bloated feeling, to hot flashes, and feeling cold as well, I remain at their mercy, and vigilant that they are tied to the meds.

The science of how a cell locks on to cancer cells and blocks them from feeding and turns them against themselves resembles a Lego assembly or a puzzle without a perimeter. One end fits another and sends a signal to show the fit. That fit means the cancer cell is compromised. One med is cut and tailored to latch on to the end of a cancer cell and prevent that cell from sinking its teeth into a healthy cell. Again a signal is sent out to show that the block is a success. The cancer is blinded by the shine (a trick) of the med and it turns against itself, and kills itself. Which protein, and which proton, and which enzyme are a matter for science. The result is a body starved of testosterone.

Science warfare tricks my cancer cells to turn their arsenal on themselves; science blocks all the food cancer needs to multiply. I bow my head to science and step aside. At the chemical-molecular level my meds send out waves of attack against the cancer, all for my benefit. Medicine is in the crease for me as my primary bat, the one destined to send cancer sailing out of the cricket stadium and beyond the boundary of my body. With this in mind Debbie and I dress and drive to the hospital, for my pre-op appointment. There is a song in my heart as I drive into the belly of the COVID-19 beast, invisible creature that shifts into many manifestations, present in all the sick palaces of hospitals where sick people congregate.

I offer a prayer, made aware by the news of the statistics of the disease weighted heavily against poor, and black and brown people. Help them. Make them breathe easily and unaided again. If I join their ranks, help me. The lanes shine on the I-5 (locals insist on the definite article every time they mention this motorway), magically free of congestion. Overnight rain has washed the city spectrally clean, and I imagine, fresh.

At the hospital in Westwood, we find a parking space in no time. The parking lot is more empty than full. Usually, I would have to set aside time to cruise around the basement floors and wait for someone to show up, and follow them very slowly in my car as they walk to their car and grab their spot. Not today. We park near the hospital doors and stroll in with our masks on, two painter's masks that I dug up in the shed, and sprayed with disinfectant, and left out in the sun. We're greeted by two masked figures in hospital scrubs. They wear gloves as well. The man holds his thermometer to my forehead and the woman does the same to Debbie. They ask us if we've had a temperature or any flu-like symptoms in the last week. We say no. They wave us into an empty hallway. A few souls wander in masks. And nurses at stations, kitted out in masks, gloves, all looking dazed in their slow movements, which we adjust to with a similar shuffle. We search, wide eyed, the many department signs for the right one that would dissipate, so we hope, this scene of wandering, aimless souls, and replace it with the mayhem of a recovered routine.

We take the elevator by pressing the call button with the retracted nib of a ballpoint pen. The lift opens to a floor that is vacant of human traffic. The sign for internal medicine, where I am to be assessed, is arrowed to my left, and we march on in that hospital post-op shuffle, as if afraid that imaginary stitches might burst and our bodies splash onto the floor. Our extreme caution at being in a diseased space, one hijacked by COVID-19 and barricaded against invasion, leaves us slow in our thinking, unable to speak and more than a little afraid. The corridor is blocked by a hospital clerk, masked and gloved; she asks me my name and appointment time. I begin to fill in a form, we stand rather than sit, and I use my own pen. I take out one of my antiseptic wipes from the clear ziplock plastic bag, and I wipe the A4 clipboard all around its frame as if casting a spell on the thing rather than cleansing it with any real effect.

The questions are all ones I have answered many times in the last four months. Do I smoke? No. (Though I always want to write, Never tobacco.) Drink? Yes. How often, and how much? Not a lot and not at all since toasting in the New Year. And then the ailments, all of which I am pleased to answer in the negative:

heart, kidney, diabetes, shortness of breath, headaches, all negative. Today I know that the operation is just two appointments
away and in a little over a week. I repeat my answers in a spell
that I cast to protect my body after the anesthesiologist switches
off my mind. A second nurse asks me to follow her and I say that
my wife is with me and she asks if Debbie is symptom-free as
well. Yes. I am weighed. 164 soaking wet, as they say, that is, fully
clothed with boots and raincoat. Take off five pounds, give or
take a pound of clothing. I feel heavy.

The nurse directs us into a room and she takes my temperature
in my ear and my blood pressure, one hundred over seventy-three,
pulse sixty. All good, she says. How do I feel, she asks. I say tip-top
except for the scourge of my cancer. She says she needs an elec-
trocardiogram (EKG) and would I mind taking off my shirt and
putting on the hospital gown with the open side at the front. She
asks me to lie on the gurney. She pins glue nodes to my left and
right breasts and two more below my chest. She attaches sticky
wires that lead to her machine and she starts to take readings of
the electricity of my heart. I close my eyes and breathe deep into
the area I imagine as bottoming out at my navel. I see the jars of
my lungs, two freestanding, tall red clay containers, and I pour
air into them in through the twin portals of nostrils and out and
in. I picture a bucket that I have fetched from a well and brought
back to the house in Airy Hall to pour with a steady tilt into the
water barrel at the bottom of the stairs, which leads up to the
kitchen.

All finished, she says, and I open my eyes. She pulls off each
of the adhesive nodes and the tape attached to my skin and I ask
if she sees anything unusual and she says it all looks good to her
eyes but she is not the doctor and she laughs. Just then the doctor
walks in. He looks about twenty-five, with the face of a teenager.
So fresh and clean and in his light green suit and light blue mask
and dark blue gloves. He looks at my chart online and says I appear to be very fit. I nod and smile. Though I remember that the
smile is behind my painter's mask and needs to be exhibited by

my eyes. I mention my note. I ask the doctor for a drug to help me with my enlarged breasts. He looks at my chest. I tell him that the subtle growth is around the nipples and on the sides nearest my armpits. He says he will call the resident doctor since he is not qualified to prescribe, only consult. He leaves. I put on my shirt but do not button it, and wait and the doctor appears. She is almost as young and she nods as I explain about my request. She glances at my chest and she says my doctor has to be the one who writes the prescription since he was the one who began the original medication. I nod. The doctor wishes me well and takes her leave with the young intern.

A nurse tells me to dress and please provide a urine sample and take it downstairs to the place where my blood will be drawn. I know where to go. My blood was drawn there a couple of months ago. She hands me a small container and a clear plastic bag and she steers me to the bathroom. I open the door by pressing on the handle with my elbow and I push the door wide with my foot and scoot into the bathroom. I need to pee. I empty some in the bowl, stop, fill the little container, and complete the process. I seal the container in the plastic bag and wash my hands with copious amounts of soap and water. I dry and use the tissue to open the door and my foot to widen the door for my quickstep exit.

I summon the elevator with my ballpoint pen. We walk, with quick steps this time, to the pharmacy and blood room. The waiting area has chairs labeled alternately with signs that say DO NOT SIT, and empty ones so orderly they might be occupied by ghosts, which create the six-foot barrier that is de rigueur these days. The phlebotomist is so efficient that she answers my question about how things have been in her department and completes the pinch of bursting into my skin and extraction of a capsule of blood in about two sentences. Debbie pulls my urine sample from her coat pocket where she hid it (I don't have pockets with sufficient space) for the short walk between departments, and some urine has leaked into the bag.

The phlebotomist won't touch it. She hands Debbie a clean

bag and says to drop the sample in the compartment that's in the bathroom. Debbie asks for directions to the bathroom and heads there for the changeover of my urine sample container from a wet to a dry plastic bag. The nurse bandages my arm and I compliment her on her seamless draw of my blood. She says I should tell her supervisor, who happens to be standing outside the compartment where I'm seated with her in close quarters. I say, really, yes, you are an excellent phlebotomist. Debbie returns.

Next stop the pharmacy. I have to pick up a renewal of my tamsulosin (brand name, Flomax). I call my doctor, and the receptionist who answers for the doctor tells me that he is working from home and she will contact him. I say that I'm in the hospital and live a half hour away and ideally would love to pick up a prescription for the drug to tackle my breast problem. She says she can see in my file, my note to my doctor, and she will page him. She warns me that it may take a while for me to get a response from the doctor. As I queue for the renewed drug, I hope to hear about the new one. Alas, the call comes to me on my drive away from the hospital.

We decide to stop at the university and pick up some books and papers from my flooded office for my spring course. Two months ago the builders boxed my books and tore up the floor and cut open the walls to remove the insulation. I see an open door. People working on the office next to mine. They promise to get to mine next. I take my leave of the abandoned campus, so many buildings standing vacant as if contaminated and earmarked for demolition. COVID-19 has devastated the city. People have scuttled away from all their stations of productivity.

We head back to the hospital to pick up the tamoxifen. I am told to wait for twenty minutes. We decide to walk to the local supermarket to buy cat food. The cats have hard food but they tolerate it and prefer soft food. We add bananas and yogurt and yeast, absent from most shops, to the list. Yeast, for some reason, cannot be found at shops. We wonder if everyone in the city has taken to baking bread. Debbie's daily loaves have filled the house with warmth. The moment each loaf is ready we crowd around it and cut doorstop slices, and slap on butter that melts and runs off, and has to be caught from dripping onto the floor by the outstretched tongue, or by twisting the slice left and right. We leave less than half of the loaf for the rest of the day.

We collect the tamoxifen from the hospital pharmacy and drive home: a miraculous straight run interrupted by only two red lights. I gear up for my body memory of all lanes in the road full and of sidling into spaces with just enough room for my car. None of that conflict materializes. I could close my eyes and cruise home unscathed in a stricken LA. Horn use is seen as too much remonstrating for an empty road. I notice all the patchy road markings that try to keep traffic orderly, the white and yellow lines, the chevrons, and all the potholes that look so small with plenty of places to go. At the house we take off our coats and shoes outside and step indoors. My son and daughter meet us just inside the door and they want to hear all about the excursion.

My daughter directs a can of spray disinfectant at Debbie, who protests in all seriousness with "Don't you dare" and "I am not joking" at a volume that restrains Liliana and amuses Nicholas. We tell them that the hospital is being run like a naval ship and that we feel confident the people working there can control the spread of COVID-19. We don't say that we feel we dodged a bullet and with two more appointments must return to the same space, and hope for the same positive outcome. This is life in a casino at Vegas, as we make the rounds and hope for luck in a gamble designed to strip our asses bare. What convinces us that we can win is the same mindset that makes us set out on the journey in the first place. That we of all people will be spared what so few people evade. That the extraordinary care exercised by us will exempt us. How else do we leave the house? Why would I stay home and give up vital ground to the cancer? I believe I can win this medical tussle.

Tamoxifen at 10 mg twice a day convinces me of that fact. The drug blocks estrogen production and stops breast growth.

It starves those glands that grow because of the drugs I take or due to the spread of the disease up the lymph nodes. Either way tamoxifen is my soldier, even with its many side effects, more hot flashes, headache, stomachache, and risk of hives and swelling of the hands and feet, and difficulty breathing (this last one of some importance to me). With this drug my prostate cancer is fully disclosed as a whole-body affair. It was never just about the prostate anyway. Things started in that place and soon the party spread and enveloped the entire block.

I feel that any fight between my cancer and me is destined to become a brawl pulling in sympathizers on both sides. It was always my intention to conduct a multifaceted campaign in keeping with cancer's quantum behavior in my body, leaping from one place to another, and with chemical and biological frontiers to its incursions in me. There can be no decency or gentlemanly antics here. This is a rumble. I knew that the minute I heard it was cancer, with all its permutations and final result if left unchecked or caught too late in its rampage. In my drive to the hospital I see how COVID-19 alters the city and wants to take its inhabitants to the brink, so far in fact that the city cannot recover from the disease. All the busy spaces of the city emptied, to starve the disease and turn back its progress. I throw all manner of pharmaceuticals (plus my planned surgery) at my cancer to starve it, extirpate it, bring me back from my dance to the brink with the disease, leave me scarred but alive.

The side effect of flatulence is another matter. I live in the age of toilet humor. I deplore it, from PG- to R-rated versions of it. Yet here goes. Nothing should faze me, right? Wrong? There is nothing more discomforting than the urge to expel gas and find that the act must announce itself like the big bang. Thank you, meds. You will cure me of my cancer and kill me with embarrassment. If I make a sudden move, bang. If I stand and pee there is a stream of noisome air to accompany the flow of urine. If I'm in the middle of talk with Debbie or the kids, the urge to break wind mounts in me and I can just about string a sentence together and can't wait to bring the exchange to an end so that I can find a bathroom to whistle in and release the poisonous side effect of my meds. I feel bloated all the time. As if the meds were inflating my intestines, minute by minute, and I might explode if someone plugged my anus.

As a teenager I might have enjoyed this condition much more. Back then we tried to manufacture air and grab the nearest person's hand and thrust it at our bottom in time to collect the blast. After a chemistry class, one friend lay on the ground, arched his legs over his head, and placed a lighter to his school uniform to prove his theory that farts were flammable. The result was a wet firework. Nothing. I should smile more as I fart and deny cancer the pleasure of thinking it has something over me. Maybe I'll take to lifting one leg or other off the ground to mark the event. Maybe shout something like "Fire in the hole" before a blast.

It could be worse (it can always be worse), I console myself. I wake in the small hours a lot. I trudge to my desk to write, alternate between sitting and standing, and regard my cancer, pay it the attention it craves and deserves, though not in the way cancer might welcome. At least not in the way I try to belittle it and diminish its importance in my life. My psychological fight with cancer shadows all other fronts shared by us. I feel most empowered at these moments, most in control of what I'm doing to control my cancer, when I confront my mood about my disease. Sleeplessness is a corollary of worry about my disease. I work by standing at my desk (ever since the public notice that said sitting was the new smoking), ready to invite sleep back into my bones with songs of enticement in the shape of these descriptions of my life with cancer.

More than narratives, enriching as they are, I need to write actual songs. Lyrics for a boom box voice, lines to be belted out at the top of my voice and no room to breathe in my stream of delivery, my ears and pores inundated by a fire hose of stimulus. To declare my energetic opposition to my cancer, my readiness to fight it, let the cornered and caged body and spirit, hemmed in by cancer, sing and dance in a shindig start to my battle strategy. For cancer is a mood in me of gloom, of stasis, of lying down in its tide and allowing it to drown me. Cancer wants me living, but dead in my fight against it. Cancer thrives in winning my spirit, the best of me, before it wins my body, the rest of me.

Hence my party mood, rather than a solemn or ponderous outlook, and search for mantras that might literally part the waters of cancer's onslaught of me. I don't mean to say that my body is second to my soul and consciousness. Only to acknowledge that cancer stages its onslaught against my body first with secondary attacks on my mood and outlook. Cancer's main troops are biochemical. I know this from my embrace of a drug regimen and surgery. Also, I know that how I feel about having cancer shapes my ability to recover from it. How I fight with cancer determines my prognosis. Each day with cancer becomes a ritual of battle and choreography, of song and dance. In the middle of an injection into my butt, and among the swathes of cloth of hot flashes that threaten to stifle my breath, reside these songs and dances. The long-needled, stork-on-one-leg dance of the leuprolide (Lupron Depot) injection as it sinks into rump flesh and my ooh-ah song that shadows it. The hot flash twist and partnering shout of a canticle. The bloated boogie-woogie and the boogie-woogie chant. The involuntary windbag sax warm-up, coupled with my Coltrane freestyle whistle.

9

SURELY I'M TO BE SAVED

My chemical castration is complete. It took three cuts. (Fingernail applause, burst-hydrant crocodile tears, world's smallest violin played with one pincer by that literate crab in Walcott's *Omeros*, begin rendition of my self-pity blues.) Bicalutamide made the first cut. One 50 mg tablet each day. I needed something to stop my male hormones from feeding my cancer.

Simply put, bicalutamide blocks testosterone and dihydrotestosterone (DHT). Male hormones, or androgens, rely on the testes to produce them and send them around the body to stimulate various organs to function in particular ways. Testosterone heads out in search of receptors in cells to join up with and trigger these functions. An enzyme converts testosterone to DHT (associated with hair loss). In my case, testosterone helps me work out longer and harder to build muscle mass, and I have a sex drive, thanks to the properties of testosterone as it meets my muscles and brings along with its glad tidings key chemicals that assist my muscles in those particular ways. Bicalutamide's antiandrogen activity stops that work by latching onto the androgen cells, in effect covering the ends of the cells that need to be unimpeded in order to grip and attach to the receptors of the other cells and deliver its good news.

If you think of one aircraft refueling another in midair, the aircraft with the fuel extends a long, hollow pole with an end that fits into the open end of the jet that hopes to receive the fuel,

that ball-and-socket fitment allows fuel to flow from one aircraft
to another. Think of bicalutamide and Lupron Depot as the inter-
lopers that obstruct the ability of the refueling aircraft to join the
other craft that needs its tank to be filled. In the body the result
is that bicalutamide and Lupron Depot shut down the production
of testosterone and its offshoot, DHT.

Leuprolide acetate (Lupron Depot) in the form of an injection
made the second cut. For the appointment I wear my best under-
clothes, no frayed threads or faded fabric on my boxers, no cuddly
looking mini balls of cotton, those proverbial pills, on my cotton
socks. I take a long time in the shower. I cream my skin to hide
the patches that start to look ashy and dry an hour or so after a
shower. The COVID-19 restrictions make the drive nervous for
me. You have to keep your distance, wear a mask and avoid public
gatherings with hospitals—right where I'm heading—as number
one among venues where the virus festers. Unsure of what I'll
be told and trying to avoid the usual cut-and-weave driving of
LA, I try to be gracious as cars form adversarial relations with
each other and break them just as fast to take up with other cars
nearby. I allow my car to be overtaken at speed and tap my brakes
without honking as cars pull in front of me way too close to my
front end. The blue sky displays a canvas of warmth and frolicking cloud. The odd crow and seagull flick across it. Parking is
not easy. I have to wait for the reverse lights of a car as the driver
takes some time to reverse out of the space. No worries, I tell
myself, at least I have a space and I am early for my appointment.

Nuclear medicine is in the basement of the hospital. Chernobyl
comes to mind, its reactor cores deep in the ground that melt and
belch up into the domesticated air of its citizenry. It makes sense
to bury the poison of nuclear medicine. It has to be doled out in
minute quantities to kill things in a place where it causes even
more harm than the thing it is meant to cure if the doses dare
exceed prescribed levels.

The nurse is named Angela. I'm in the city of angels. Surely I'm
to be saved? Angela explains the many side effects of the medi-

cine, principally the hives, or swellings or difficulty breathing, that should they occur I must call my doctor right away. The drug, all 11.5 mg of it, comes in powder form, which is in a capsule. She inserts the capsule into a tube and adds a clear liquid, saline, to the mix. She shakes the tube. Adds a long needle to the end of it and tells me to pull up my shirt and pull down my boxers. I wish Angela's angel dust concoction the luck of a warm hand with dice in Vegas. She tells me to expect a pinch. It is more than a pinch, more like what an aunt did to me in Guyana when I went against her orders: she gathered a bit of my flesh on my arm or ears or back or leg in a pincer move of clamping thumb and index finger, and twisted it. My aunt's move made me howl and hop away from her as fast as possible and left me with a sore spot for a couple of days. The needle was my aunt at work in slow motion. I gritted my teeth and winced with my face turned away from the nurse, who asked me to relax my buns.

Leuprolide acetate is a synthetic protein that overstimulates the production of testosterone. Leuprolide targets the anterior pituitary gland, which produces the hormones that stimulate the production of testosterone. Lupron Depot floods the anterior pituitary and the result is to desensitize the gland and undermine its function as a regulator of testosterone. More specifically, the hypothalamus receives the message of a flood of Lupron Depot in the body and it sends the signal to the anterior pituitary that there is too much testosterone present and it should cease and desist, which triggers the response of fatigue in the gland from overproduction to a drastic reduction of testosterone levels in the body. The body reacts to the stimulus as if flooded by the hormone and ceases production of it. Testosterone stocks in the body decline as a result of the presence of Lupron Depot. My injection lasts for three months, thankfully. The hormonal disguise circulates in my body, mopping up testosterone. By the end of its prolonged release I should be free of the major source of my worry, my prostate, and well into bouts of radiation and chemo as needed in a mop-up operation of my own.

This is the last thing my cancer wants to hear from my body, its food source on many fronts. The site of the cancer atrophies as a result of a lack of testosterone, though not by much. The damage of the cancer continues in its spread to other areas. Lupron Depot happens to be my Anansi. My Brer Rabbit as well. What tricks the two of them play to fool my testosterone stocks and deplete them! I say play on. All I carry is a sore spot on my right rump that lasts a couple of days. I picture the deployment of the drug as waves of angels spreading their messages of goodwill throughout my body and reducing my prostate-specific antigen (PSA) test result from its fantastical reading of 256 when it should be way below 1—yes, 1.

Tamoxifen dealt the final death cut to complete my medical castration. At 10 mg, twice a day, I find it a palliative. Every time I lift a tablet to my lips I feel a shot of goodness run through me in my belief that some useful action has been set in motion to strangle my cancer. It is like tilling soil. That sounds too grand. More like the raised vegetable garden (two eight-foot-by-three-foot beds) that Debbie and I built last fall from planks of wood nailed together and lined with tarp and topped with twenty bags of a soil mix, and seeded with lettuce, tomato, basil, and thyme.

Tamoxifen. If only I were a man at ease with my body no matter its permutations. Instead, I baulk at the tenderness around my nipples and the slight swelling about the size of a dollar coin or English fifty pence (though not an equilateral-curve heptagon, that would be too much). A strip of engorged flesh runs along the outside edges of both breasts. At a glance I look like someone with enviable pectorals. Up close they tell a different story. I see the new cartography of my body as cancer territory. Sensitive to the disbelieving probe of my fingers, the swelling dearly wishes to pass as just my body on a growth spurt. But I am too old for such generous displays of physical prowess. I know the denial of testosterone in my body brought about by the combined onslaught of Lupron Depot and bicalutamide has led to the dominance of estrogen. Enlarged breasts derive from my estrogen, given free rein in me in the absence of testosterone. Damn right, I need something for that.

As I said, I wrote to my doctor saying that I noticed the alteration to my chest, and I wished to curb it. Debbie's research helpfully found the drug that works to inhibit breast growth. I added it to my note to the doctor. He dutifully wrote the prescription. In fact, he had mentioned the side effect on our first meeting when he prescribed bicalutamide tablets and the Lupron Depot injection. (Debbie suggested tamoxifen as the likely fix if the need arose.) At my health web portal I dug into UCLA's information on how the drug works. The patient information tells me how to pronounce the name and how to take the drug and what to look for if things go wrong for me. Though useful, the pages for patients seem preliminary as far as learning about the makeup of the drug and its pathways of operation in the body.

Tamoxifen blocks estrogen and treats breast cancer, and acts as a prophylactic as well. Among its many side effects is the counterintuitive possibility of more breast swelling (as if I needed more of it and vaginal discharge (which is not my worry). The hot flashes, which wake me and stop me midactivity several times in the day, occur in 70 percent of men. Signs of tiredness and fatigue and a bloated feeling, some weight gain, thirst, and cravings. All plague me to such an extent that I begin to measure out my favorite almond yogurt into a four-ounce container that I've saved, rather than trust my eyes and scoop it like ice cream from the large container into a small bowl. As I serve myself I try to add one spoonful less than usual of Debbie's culinary delights (that have multiplied in excellence with COVID-19's enforced housebound rules, and have become a major challenge for me, for being a major refuge), and I always attack the salad as the go-to filler of my famished urges. Nevertheless my love handles inflate from neat handgrips to unwieldy handfuls of corpulent excess. I find her quiche the most tempting of all. She adds an array of cheeses to her mix, Swiss, sharp cheddar, Gouda, and broccoli. The crust is just so crumbly and yet adhering to the pie (is pie the right term for the contents of a quiche?), with a slight sweetness to it and a little bit of chewiness to the multiple cheeses in play. Not to mention the oils sweated by the cheeses. Nor the way a salad with tomatoes from the makeshift garden compliments that quiche. I always go back for more with the rationale that I began with a small slice. I try to chew each mouthful sixteen times to abate that unquenchable sense of needing more, always more, like a gormandizing version of Oliver Twist.

Part of my tamoxifen blues rests in a psychological sense of the neutrality of my gender. I feel neither male nor female. My crotch attached to clear principles of pleasure along a masculine trajectory has retreated into pure functionality. I hold tamoxifen responsible. My Anansi savior and my crucifix, with the bonus of bouts of hot flashes, add an image of me tied to a pole turning over a fire. Brer Rabbit tamoxifen. Two tricksters in one drug, present for dual application by me, and going by the long list of side effects, my cancer too. What began in my prostate now languishes far from it and conducts skirmishes in my breasts. I think of the keys of my spine along which the cancer must sing its blues progression as it climbs to my heart and brain.

The Nicholas Brothers, in my body memory, work their tap and acrobat dance for me. I rename them Anansi and Brer Rabbit. I hope they work as if doubled for my cancer as well, though I know that the trip up my spine along my lymph nodes resembles the choreography of those talented brothers. Tamoxifen, tap dance, like them. Somersault and backflip like them. Neutralize the growth of my breasts, and I will gladly pay the price of becoming a eunuch. Eat less of Debbie's quiches and cakes that are myrrh and frankincense to me. I'm caught in a tactical retreat from the variety of my life into a simpler, stripped-down version of it, still vital though lighter, still complex, if far less complicated.

Today Debbie and I braved an LA drizzle to walk the dog. A little rain cannot stop us. Neither of us is Lot's wife, a pillar of salt who had to avoid water like the plague. COVID-19's housebound rules make this walk necessary whatever the weather. The grains of sparse water speckle my glasses and sand my face, as in a breeze on a beach flung at me, that I twist my spine to turn my back to, and save my face. I wish for rain to lather me. With the summer nearing, this rain will be the last for many months. Let it not be my last. Make it a baptism of the many days ahead with or without rain. So that I live to see the city find its feet one step at a time and one day after the next.

Tamsulosin is exempt from this hatchet job on the grounds that its function of relaxing my muscles to help me pee, while it indirectly shrinks my prostate, provides a critical service. I take one 0.4 mg tablet at bedtime. I sleep all night thanks to it. No more trips to the bathroom twice in the night. Tamsulosin cannot be a blues of my despair. More the jazz of my survival, it remains a testimony of likely reparations paid to my spirit. There is a reverse dance between my cancer and this drug, a dance that follows the drug's Nicholas Brothers gymnastics at the site of the cancer to uproot it. The reverse dance is a backward journey to drive that cancer away from my breast and back down my spine to where it started in my prostate. The dancer must be someone as good as Alvin Ailey. Or simply my brother Greg, at Ballet Rambert in 1978 or '9 in a *grande jeté* that I swear he held for a whole second longer than all the other boys around him so that he floated across the stage and high above those boards, coming down on his lead leg, his right, like a feather loosened from a pillow.

I have more time to devote to my death with so many assets on my side attacking the size of the cancer and reversing the ground gained by it. Today I undergo my prostate-specific membrane antigen (PSMA) test. This test provides the eyes that the surgeon wants in order to operate on me. Today I give him his eyes. I wake at 4:15 a.m. worried about the six hours, when I have to be nil by mouth, before my noon appointment, except to take a sip of water if I have to swallow any meds. There are two tablets, the tamoxifen and the bicalutamide, that I consider knocking back early to avoid water (as if I were made of salt) and preserve my six-hour fast.

I will my body to make this penultimate stride to the surgery after a phone call from the hospital that asks me to take a
COVID-19 test two days before the operation. If the test is negative I am allowed to go under the knife. If it is positive all these
last four months of strategy and worry come to naught, the operation will be postponed and rescheduled and I will have to be
tested again before it to be sure I am COVID-19-free.

The PSMA shows the exact paths taken by my cancer. My body
should light up with it and all the surgeon has to do is collect the
shining gems of my illness, Hansel and Gretel style. Of course he
can go only so far into my body before he has to give up and exit
and close me up. The good news is the PSMA picture of my cancer will be utilized in any radiation and chemo treatments that
follow the surgery. It is my word of the day. PSMA is my song put
to the tune of the Village People's "YMCA." Here is the song in
full for a sing-a-long.

P-S-M-A!
I want to have it now.
P-S-M-A.
For the surgeon needs eyes
For my cancer's disguise
'Cause I want to live
And have my life back.
Help me sing it now.
P-S-M-A!

All I have to do is work out the choreography for it. I must ponder that *P* as a dance move. How? *S* is a doddle. Try this. I want
people to clasp their hands as if in prayer and raise those clasped
hands above their heads and bring those hands down like a snake,
yes, down like a snake, in the shape of an *S*, go, in the shape of an
S. The rest is easy thanks to the Village People.

The PSMA machine has a magnetic resonance tube and I am
fed into it on a gurney that the tube moves up and over me, and

it reads the nuclear fluid injected into my veins to see which parts of me have absorbed that fluid. There are markers in the radiation that target the cancer cells or the antigens manufactured by the membrane of my prostate. Wherever those cells have migrated, that radiation will find them and latch on to them and send out a message that the imaging machine reads and maps for the surgeon. There is a different tune for this search-and-flush-out process of my test. I hear a melodramatic tune without lyrics: the *Mission: Impossible* soundtrack as the chemical is injected into my arm and starts to seek out the cancer.

I might end up gamma-super-powered after all these infusions of radiation. It could be my superpower, a bit like the Hulk but without the ugly. A new cancer might spring out of this nuclear bombardment of my body. When I think of the treatments that involved radiation, what comes to mind is history. In a poem by the Guyanese poet Grace Nichols titled "I Is a Long Memoried Woman," Nichols imagines the Middle Passage from the perspective of a woman, a terrain previously the domain of male poets and fiction writers. There are many memorable passages; for instance, "it isn't easy to forget / what we refuse to remember." Its apparent tautology invokes one big drama of the Middle Passage, that of willful forgetting. As a mechanism, forgetting achieves the opposite of its intentional amnesia, because the forced part of it serves to impel memory. But for me the telling phrase is when the poem's narrator declares, "I have crossed an ocean / I have lost my tongue / from the root of the old one / a new one has sprung."

We speak in tongues. For me, what is new is that which I wish to stay news. It concerns the lessons that I learn out of all the pressure of my symptoms, their diagnosis and treatment. Cancer instructs me about my life even as it seeks to annihilate me.

There is a hip-hop chant for my penultimate PSMA appointment. (Just in case my Village Peeps are not enough—when are they ever anything less than more than a handful!)

Big-up PSMA! Hip-hop hooray!

What have we here today? We got PSMA!

There is a cheerleader quotient to my choreography with my cancer. I am on the sidelines championing another version of me in a contest with cancer. My cheerleader self is kitted out with pom-poms and butt-creased shorts. I have multiplied into a troupe. We semaphore with our pom-poms and chant our PSMA songs. The version of me in the game against cancer is an amalgam of Muhammad Ali, Claudia Jones, Toussaint Louverture, Sojourner Truth, Bruce Lee, C. L. R. James, Ma Rainey, Bob Marley, and Ip Man. I know that is quite a cut-and-paste job of radical innovators. I need every corpuscle of their bodies to help me in my contest with cancer. As my disease morphs, so I call upon my heroes to step up and help me with my fight. As I remember them in their fight in their history, so they help me with mine.

My memory is invention. My experience of history (How, you may ask, can a finite body experience the long curve and straight line of history, is that not an oxymoron?), as I glean it from education, research, and life, makes history a living thing. My brief history with cancer makes my cancer and me living entities within history. As long as I keep the two (my cancer and me) in history I stay living. I am not consigned to a dead history. I remember in order to live. I hope cancer, despite its extensive arsenal, has no memory. As it duplicates my skills to counter me with Anansi and Brer Rabbit and the persons out of my personal collection of history (and fable, myth, and magic as well), I want cancer to forget the making of my history with it as that history is being made. I want my cancer to be unaware of our current, shared flux as an event in an unfinished story.

The magical component to all this stems from my upbringing in Airy Hall, the Guyanese village where I spent my childhood years. Though it was a small place, it had one of everything: one drunk, one madman, one shoemaker, whose workshop doubled as a preschool taught by his wife, one corner shop for dry goods, one bakery, and a midwife who handed out homeopathic remedies for all manner of illnesses. As a child in that place, I grew to

believe in things unseen as forces that shape life. I say the word
magic not to belittle but to keep invention at my fingertips and
bring laughter on board. I could call it by its other name (it has
many names) obeah, as well, and the scene of levity turns deadly
serious. I could label it all as superstition in the absence of hard
scientific fact as a way to put that childhood period in its proper
place. If I did that I would be a fool. Not the good fool of play and
mischief for the sake of invention but the fooled, the hypnotized
and duped.

Airy Hall seemed to promote the spirit world in part to inform
and safeguard the material world. Our days outside ended at
nightfall and our days began early at the crack of dawn. The diur-
nal cycle was accompanied by the cycle of the spirit world. Spirits
good and not so good ruled at night, they patrolled the dark and
frolicked in it. Material things ruled the daylight. During the day
our behavior was informed by that nighttime lesson of obedience
to guidelines of the spirits. If a crow landed on the house, that
was a bad omen of imminent news about a death or dying relative
or friend. If a black cat crossed your path, that foretold a not-so-
good outcome to your journey, and made you guarded for the
rest of your day.

The list, though long, is by no means exhaustive. At night we
gathered around a gas-lit lamp with its soft sphere of a wick under
a glass shade, to talk about the workings of spirits. Our eyes widened and jaws dropped to tales of children taken in the night by
supernatural forces. We knew that to venture out into the thick
dark that made the trunks of trees and their limbs join hands to
form a wall would be inviting death. We also looked up for long
periods at the night sky to marvel at the patterns of light as we
waited for a star to pitch so that we could make a wish by it. Each
childhood mishap was credited to the machinations of the spirits.
But so was all our fortune. All our attention and concentration
grew out of this focus on spirits and talk and thought about them.
They figured in our dreams as well.

Cancer has nothing like this world in its arsenal. Cancer's

mechanism relies on chemistry and time-locked genealogies, marvelous building blocks for sure, and vulnerable as a result to uncertainty, the numinous as magic. If cancer exhibits lockstep progression, I may be able to alter that course with inducements of magic, fable, myth, and the story component of his/her/their story. I redouble my effort to build alternatives to cancer's march to an early end to my life. Cancer's direct assault calls on me to absorb its energies and divert them into more creative ends (beginnings) for me. As cancer drives forward in my body, so I twist and shout to evade it.

*   *   *

There is a reggae song to go with the other tunes of my resistance to my cancer. Just as there is an epidemiology for my disease, there a matching epidemiology for my resistance to it. In 1976, Tapper Zukie, a Jamaican DJ, recorded an album in London titled *MPLA* (the Mozambique People's Liberation Army). That title track, "Dub MPLA," an exemplar of incantatory deep dub, easily works with PSMA substituted into it, along with some words about my condition and my struggle with it. After I say "PSMA," you have to hear a heavy bass line, six beats that are 1, 2, 1, 2, 1-2, slow, slow, slow, slow, quick-quick, or *boom, boom, boom, boom, boom-boom*. It is hexameter if we hear every sound as a stress ('cause you feel every pound of the bass). It can be construed as pentameter if we take each of the first four numbers as stressed monosyllables, and assume that the last two numbers concede a stress on the second number, rather than counting them as two unstressed syllables delivered in rapid succession, or as two stressed ones of equal weight. So much for the grammar of my resistance in exact countermeasure to the grammar of cancer in my Black body.

I say this about the two grammars (for cancer and resistance to it) and their respective epidemiology since my ear may pick up not hexameter or even pentameter but iambic trimeter, with the third pair delivered faster than the previous two pairs. Whatever you settle on for its metrical beat, the rhythm pans out as roughly similar in its buckling effects on the spine, hip, knees, and other bones, in its acceleration of the heart and blood circulation and in its exhilaration of the spirit. You have to imagine my close-cropped hair and receding hairline as magically recovered into copious swirling dreads, possibly red ones. I perform a Bob Marley skank (in those days *skank* referred to a reggae dance) of hips dipped and each leg bent in turn as I hop from one foot to the other, and shake my head, and as I chant "PSMA," to bring down the Babylonian growth of my cancer.

A pom-pom is insufficient as a prop. I need maracas and a tambourine. I need the many strings of multicolored beads of a New Orleans Mardi Gras, and a shirt from Trinidad's carnival and the headgear of Brazil's. Add to all that bacchanal paraphernalia those voluminous sound systems of London's Notting Hill Carnival. Let's party and let the games begin. Both. Dear cancer, may I have the privilege of our first dance? Hey, cancer, want to come out and play? I have this feeling that today will go my way. One of those good days that the rapper Ice Cube dreams about in his track "It Was a Good Day," ironic, braggadocio, and ponderous in turn about life in South Central LA, where all the life-threatening things that routinely happen magically do not, until the close of day bursts the bubble of that dreamtime with the same old, same old helicopter (ghetto bird) overhead, and multiple squawking squad cars with militarized cops.

So it is that we hit Washington in Mid-City and find nothing on the streets, a clean sweep of asphalt heading west and shining with the rain as if the sea began at my door right here in Mid-City. Debbie wonders how we will go back to jammed streets after this loving emptiness. The left onto Crenshaw yields the same grace: few cars, little foot traffic, someone selling face masks where they once sold flowers. The right onto the I-5 and it is the same, no turnstile of lights to feed cars onto the near gridlock, just an easy slide down the ramp and ease out left into sparse traffic. We sail to my appointment. We tack lanes of the sea. I do not drive. The car conveys me.

With the air so clean and washed now by rain these last two days, there is a lightness to the already well-lit place, less resistance offered to my car, more invitations sent to my lungs to trust and draw deep. Even the lights hold us for shorter periods, their green with a polished look, their red looking more apologetic. There are spaces galore in the hospital parking lot. We don masks in our seats and emerge from the car disguised in broad daylight as if about to execute a bank raid.

A nurse at the door points to a newly added sign that lists COVID-19 symptoms and she wants to know if we have anything on the list, coughing, runny nose, fever, difficulty breathing, we shake our heads from side to side for each, and speak loudly with our mouths comprehensively covered, and we smile with our eyes or beam goodwill with them. The nurse holds a temporal artery thermometer close to our foreheads and waves us into the hospital. We march on, less a march, more a saunter. We are early and I say to Debbie that if I move faster I might pass out from lack of air thanks to my constricting mask.

I use a ballpoint pen to summon the elevator to the basement that houses nuclear medicine. Debbie remarks that the isolation in the basement is perfect in case of a Chernobyl-like accident. Funny you should say that. I was thinking the same thing and how I was about to introduce that feared chemical compound into my body voluntarily. Debbie has to leave, new policy, only patients who need help can have someone with them, and since the whole thing should take three hours it makes no sense for her to wait in the car for me. She wishes me luck and heads for home. I promise to keep her updated.

There is just one other person, besides the male receptionist, in the waiting room. Alternate chairs are labeled as not for use to enforce the safe distance between patients. The other person is a young woman with short hair and baggy black clothes who does not look up from her phone, which she addresses with two hands. She has a walking stick next to her seat. The fluorescent lights bleed my brown skin to resemble her whiteness, and my old middle age seems less distanced from her twentysomething youthfulness in this blanched light. It is as if the waiting room is lit by the nuclear particles that both of us need to send around our body to highlight our disease. The introductory exterior light means to lull us into making the transition to imminent interior bombardment.

Since the procedure is experimental, I have a lot of reading matter, mostly disclaimers in case I die or become disabled, though this rarely happens, going by the stats (one in one hundred thousand), and a lot of consent to grant the experts in various branches of the medical profession access to my file. One part of the test is known and in abundant use at over twenty thousand hospitals worldwide. But the tracer is the culprit in need of research. The friendly head of nuclear medicine research, and professor and surgeon (he offers his card in one hand and his elbow for me to bump), tells me that the tracer is already approved to show cancer in the brain. This prostate application for the PSMA test, though it utilizes the same chemical imaging technique as the PSA test, is not approved. The professor says that they came upon it accidentally when a patient with both brain and prostate cancer was given the tracer for the brain and it showed cancer in the prostate as well. He thinks that approval is inevitable given the high accuracy of the look for the surgeon that the trace drug affords and because it is approved for another procedure; that is, it's not truly experimental. They just need the numbers of patients, he tells me. I feel like I am doing some good for medicine. I hope the medicine will reciprocate.

The approved part of the test is the conventional position emission tomography (PET) machine, which provides a magnetic resonance pictograph of the body's interior with a chemical highlighter taken orally or intravenously to sharpen what the radiologist sees. PET maps inside the body by bouncing magnetic sound waves off the organs, which are highlighted by tracers that the machine's waves find, just as homing coordinates might re-position a satellite remotely. The unapproved part concerns the tracer, called 68Ga-PSMA-11. The first number is the chemical chart placing of the gamma rays. 68Ga radiation has a short half-life of six hours or less. It is ordered up from the manufacturing lab the moment I pay for the test. A special delivery of a lead-clad, outsize sandwich container brings it to me. The radiation sits in its cozy stainless-steel canister in the room to attain room tem-perature, though the nurse tells me that it will feel cool running up the vein in my arm since my blood is warmer than the room.

Somehow children crop up in my talk with the director-professor-surgeon. We agree, along sexist, cisgender assumptions, that his boy and my two sons cope better with being housebound than his daughter and mine, who appear more agitated with iso-lation and seem to need more tactile human exchanges. His boy plays games online, as do mine, and his daughter yearns to get out of the house and meet with her friends in the flesh, as does mine. A part of my consciousness wants to ingratiate itself with the surgeon to let him know I'm just like him except for my mal-ady. It occurs to me that I've taken to heart those radio reports about Black people under COVID-19. Apparently, Black men are fearful in public with their masks on their faces in case it adds to an already threatening reading of their bodies. Also, an alarm-ingly high number of Blacks compared with Whites are dying from COVID-19.

What troubles me is my need to feel as near a human as pos-sible to the head of nuclear medicine research. I view my cancer as a factor that separates me from the rest of humanity. Blackness is my marker for this noted difference in a White-run system. COVID-19 for all its pandemic hoopla has not altered the fact that race plays a big role in who gets to live and who is left to die. I should twin race with poverty. The poor and homeless face the brunt of the effects of COVID-19. Add to this fact that Afri-can American men are more likely than White men (of European descent) to contract prostate cancer and perhaps my paranoia is justified after all, is not in fact paranoia but a fair assumption.

I wish I had fewer things to worry about. It makes sense that cancer would co-opt many things on its side to overload me with anxiety about having it and weaken my resolve to fight it. A nurse comes in and she delights in her driving time to work cut in half by COVID-19. She asks me to pick an arm for the intravenous site. I roll up my right sleeve, remembering that I gave blood last week from my left arm. I do not want my veins to look like I imagine heroin addicts' arms to be—laddered with bruises from the assault of countless needles. I fear the collapse of a traumatized vein.

The nurse barely makes contact with my skin. Gloveless, she wears a plain, thin gold ring on her left thumb. Her manicured, pink nails, possibly modest extensions, shine. Her hands' butterfly touch belie the pinch she meekly warns me about before she punctures my vein. It feels more than an avuncular pinch, more like my aunt changing her mind halfway through her pincer movement on my flesh and releasing her vice to leave me with a burn that is about half the strength of her usual furious application. She pours a white powder into 1,000 mL of glucose solution that dyes the square plastic bottle ruby. She says I have forty-five minutes to drink it all. I reply that I'll pretend it's red wine since I've not had a drink in months. She raises the gurney on which I am seated so that I can put up my feet and recline, and she departs. I check my phone but cannot get a signal in the nuclear basement bunker. I imagine cement poured over days by a convoy of trucks with slowly rotating payloads lined up both sides of Wiltshire Plaza and snaking for a mile along these Westwood streets.

Left alone, I pour the sweet, red water into a paper cup and drink. Room temperature below ground means cool, so that I feel this burgeoning refrigeration of my body that offers nectar to my disease, for it to sip, lose its camouflage, and reveal its encampment in me. The masking effect of the sugar does little to disguise the medicinal taste. I read the long handout about the test and stop after every paragraph to take a gulp and after several of those, stop to refill the cup. I note, without wanting to, how more plastic shows than drink and soon less drink, that makes me wonder if I have one or two more pours from the bottle for me to drain it. I am helped by the fact that six hours ago I took my last drink, early-morning coffee that I woke in the dark to enjoy, making me wonder if I faced a firing squad and they offered me a last cigarette whether I would decline it for a coffee or in addition to a coffee, since to drink deep of the air that I was about to lose makes a delight and a delicacy out of a cigarette. Or would it be a spliff and a coffee? Coffee first. No doubt.

The nurse returns and congratulates me on finishing the drink, she says quite a few people find it impossible to get to the end. I think, Now you tell me I could have left some, when you gave me the impression forty-five minutes ago that I had to drink it all. Sneaky. She directs me to the lavatory to empty my bladder. I elbow open the bathroom door, a long lever curved at the inward-facing end, and use a napkin to turn the lock on it. I dispose of the tissue and pee. It is clear. And not as much as I expected given how much I took on board. I thought ahead to the time when the urge to go again would make me have to ask someone or other to point me to a bathroom.

To keep me at the sink for the recommended twenty seconds with the water running and me rubbing my hands, I recite Langston Hughes's "The Negro Speaks of Rivers," for its bravura packed into two musical nuggets for stanzas. The poem's trance-like opener that repeats at the poem's close is as nimble as water. The water in the refrain matches the flow of the tap. The smatterings of soap, water, and twist and turn of flesh might be the poem's metrics and shifts of the speaker through the emblems of ancient African civilizations to the ancient Mississippi, to link Africa with America: As I dry my hands, I think for the second and final time:

"My soul has grown deep like the rivers."

I exit with the same tissue trick to unlock the door and to push down the door handle, and with my foot, I jam the door and widen the opening with the help of my elbow to keep the door wide for me to slide sideways through it. The nurse meets me outside and she sees my maneuver and says with a smile that everyone is doing that nowadays.

The PET-CT scanner takes up the room: a long gurney engulfed at one end by a big white tube, the size of a tractor tire. Everything is painted white with the odd pastel tone that is so saccharine in a room but denotes sterility. She tells me to take off my pants and put on a white pajama bottom that has faded lilac-like flowers on it. The pants are big. I ask the nurse if I can keep my underpants on. She says yes, and exits smartly. I mean her moves are economical, as if edited by her before she does them. I take off my shoes, my trousers, and pull on the huge pajama bottoms. They gather at my feet. I wait for a moment and she returns. Can she see me change? I expect the room to be wired for everything, sound and image present in the walls as well as in the PET-CT scanner.

I lie on the gurney and she makes me scoot up to rest my head on a pillow. I tell myself to relax and she offers me a warm blanket, which she spreads on me. I marvel at its warmth. She says they keep the blankets heated because the room needs to be cooler than usual to keep the machine cool. She offers me a second blanket. I say yes, keen on the cozy feel of a warm cover gently pressing on me. She takes my arm and flushes out the IV with saline. Then she adds the gamma nuclear concoction to the IV with a warning about the slow crawl of the cool liquid up my arm that spreads into my chest and up my neck.

This is medicine at work, an invasive force with a signature arrival no sense can ignore. However I wish to see my cancer, as a dance, a play in perpetual rehearsal, a healthy dose of insecurity that negates the bombastic ego, this machine that covers my body now with my arms raised over my head looks nothing short of a battle cry and charge at an enemy. I hold my breath as the intercom voice of the nurse instructs, and the machine spins, with a red and blue light and the lowest imaginable whir, and I breathe out when she says that I can. This happens three times. The doughnut moves along my body, stops, and works some more.

Cancer, if you can hear me, now hear this: A clarion plays on my behalf that hopes to drive your forces back and out of me. Chemical numbers assembled in my body now distribute gamma rays, the most destructive form of battle of the modern age if we take Nagasaki and Hiroshima as benchmarks. 68Ga radiates inside me in waves that stop just short of washing my bones clean and purifying my blood. Instead they seek out and leave an identifying mark on each and every manifestation of my cancer in the most efficient reconnaissance ever. I cannot ask for a bigger advantage than to have my enemy under spotlights.

The weird thing about being nuked is that there is an assessed safe level to the process. I find it hard to believe that a portion of the radiation will not stray into my brain or spinal column and stick there for long enough to start a new crop of my disease. I conjure the image of a trusty flu shot—planting the very thing in my body that I hope to evade but in safe quantity to trigger my inoculation against the virus. Gamma rays work like this for me. Be the guiding lamplight for my surgeon to see his way around my insides.

I swallow pooling saliva and grit my teeth as nausea shimmers at the margins of my senses. In my effort to think of something other than vomiting, I imagine the theme music to *Hawaii Five-O*, the seventies television series syndicated in the UK, in which a long boat of Hawaiians muscle-paddle on one side of the wood craft and change sides, in unison, making a splash to the finger-clicking, head-nodding theme song. It works. The announcement of the end of the session, this time by a male technician, brings the machine to a stop and the door of the room opens and he enters and stands next to me. He talks about me sitting up slowly and gathering my clothes and dressing in the next room and in the middle of his talk and fiddling with blankets and examining my arm he pulls off the plaster and detaches the IV in a quick swipe. I say nothing but I inhale loudly and stifle a comment about the unexpected pain since I'm sure he thought it was best not to warn me about it. I decide as a consequence that I'm one of those people who prefer to be warned about impending pain rather than be surprised by it.

He opens the door and points to the changing room and bathroom, and the exit sign for the waiting room, where he tells me to wait for about twenty minutes while he burns a CD for me with a copy of the 68Ga-PEP-CT scan. I feel a slight headache and lethargy as from a long workout on the stationary bike. The nuclear test works its quiet ministry inside me and exacts a toll on my body. I pee copiously, seemingly more than the 1,000 mL that I took on board. I find the waiting room and it is empty. One lone figure passing through the room pulls a sleeve over a hand to open the door and disappear. I pick a chair near to the front desk, where the clerk is on the phone constantly.

Where is the air that I am breathing now in this basement filtered and generated? What if COVID-19 in its next iteration finds a way to travel in molecules attached to this air? I look around at the physical space and imagine it coated in the virus. I have a ziplock sandwich bag with four sheets of disinfectant wipes in my jacket's left side pocket. I reach for it and sink my hand into the wet interior of the bag and wipe my hands together. I bring my wet hand to the front of my painter's mask and hope my touch neutralizes any virus on my mask. I text Debbie to come and get me and return my attention to my phone, which works in this part of the basement by some miracle of design that admits phone signals. One of the many operations in my life that I will need another lifetime to understand how it works, but for now I accept its friendly fire of magnetic rays into my eyes and ears.

The technician appears sooner than anticipated and delivers the CD to me. I thank him and he wishes me well. His parting gaze is a look I have come to recognize in nurses and doctors who deal with me. Knowing the details of my file, they look at me as if seeing an astonishingly limited numbered of days of life emblazoned on my forehead. It is a look of pity and warmth and it stops just short of commiseration. It is a look that I fear the moment I catch it, and immediately following my fear, this rage surges in me, rage mixed with defiance, that declares I will live a long life and prove them wrong.

It is early for my ride to arrive but another second in that basement will be the death of me. I hurry away with a quick parting greeting to the receptionist, who waves while still on the phone and whose eyes I avoid just in case his smile is a knowing one about me. I summon the lift with my ballpoint (nib retracted) and exit with big strides and step from the automatic doors into the broad day. My energy returns a spring to my steps. I must be glowing right now. If a machine could pick up the radiation in me it would buzz loud and long. If I clasp something like an egg I might boil it hard in its shell with my gamma ray touch. If I stare at a brick wall perhaps I can see through it to the other side.

I phone Debbie as she drives past me on the other side of the road with a divide full of plants that hide me from her. She pulls over and I cross at the lights and hot-step it to her. I tell her I am nuclear. She scoots around the car to the passenger side and I fold into the driver's seat. She has a banana, an energy bar, and a whopping slice of her walnut-and-caramel cake for me. I thank her profusely and drive one-handed as I gorge.

Debbie mentions that Liliana has an online debate competition beginning in thirty minutes. Ordinarily this would have been impossible for us eight miles from the house at this time. We reach home in just under twenty minutes. Liliana is delighted to have us at home. It is her first online debate, brought on by the enforced isolation of COVID-19, and no one is sure how it will work out. I tell her everything for me went according to plan and that I have a CD of the result though no way to understand what's on the disc. Between one debate and the next as the judge adds up the scores of the student entrants, we get Nicholas to load the disc on his computer, since my Mac cannot read it. What comes up is a shape of my body with a line below my crotch area and another at my neck to demarcate the lines of inquiry of the scan. The second image is a series of sections of my body looking at it as if I were cut in half and a machine had traveled up my body shining a light on everything. The image is mostly shades of gray (less than fifty), and apart from the clear shape of kidneys and pelvis, we are not sure what we are looking at on the screen. I tell them in our confusion over what we are staring at that a dark gray pinpoint at the bottom of the body shape surely has to be my rectum. They laugh. We give up. I tell them that I'll report back after my talk to the doctor on Monday about the results. Now that my doc has eyes to find his way around the inside of me, I can ask him what the radiation reveals about the spread of my cancer.

10

HELLO, MISS CORONA.
MEET MISTER CANCER

I did not in a month of Sundays ever consider this Sunday to be my last Easter. Yet here I am forced to mull over that fact as a distinct possibility. I face a major surgery. I have a deadly condition. In this mindset I return to Easter in Airy Hall, the best rendition of the occasion in my life. We sang the hymns at Sunday school.

Yes, Jesus loves me,
Yes, Jesus loves me,
Yes, Jesus loves me,
The Bible tells me so.

We also sang,

Someday, someday, I'll go where Jesus is,
Someday, someday, I'll go where Jesus is,
Someday, someday, I'll go where Jesus is,
For I'll be brought up to meet him,
Brought up to meet him,
Brought up to meet him in the air.

We listened to the scripture and the Psalms. My favorite remains Psalm 23. I left Sunday school with my dozen-and-more cousins with winged feet that made us skip along the side of the dirt road all the way home, some of us still singing one or other hymn.

We skipped home looking forward to the day. All during the previous week (except for Good Friday) uncles would call each of us in turn and measure us for a homemade kite. We watched as one of us was called up to stand still in front of two uncles. They looked the child up and down and glanced at each other and nodded and they waved the child away and picked up pieces of wood and marked those pieces. It seemed an age went by as others came under the searching eyes of my uncles. Then came my turn to be measured for my kite. I stepped close to them and they held up my arm, since I was very skinny as a child, to gauge what if any muscles clung to my skin and bones. They shot each other their knowing glances and picked up a small piece of wood and marked it up and waved me away.

The wood earmarked for my kite seemed so much smaller than the others. It might be because it shone brightly for me with my eyes on it as mine. One uncle used his cutlass to cut six strips of greenheart wood for the frame for the kite. Another uncle used his chisel to shave each piece of wood smooth and thin. That light scrape of the wood sent fragrant curls from it floating to the floor around my uncle's bare feet, and made the wood so thin it could bend a long way without breaking. My aunts came into the picture with hammers and little nails, and rolls of colored paper. They drove nails, with little taps, careful not to split the wood, into the middle of the wood frame. If a piece of wood split accidentally down the middle or into two pieces, it made us suck on the air as if pricked by a needle, and our aunts stopped what they were doing to stare at the ruined wood and they sucked their teeth irritably and tossed the wood aside and had to ask one or another uncle for a new piece, which slowed the process. My aunts cut paper shapes, mostly diamonds, from colored paper, which was kept from creasing by rolling the sheets loosely like bolts of cloth. They angled thin paintbrushes dipped in glue onto the ends of each piece of paper and onto the wood frame. They used their fingers to press on the glue and stretch the paper on the frame. They rounded their lips and lowered their faces close to the wood and paper and glue and blew on it. I could smell the perfume of glue and of shaved wood, the fine dust from the paper that made me sneeze.

My aunts and uncles worked on our kites all week between their usual chores. By Thursday's close the kites piled up, stacked in corners of the workroom. Each with our name on it, not written, but in skeletal form, made just for our frame to handle. Each linked to one of us changed us as never seen before, wood and colored paper, with a tongue and a tail and a ball of twine on the end of a stick, propped up against a wall. We went to sleep talking late into the night and had to be shushed several times by a grown-up, and slept fitfully and rose early.

The adults were up already. Plaited loaves of Grandmother's baked bread were spread on the table to cool and taunt us. It was Good Friday and nothing could be done that was not already a thing to think about and refrain from doing. We had to ponder the ultimate sacrifice made on our behalf by Our Savior. We had to ignore those kites, newly minted for each of us as if the materials were withdrawn from each of our bodies. My grandmother could see everything because she never slept. So it seemed, awake, as I nodded off trying to stay up with her, and up and about the house before me even though I woke especially early just to catch her in her bed. She banned us from going near the kites and said we should not look at them since they were there to tempt us on Good Friday, a day of rest, when nothing should be done, not even fly a kite in anticipation of Sunday. No room for anything on Good Friday but grief and the lessons of that monumental hurt.

We believed in what happened to Christ, for we knew our kites would rise as emblems of his soul, ascending from the gravity of this world toward a more ethereal existence, paid for with his life, sacrificed on behalf of us lesser mortals. The string that we held on to presented to us the chance to join Christ in his heaven, as we'd sung in Sunday School, and as we held on to our kites, each seemed to be one of us up there, something that stood for us, small bits of our being, kites that encapsulated our bodies, our souls, no less, us flying on the end of as a long navel-string, sent up to meet His majestic ascendency. That was our Sunday. There was a great show of finding a clearing away from the next person and raising those kites in the breeze. We stood up and pulled on the strings and swung the kites' tails from side to side, and their tongues sang in the breeze. We were airborne for the first time and for the rest of our lives. Our kites joined us to whatever forces dwelled out of reach.

And so this Sunday—if it is to be my last Easter—I want nothing more than to be with Debbie and the children and stay around the house. This version of Easter, cramped by COVID-19, and entirely secular, I wake early with Debbie, who hides chocolate eggs, positioned in partial view, for our thirteen-year-old daughter to collect when she wakes. Our two boys, young adults at twenty-two and nineteen, want the chocolates without the hunt around the house for them. I sit in the quiet of the living room and write this and hear the start of birds as the night thins and retreats and light begins in the east, as the things in the world that the night welded together begin to separate into their names. So that I can say tree, flower, car, house, grass, bird, fence, road, and each of them becomes, if not holy, infused with spirituality.

If only it could stay like this, a pristine memory of ritual, compliance, patience, and concomitant reward. Of seeing those kites being made all week, and watching them on Good Friday as we thought about the supreme sacrifice that was made on behalf of us all, and finally flying the little pieces of our lives on Easter Sunday to commemorate His rising.

One cousin had to disobey the golden rule about Good Friday. It was inevitable that someone in our midst would succumb to the temptation to fly a kite and break our grandmother's ban that forbade us to touch it. That cousin remains a hero to me for his valiant effort and spectacular failure.

On Good Friday we rose early. At first this Good Friday seemed

like all the ones before it. We ate fresh bread, buttered, with cups
of sweetened tea for us to sip loudly and dip the bread into and
chew long before swallowing it. We talked fast, as if talk would
run out. We saw our kites. Adults reminded us several times
to think about the significance of the day. His sacrifice. The re-
quirement that we lie low in honor of that sacrifice loomed large.
Everything was done in hushed tones and with penitence as the
guiding force for everything. I felt like I had to tiptoe around the
house.

My cousin behaved like the rest of us. There was nothing to
telegraph his intention to disobey my grandmother. No one had
ever rebelled against her orders about Good Friday. We completed our chores with a lot of talk about our kites and about the
unbearable wait for Sunday. We said we would outfly each other
by miles, that our kites would sing the loudest and that the color
of the tails of our kites would stand out the best from all the rest.
My cousin may have nodded his assent rather than contributed a
boast of his own, as another cousin pointed out afterward, as if
that reserve were some sign of his rebellious intentions, but I did
not notice. It was hard to get a word into the mix with all of us
brimful of words about what they and their kites would do come
Sunday. A nod was as active as the younger cousins could get in
those conversations.

We performed only essential chores on Good Friday. We had
to fetch water from the standpipe positioned in the middle of the
village at the bend in the one road into and out of it. We walked
fast with our empty buckets and talked the most on that outward
journey. On the way back we focused on the walk with the buckets full of water that we tried our hardest not to spill onto the
parched red sand. We emptied the buckets sometimes with the
help of an adult into the water barrels stored at the bottom of
the steps that led from the kitchen.

I do not remember which one of us noticed my cousin. Someone called to the rest of us. We could not believe our ears. So-
and-so was heading into the field with his kite. What? Did you

just say what I think you said? Am I hearing things? A commotion sprang up right away. How no adults caught on to us and intervened fails me to this day. Sure enough, I looked out the crowded window after elbowing a bit of room for myself, and there he was, unspooling some string and starting the pull of the kite to coax it into the breeze. Had he gone mad? He was acting in direct contradiction of our grandmother. She was known as the one adult who when she said a thing, that thing had to be done or else. She could not be disobeyed. There would be some unpleasant consequence if someone, big or small, disobeyed a direct order from her. Yet here he was, my cousin, in the field close to the road starting up the engine of his kite in a brazen disregard of our grandmother. What would happen to him? I wondered this even as I willed him to hurry up and get the kite off the ground. The long tail still dragged even as the kite dipped and climbed and dipped and climbed some more. He tugged at the string and released some more of it and stepped back and tugged. And so the kite climbed as if ascending the rungs of an invisible ladder.

We were on the verge of cheering for him. For there he was, flying a kite on Good Friday against my grandmother's wishes and not a thing happened to prove that our grandmother should never be disobeyed. I was about to stick two fingers of each hand, the middle and index fingers, into my wide mouth and whistle with everything in my lungs, topped up for the action. Just at that moment my cousin screamed and released his kite, just let it go, the very kite that was made in his likeness, and he crouched down and grabbed his right leg. He kept screaming. Everyone ran to him. I was left behind by the better sprinters, who tore down the steps that led into the yard, taking those steps two or three at a time at great risk of tumbling onto their heads. I held the banister with a sliding grip and looked at each step as I raced down with hardly a touch of the balls of my feet.

A couple of grown-ups were crouched beside him as we gathered around. He kept screaming. The adults held his hands away from his leg and one of them tore off his own shirt and in one

move of pulling his arms apart divided that shirt into two strips
for a bandage. I crouched down and peered though several legs
and caught a glimpse of my cousin's injury. A long piece of greenheart wood stuck out the side of his calf and it appeared to have
penetrated his heel. There was some blood but not as much as I
expected. Another uncle scooped up my cousin and positioned
him sideways on a bicycle and rode off to the nearest town where
there was a hospital. My cousin was still bawling as the bicycle
disappeared around the bend.

My grandmother walked back into the house. We followed.
We stared at her from a safe distance. We did not say anything
about our kites. Our cousin returned bandaged and with a crutch
some hours later. He offered a weak smile. My grandmother took
him into her room, a special vanity and bed and rug on the floor,
that we entered only if told by her to fetch her something that she
needed from it, or else to polish the wood floor. She closed the
door and uncles and aunts shooed us from the hallway.

My cousin came back to us with a look of peace about him and
so very tired that he kept yawning and before we could get anything out of him an adult steered him away from us and straight
to bed to get some rest and to heal. That is what the adult said to
us. *Stay out of the room and let the boy get some shut-eye.* The grown-
ups said that my cousin's accident was sufficient punishment for
daring to fly his kite on Good Friday. My grandmother did not say
anything. She didn't have to. We all knew not to disobey her no
matter how strong the temptation. We believed the wait for Easter Sunday was worth more than the risk of breaking our grandmother's rules and ending up in a terrible accident. And when
we ran out on Easter Sunday with our kites and filled the sky
over Airy Hall with them, we forgot all the reasons why someone
would want to rebel in the first place.

All these years later I carry that incident from my childhood
in Airy Hall as if to prepare me for what could be my last Easter before I die, though I am not ready for Liliana's slow-motion
way of going about her hunt for the eggs hidden in the living and

dining rooms and bedroom that serves as a music room. Liliana takes some time to dress. Debbie and I are seated in the living room, feet up on the coffee table, twiddling our thumbs. I shout up the stairs that it is Monday already. Nothing. Debbie adds that the eggs will hatch. Again nothing. We make small talk. Nicholas walks in with his favorite poncho, the one he wears with his friends from high school, all of whom bought one. He takes his basket and smiles at the contents. Liliana appears at the bottom of the stairs. I expected full makeup and a ballroom gown. She is in her best fatigues, no makeup, none needed. She looks beautiful. Hers is the kind of effortless beauty of form and appearance that other people have to spend hours to orchestrate.

I tell people that Liliana was sent to us by the gods. That after our two boys and a gap of five years it was a shock for the sonogram to confirm her sex and we questioned the radiologist in disbelief, and she laughed and showed us the indisputable evidence and we cried.

Liliana walks from mantel to side dresser to sofa and picks up chocolates and other candy and adds them to her basket. We call her back to sweep a place where she missed something and she obliges and expresses surprise at what she finds that was always there staring her in the face, more chocolate. Soon her basket fills. Soon Sunday settles into its COVID-19-altered name in a week of Sundays thanks to the virus. A lone jet, sounding like a vacuum cleaner, passes overhead. One car, then two, drag rubber along tarmacadam with a sound of sandpaper on wood.

*   *   *

My pre-op orders me to take a COVID-19 test. It is the last hurdle to the physical ejection from my body of the major site of my cancer. The pre-op test before COVID-19 amounted to a stress test of the body's ability to withstand anesthetic, the heart's electrical efficiency, and a cardio assessment. I met those criteria. Now COVID-19 presents itself as if to bar my entry to the café where the healthy sup. I protest even as I see how I am a small piece among millions who are at the mercy of the contagion. I see COVID-19 for all its pandemic claims, as no more than an incarnation of my cancer—in this case society at large grieves with me, as we are both under "heavy manners" (as we referred to despotic authority in those bygone days of my London youth) from one thing or another, that is none other than the same thing, which is cancer.

It is this conflation that I insist on that needs some explanation. The death and suffering across the world from COVID-19 dwarfs my calamity with cancer. A sense of grace tells me that I should accept the fact that I am one person among a multitude of people in great distress at this time. Of course, I count, but for much less. I need to demonstrate a sense of proportion even with my affliction taking its toll on my ability to think in an even-tempered way. I should see how the millions of infected souls outweigh my struggle to extend my life against the petition of cancer to shorten it. But a part of me believes that my cancer would dearly love that too. My cancer wants me to put my fight with it second and focus on the bigger fight of COVID-19. The less time I devote to the fight with my cancer, the more it thrives in me. The more I attend to the pandemic of COVID-19, the better for my cancer to progress without my surveillance. COVID-19 is an agent of my cancer. It is one among many curveballs pitched my way by my cancer.

If today's test result comes back positive, it means the operation cannot happen in seventy-two hours. And in a climate of physical isolation, who knows when the medical team could reconvene on my behalf. I am just one person. Thousands have died from COVID-19 and the routine at every level of society has been upended. People will suffer the consequences of this enforced and necessary isolation for years to come. It is the plague of the digital age, I have read and heard. My cancer should shrink into perspective under that magnified gaze. I should even be courteous enough to put off my surgery myself, without bothering with

any tests, to allow the experts to assist in the struggle to treat the
COVID-19 afflicted.

For me to bow to the excesses of COVID-19 would be for me to
surrender to my cancer. It is that plain and simple. I have to fight
it because this is a fight for my life. If I have COVID-19 dormant
in me—I do not exhibit any symptoms—that means I cannot take
the next best step to halt the progress of my cancer. That leaves
me a walking dead. I may recover from the novel coronavirus,
if I have it, and, in effect, I will have signed my death warrant
with my cancer. The urgency to remove the prostate and the surrounding lymph nodes feels the same with or without COVID-19.
Of course I try to do both—attend to my cancer and COVID-19,
as twin demands made on my family and me, on society and its
future. I see a version of me inclined to die for the bigger cause of
a stand against the novel coronavirus. I mean, not fight my cancer
in this willful fashion by insisting on treatment in the midst of a
pandemic, and devote myself to richer days with my immediate
family. Someone else might decide not to fight the advance of
cancer in their body on the grounds that the wider war that is
being waged against the novel coronavirus takes precedence. Not
me. The binary is a false one. My family members do not benefit
from my early demise from cancer if I devote myself to fighting
COVID-19 with them. We are a unit doing our best to stop the
spread of the disease. We are isolated at home. We shop when we
absolutely have to. Our online lives have grown exponentially as
we keep up with family and friends.

I want to put the test behind me and continue my preparation
to face the first surgery of my life and the biggest challenge to
my longevity. COVID-19 is only as big a threat to me if the test
returns positive and cancels my surgery. In this sense COVID-19
shows another face of my cancer.

I wish there were a song for this. It would be great right now
to muster the ability to laugh (by the calypso satire of Trinidadian
picong) at both COVID-19 and my cancer. I can't at the moment,
though I look ahead to the distance and perspective that will

bring me the added imaginative arsenal of wit and laughter and a quatrain or two of excoriating calypso.

I get prostate cancer
It wreck my calendar
COVID-19 join the gang
The two make big bang

* * *

At this stage of the run-up to my operation when I will lose a part of my body to my cancer, I have a routine. Stuck in the house, I find any occasion to go out an opportunity to dress up. For the COVID-19 test I wear my best jeans (the brand of which shall remain nameless, since it is the fit more than anything that enthralls me) and a shop-pressed shirt and good shoes. I shave as well. It's a drive-thru test. Debbie accompanies me. The university hospital is nineteen miles away at Redondo Beach. As we drive we talk about one of my early experiences soon after my arrival in the US with the notion of drive-thru. In Maine, I saw a sign that said DRIVE-THRU REDEMPTION. I asked Debbie if it was religious. If those who have sinned could drive up to a window and be absolved. Through her belly laughter she said it was for the return of cans and bottles. Two empty highways later we arrive at the hospital. I have a long paragraph of special instructions that I printed from an email about where to drive on the hospital grounds to receive the COVID-19 test.

I turn into a lane that is not the main entrance but one of the side entrances that takes employees to the parking garage. I remember to pull on my mask. Instead of entering the garage, I am asked by the man and woman at the guardhouse positioned on the property two steps from the sidewalk if I am there for the COVID-19 test. I say yes. What is my name? I have to say it twice for them to understand me through my mask. "Welcome, Fred," the guy says, in a chipper way, as if I am there to collect lottery winnings. The woman tells me to stay right and follow the road all the way to the back. The man adds that I will know to stop when I see another guardhouse.

Debbie and I comment to each other on how long a drive albeit at a crawl pace that road turns out to be as it snakes around the back of the building, as if taking us to an isolated spot, the kind of removal that a bomb squad performs before they blow up a suspicious package. The guard there sports a broad smile and welcomes us. He wears a mask as well. That is how big he smiles, the kind of smile that spills out of the corners of a mask. He speaks to me at a couple of feet away from the passenger window, where Debbie sits. I say my name. He repeats it with an entirely different pronunciation and confirms it on his clipboard. He props a walkie-talkie toward his chin and says into it that I am there. A nasal reply sounding as if the person held her nose to speak blasts out of the walkie-talkie. The guard takes the number one printed on plastic-covered letter-size white paper and pins it under my passenger-side windshield wiper. He tells me to proceed along the cones that lead out of sight until I come to a tent. I thank him and look ahead and drive at a crawl. The blind left turn reveals a white tent the size of a single-space garage with open sides. I drive in and a man in a security uniform and mask signals for me to stop beside him at a white line with a large stop sign. He tells me to put the car in park and switch off the engine. A nurse at a table about six feet away asks me in a shout what my date of birth is and to state my full name. Another nurse with a mask and visor too (it looks a little like a welder's but made of clear plexiglass) has a small vial in his hand and long prod modeled on a Q-tip but longer and with material on just one end and rather more of it than one sees on a cotton bud and with a firmer, more compact look.

He says to look straight ahead and hold my chin up a little and not to move my head. I lean back on the headrest and offer my nostrils to him. He reaches into the car with his gloved hand and sterile gown-covered arm and sticks the probe up my nose, so far up that his fingers almost touch my face and I feel this

tremendous shooting pain behind and between my eyes, so much
of a shock that I involuntarily shout, Ouch! He retracts his arm
and dips the stick into the glass capsule labeled with my details.
A fat drop of water bounces out of my left eye above the nostril
that the nurse drilled into, and my right eye blurs with water. My
nose waters as well. I become many spigots, many fountains of
responses, none of them under my control. I inhale deeply a few
times and Debbie and I laugh as I pull off my specs, dry my eyes,
put them back on, and drive away and search out decent words
for "What the fuck?" It takes me a mile of road before I remember
that I have the mask on in the car. I take it off and stuff it into the
storage side panel of the driver's door, knowing that I will need it
for the hospital stay.

I had better not have that virus after the unpleasantness of the
test. Did the male nurse stick the probe in too far? Why did it
hurt worse than the Lupron Depot injection into my butt? Maybe
I have more nerves in my nose than I think. The two highways
are a dream drive that flirts with my ability to see just how little
of my attention I can sink into the task of driving home. There is
no time for speculation before I exit the highway and make the
couple of turns home. The area behind the upper bridge of my
nose throbs like a stop sign at a pedestrian crossing. I imagine the
beat matches the rhythm of my heart.

Back at home an email pops up that says in the heading that
it contains my PSMA test results. For security reasons I have to
log into my UCLA health portal to access the two PDFs. I call
Debbie to be by my side as I open the mail. One is the confiden-
tiality agreement that I signed, which gives them permission to
use their findings as a teaching tool, the other details what the
gamma highlighted. I speed-read to the story about the lymph
nodes. They have taken up the gamma rays throughout my body,
which means the pathogens that specifically identify the cancer
in my prostate membrane have migrated throughout my body,
principally in the lymph nodes, which regulate infection and
cleanse the body of impurities.

Last thoughts cross my mind. Single words and images of people charged with a sad feeling. *Fuck. Christ. Wow.* Followed by my children, Debbie, my brothers, mother, grandchildren, and friends. All of it, and them, seen and felt at high speed. This is it, I think. My pulse speeds up and I start to breathe as if I'd sprinted to catch a bus. The lights around me increase in brightness—all the day and everything in it suddenly made big and bold and up close. I blink back what must be water brimming my eyes and turn my face away so that Debbie can't see me. I summon my bits of classical music and jazz that I've been listening to a lot lately since it helps settle my mind and body.

I wonder if the surgery can do more than remove the prostate and some nodes that are nearby, and whether I'll end up having chemo and radiation anyway. It's a worst-case scenario. The lymph nodes once they become replete with cancer succumb very quickly to the disease, and the prognosis gives the person about five years of life at best. Do I even have as much as those five years to live? It is sixty months, two hundred and sixty weeks. How to maximize 1,826 days, assuming I have that full calendar at my disposal? Write and read, meditate, and hang out with loved ones. And for hours, all 43,841 of them, I am a rich man. Let me go to minutes and be a multimillionaire of my mortality, 157,784,760—and if I write those words, they hold the promise of more time: one hundred fifty-seven million, seven hundred eighty-four thousand, seven hundred and sixty minutes.

I never thought I had inordinate helpings of time at my disposal. I saw it simply as a deferred condition of my mind, the least of my worries as I plowed on with my ambition and with paying the bills and enjoying family and friends and the city. I pushed away the idea of time as limited and finally about to run out as property held in common by humanity and therefore canceled as a specific thing for me to worry about. If everyone dies sometime, what is there to agonize over? It is only with the subtraction from it by my disease that I jump to my feet in protest and cry foul. I have come to terms with the idea of an inevitable death. I have not come to terms with death made into an earlier prospect by cancer.

Hello, Miss Corona
Meet Mister Cancer
You two make a team
Of nightmares from dreams

Cancer, you are a thief of my time. You have broken into my body and headed straight for the vault where I store my years, and, cancer, you have helped yourself to a couple of decades. You see, cancer, without you in my life I saw myself in my mideighties before I bowed out of this body. Not in my early sixties and threatened with not seeing sixty-five. For this reason I strip naked and stand ready in a gladiator's arena of medicines and mantras to fight you to the end. I have a thirteen-year-old daughter. It is her face that I see when I think of my early death. I think of my sons and Debbie. I never wanted to leave any of them, not this preternaturally early. And so, my cancer, you are my only opponent in this arena. More than COVID-19 or the chance of a natural disaster, it is you, cancer, that I fear and for which I stop everything in my life, and prepare to battle.

So tonight I stuff myself. As I work in the living room, I hear the Morse code of the chopping board extemporizing for an hour in the kitchen where Debbie dices and slices potatoes, carrots, tomatoes, onions, basil, and garlic. Coriander hangs in the air like pollen. Soon I help myself to two servings of Debbie's curry, which perfumes the house from pillar to post. The omnipresence of curry in the air creates the illusion that I am eating through my nose, inhaling the benefits of Debbie's delicious meal as much as chowing down on it. I round off stuffing myself with a hefty slice of her sponge cake frosted with a light blue frosting and sprinkled with chocolate shavings, which is the epitome of a speckled bird's egg. I drink two eleven-ounce cartons of unadulterated coconut water. I belong to a brigade of gormandizers, bacchanalians devoted to sensory excess. Oh to induce vomiting just to start this overindulgence all over again!

Stuck on the sofa with a rotund belly, I delight in a bloated feeling of my stomach's skin distending in slow motion. It is as though I ate yeast that continues to work in my gut by swelling everything in its purview. What contentment truly earns its name without going to the brink and over the brink? My brain draws its blinds of discernment for nonchalance toward fate. My muscles forget what muscles forget when doused with salt, fat, and sugar. Tomorrow I fast.

11

THE MADDENING PAIN

Morning coffee. How good of you to haul me by my nostrils out of sleep as your maker, preset to brew at five thirty a.m., fills the house with your genteel aroma. Fill my cup, the lash against porcelain gradually muffles as my cup brims. Today you are my only indulgence as I prepare for tomorrow's surgery. My palate riots with delight. I pick up traces of clementine and apple in the coffee as well as fragrant wood such as the eucalyptus.

Debbie and I take the dog for a walk. This is my last morning of walking the dog with my prostate intact. I lost teeth in the past and should think of this organ nestled below my bladder as another of the things Bishop talks about in her villanelle "One Art." Her list moves from the physical to the psychic, the stakes increase as the villanelle progresses. Bishop's ultimate loss turns out to be the greatest sacrifice of all, love. Mine pales in comparison. The chance that I may not wake from the anesthetic amounts to hardly any risk given my good cardiovascular health.

The dog pulls me along as usual. My eyes flick from one thing to the next. Could the light be cleaner today? The morning bounces off windshields with an extra spring in its heels. Flowers appear washed by this light, their colors intensified so that yellow and red and purple appear raised above the petals and almost independent of them. There is a thickness to the colors and an extra-sharp point to each inflection of red, yellow, and purple. I drink deep of the morning, holding my lungs full for a second that lasts a step or two before I exhale. Everything appears to be still, no breeze, none of the branches at the tops of palms waves at me.

Should I be thinking at some point that this may be my penultimate walk?

No, that would be morbid. You'll get through this.

I feel a giant clock is over my head and it's counting me out.

I know you must feel terrible. But you have to believe you'll be cured of this.

Debbie takes my hand and I hold the dog's lead with the other. As we stroll, our steps are in line as if we'd marched this way for so long it was second nature to walk in rhythmic harmony. I don't mean to look at our feet. But every time that I do look down during our walk around the neighborhood and talk about a range of things, I see that we keep in lockstep.

I am running on empty, fumes, subcutaneous fat. How can I feel so hungry so early, I ask my belly, which grumbles a loud complaint that ricochets off my bones. My jaws that should work for speech for the most part, this morning grind my teeth as if to make nutrient powder. Each thought starts to operate with the ornate punctuation of a food for thought or a thought for food or just plain feed me. At some point I expect salad to decorate the trees and that squirrel curled around the bird feeder to be the pie in the oven that the sun crusts.

I think of my days in London, a couple of years, summers, during which I fasted to please my single mother, who dated a Muslim man and turned all her children into followers of Islam to please him. Ramadan among English schoolchildren turned out to be the toughest test of all. The English boys knew that I was fasting, and they opened packets of crisps in front of me and scrunched each crisp one at a time, holding out the pack to me for me to help myself. At the end they balled up the empty plastic packet and threw it at me and walked away laughing. The greasy plastic took on a smell of salt and oil just by my staring at it as it unfolded on the ground.

Just as Ramadan made me tour London, airborne with delight
at my superior triumph over the teenage cravings of my body, so
I hope this fast before my surgery will embolden me. That I may
heal at an accelerated rate. Feel pain as balm. Allow the surgeon
to find the bulk of my cancer and extirpate it—that word again.
Extirpate. Again in midseventies London, the television show
Doctor Who featured aliens called Daleks. Though they were the
bad guys, the alien species and invaders, bent on the extermina-
tion of humanity, the Daleks were my heroes. They looked like
outsize industrial vacuums ready to tidy around the stalls of an
outdoor market. Their favorite word, *exterminate*, resembles, in
loose homophone terms, *extirpate*. I turn those Daleks, their stiff
protuberances of malcontent, against my cancer, to exterminate,
to blast it into oblivion.

For now I combat a stomachache induced by the eight ounces
of magnesium hydroxide (the hospital recommends two doses,
each taken two hours apart) that I drink with a tight feeling in my
throat, after a cup of coffee. I set out a loose outfit that I plan to
wear to the hospital in the morning. When I call the hospital I am
told that Debbie has to drop me off at the entrance and leave right
away. She cannot return to see me until I am discharged from
their care. This means I wake up without seeing her. With no
visitors allowed to see me, if I have to stay beyond the one night
allocated for my surgery, I will be alone in true terms.

Let the purge begin! We all know how much a laxative disrupts
any semblance of routine, even a reality defined by COVID-19.
'Nuff said about that. What makes me think of Swift and the scat-
ological as an aesthetic for devastating satire? I am at the mercy
of my gripes. The fist of kneading pain tightens and eases its grip
a little and tightens some more. The way I peed in the sports bar
back in the heyday of whatever the body believed that it was, the
same force of that output happens from my anus as a result of the
milk of magnesia. The result on the toilet makes me glance back
the way a dog might turn quickly to glimpse what turns out to be
its tail. My stomachache subsides. The rumbles continue as I sip

low-sodium chicken broth. I take my meds as usual and wonder if
they do not just wash out of me before any useful uptake of them.

For me all this practice amounts to a purification process to
expel my cancer. Now I am in the realm of the body. Where I will
stay for days, on lockdown with my cancer, the two of us under a
dome of COVID-19. A cancer first hosted by me and now about to
take me over. If I let it. If I risk such a high degree of Keats's negative capability that I champion the cancer's right to life in me at
my expense. I take that chance and slip the moorings of my ego,
on the assumption that I stand to gain some perspicacious insight
about my disease.

Surgery under COVID-19 doubles the number of plates that
I have to keep spinning on poles, and this from my heightened
sense of enough already as I wrestle my cancer. The main battle,
surgery, never promised anything but a challenge. Surgery attacks the fortress of my cancer. Success on that front should send
cancer's troops into disarray. Stationed at various outposts in my
body, where they stand guard and propagate bad news about my
deserving status as a body near the point of being vanquished,
their presence so far from the source is testament to the fact. Surgery should sever their links to their main supplier and reason for
their existence.

*   *   *

My war with cancer is pain, grief, and death. I skip the dying part
for extra pain and sadness. You see, I am a coward in the face
of pain. I find out that I cannot think, breathe, or act properly
while in pain. What died in me is gone, literally pulled out of my
punctured torso, six wounds, with one twice the size of the other
five, all across my torso. My midriff is tender, bloated, and stiff.
Deep inside, a current of hurt surges up and out, and hits each of
those six incisions with a steady pulse. I try to breathe yoga style,
deep and slow with a pause between the two breaths heading in

opposite directions or it is the same breath sculpting me. I sink
my attention into that process. To rob my pain of the whole of me.

My cancer captured two sites, my prostate and vascular gan-
glia, a bundle of nerves that power the muscles of the penis and
deliver semen or lubricate it for delivery. Both are gone, along
with nearly three dozen nearby lymph nodes. It took six hours to
cut and clear it all.

I watch a scythe swing left and right cutting down swaths
of my cancer, pendulum to the left and clear, pendulum right,
clear, in a slow march and harvest up my pelvic girdle. My medical team of four become Anansi, whose eight limbs wield four
scythes. I need compound eyes to follow my trickster's industry.
At a microscopic level, Anansi's limbs are a flurry. Scythes de-
scribe circles in a close dance of almost touch. If one sweep of a
blade misses a wisp of cancer, a second blade swoops in to catch
that wisp and a third so that where cancer stood tall, rooted and
branched, there is fresh blood and raw flesh, its upturned ground.

I, that is, me, whose entire middle section hurts and who cannot think one thought without pain stitched into its formation,
must now recall the last four days. I hold out my hands for the
warmth of a hearth, stuck in that gesture, so that a word for cancer sounds like the word Cincinnati, and I want those consonants
to mean something more to me than an end of things; I say the
word aloud many times to test its soundness and the word traps
me in its meaning and threatens to keep me stalled there, unable
to move against it if cancer needs a course of actions to uproot
its station in the body. At some point repetition leads to transformation, I say Cincinnati and it rolls off my tongue as Sing,
Sing, Natty, probable title of a reggae hit by someone like Dennis
Brown. I could find words to fit that reggae tune to do with my
healing. That is one song that I must write once I am around the
corner of this pain and can see it out of my rearview. Right now
my cancer wants to reign supreme over me. I wish to defeat it
unequivocally. We are both still in pursuit of the throne that can

never be attained. Since the prize is the body and the body loses
if either of us wins outright.

I need to control the maddening pain. This operation against
my cancer seems like a war of attrition. I pay a price to cut the
cancer from me, the bulk of it. The doctor tried to explain the
process to me before the anesthesiologist took my consciousness.
The doctor said that he would remove whatever bad things he
encountered, which may take some time. He said that the PSMA
showed him where he needed to go. I said I wanted him to get
every last bit of the cancer no matter how long it took or how far
he had to go to get at it. I thanked him with the kind of profusion
typical of the desperate man completely dependent on another's
generosity and grace. He told me not to worry and we nudged
elbows, the COVID-19 poor substitute for a hug.

The anesthesiologist struck off a list of things that he wanted
to be sure I did not have or did not take or that might make me
vulnerable to the tool of his trade, a combo of gas and IV fluid
that should knock me out along with air pumped through a tube
to keep me oxygenated. He wore a silver lambda chain around
his open-necked shirt, and that was the last thing I noticed as he
slipped the mask on my face.

I woke to a nurse calling my name repeatedly. And she kept
asking me to keep my eyes open and "stay with her." This is the
first time with the increased COVID-19 restrictions that patients
have come back from the OR and not had a loved one able to meet
them when they came around in the recovery room. The nurse is
the substitute for that familiar. I come around to my name. The
nurse's voice is sonorous. She talks me back into my name. The moment I recognize my name, I catch sight of, simultaneously, a
sheaf of facts about me. I think I hear trumpets. Her smile is broad.
Her lips are painted red and her white teeth emit radiance. I blink
and squint. She hands me my glasses. I need her help to place the
left handle of my glasses behind my ear. There is the tangle of a
drip line attached to a bottle on a stand. The line leads to a port
at the top of my left hand. I am laughing. Feeling giggly. Elated.

I associate the levity with the relief of being alive. How did it go? The nurse says, Excellent, and the doctor will be along in a moment to tell me all about it. I look around at the wall clock and do not think it correct. What time is it? She confirms the time, late afternoon. How long did it last? When she says six hours, I ask her to repeat that and she says six again and I try to sit up and cannot.

My mouth is dry. She offers me ice chips on a teaspoon, which she feeds to me. Her nails are long and match her cherry-red lipstick. The chips distribute cool and water in samples that I want more and more of. The ice runs out in the plastic cup and she asks a passing nurse's aide for more. I swallow what feels like grief and wonder and they are succeeded by a detonation of exhilaration. I ask her as she spoons more ice into my mouth to forgive my British teeth, they are clean and healthy and crooked in keeping with my nonchalance during my youth and adult life in England for orthodontics.

She checks my vitals and feeds me more bits of ice. Again, I tell her the ice is delicious. Again, I ask the time again and again she tells me and as before I express incredulity as if for the first time. It finally sinks in that that I've been in surgery for six hours. It's after four in the afternoon. She said the operation began at a little after ten in the morning. Is everything all right? I ask, certain that for the operation to have taken that long meant that the surgeon encountered some trouble.

The nurse smiles and repeats that the operation was a success. She calls Debbie on the phone. Debbie tells me that the surgeon phoned while still in the OR, as his assistants were closing me up (with superglue) to tell her that everything went well, though there was a tricky part to it. Her phone voice is so clear I wonder if she might be standing behind the curtain that demarcates the recovery space from the corridor. I wish she could be here with me. Angelic nurse isn't enough for me right now. I start to tremble and the nurse unfolds a second blanket and spreads it from my feet to beneath my chin.

One of the doctors who assisted the surgeon appears and says that they got everything. How do you feel? I reply, Elated. I thank him. He looks at the nurse's chart and scribbles on it, says he'll see me on the ward and steps around the curtain and disappears just as the surgeon steps into my frame. By this time the light in the room looks softer, thanks to my happiness, and a glow surrounds the doctor and the nurse. I link my life to their skills. I promote them to transcendental status. They may be floating rather than standing on terra firma. I feel luck wash over me as if baptized. The surgeon speaks and I hardly hear him; more accurately, I hear him—the sounds of words roll off his tongue in full incantation—and hardly any of it makes sense. Bits of it do. I string the bits together and construe that my operation presented him with a unique challenge because my enlarged prostate, a part of it, had fused to the wall of my rectum. He says what took a long time was not the removal of the prostate but the many thin layers of it that he had to peel with care off the rectum wall so as not to perforate the wall or leave too little in place and create problems for me later on.

I thank him as much as I can between asking him more than once if the surgery was a success. He says yes, though he hopes he got all the cancer at that contact point between the prostate and the rectum. He ends by saying that I should rest and that he'll see me again soon. I thank him. It seems gratitude is my default position as I come to my senses through the avenue of ecstasy. I ask him again. I can't help it. I feel weird.

You got everything?

Yes, I got everything I could find, yes.

Yippee!

It was hard, but we got it, I think.

Fab. Thank you from the bottom of my heart.

We'll have to be sure in about three months.

Three months.

Yes, once you've healed, we'll do a blood test and see what your PSA says.

That's wonderful.

Yes, for now concentrate on healing.

You bet. Thank you, Doctor.

You're welcome, Fred.

There is pageantry to cancer. Imagine a set of behaviors that aligns with the growth of the disease and you can see how the show of cancer may grow from a one-person, no-frills event to a full production with the overblown values of spectacle. Both the show of cancer and cancer the show-off are necessary for it to register that it is there in the body. Cancer wishes to be noticed as a part of its destructive procedure. This can be enriching for the cancer and for the person afflicted with it. The cancer sees that the curtain rises and it is center stage, and there in the audience making it all worthwhile is the person for whom the show must go on and for whom the show is devised in the first place.

I saw a metaphor for cancer's workings at a West End production of *Waiting for Godot* starring Patrick Stewart and Ian McKellen. The two veteran actors have known each other since the seventies and they work like a couple in a synchronized swim, or a pair in a knife-throwing act where one throws the knife and the other is strapped to a spinning wheel. *Godot* is a dark play about the absurdity of a life that accrues wisdom only to jettison it and begins with an athletic body only to walk it into decay. As the wisdom increases so the opportunities to do anything with it decrease as the body and mind shut down. For any species it is an odd formula on which to predicate survival.

The waiting room of life leads to no end result, no point to raised expectation and no fruits from the time spent working things out as one waits. The two actors injected a panoply of non-verbal touches and signals between Beckett's words to denote a stimulus or impulse against pointlessness, as if in search of the point of it all even with the knowledge that there is no point to any of it. Some of their actions blatantly contradicted what they were saying to each other, others implied more than the words signaled. In addition, they appeared to be aware in those non-verbal exchanges and asides that an implicit contract existed between them and they were in this fine mess of life together, rather than isolated and doomed to be alone in their awareness as indicated by their speech. Furthermore, they signaled each other that they would support each other even if to offer help to each other would be just another sign of giving in to the absurd. They celebrated their longevity as well: both in their seventies and alive to witness the absurd, and there was a wealth of pleasure inherent in that fact that they had their health enough to work at a demanding play.

As a member of the audience I derived a similar pleasure, no matter the triumphalist absurdity of the whole event of Beckett's play. I was seventeen when I first saw Ian McKellen at the Royal Court Theatre in a play titled *Bent*, about the treatment of gays in the Nazi concentration camps. Gays, given pink stars and denounced as deviant and decadent, were an invisible and persecuted minority, and this was the first play highlighting the fact. (Not to take anything away from Gay Sweatshop's smaller-scale works that preceded the production at the Court.) I had seen Patrick Stewart in a number of Shakespeare plays with my high school English teacher Geoff.

Both actors, from their young and wise days, to older and foolish with it (if we take foolery to mean serious play, and in keeping with Bob Dylan's "Oh but I was so much older then, I'm younger than that now"), enact a kind of throwing off of grand wisdom for a less showy assumption of humble not-knowingness, one that goes further and is of much better use given the lightness demanded by life.

If more proof were needed, in addition to the *Godot* play, of an endless list of things that testify to life's pointlessness, the respite on offer may be that there is an escape clause from a Beckett play.*

---

* Kumiko Kiuchi, "Oxymoronic Perceptions and the Experience of Genre: Samuel Beckett's *Ghost Trio*, . . . *but the Clouds* . . . and Beyond," *Journal of Beckett Studies* 18, no. 1–2 (September 2009): 72–87, https://doi.org/10.3366 /E0309520709000284.

It comes in Beckett's stage direction to the script, written for television, titled *Ghost Trio* (1975), in which the door and window on the set are noted by Beckett to be "imperceptibly ajar." There is a story that the director crouched at that door in Beckett's presence and pushed the door against the jamb in an effort to show that the door was not closed, and was as near to imperceptibly open as was humanly demonstrable. The director must have been pleased with himself for paying such close attention to the playwright's notes in the presence of the playwright. Beckett is said to have walked up to the set door, opened it wide and slammed it shut, and said, "There, imperceptibly ajar."

Imperceptibly ajar remains just that: a perception that is at the same time acknowledged and denied as awareness. Knowing that life is absurd does not rob life of its joy. In fact, any joy gleaned under such duress is bound to be worth a whole lot more than joy derived from contentment. Wordsworth rubbed against it as a sensory fact in "Tintern Abbey," a poem that Geoff Hardy read aloud to us and acted out with great fervor, in my high school years. The crux of the poem, titled as written at the ruins of the abbey and with a date as well, centers on the sensuous memory of a poet whose university is the physical world but whose gift is an ability to extrapolate from that world into metaphysical territory, Wordsworth's fabled "emotions recollected in tranquility."

My postoperative confusion coupled with a sense of being tied to my body's register of a gradual increase in pain sends me into digressions, escape mechanisms, that help me to cope with time dragging its feet and my time weighed down by the surgeon's assault on my body, and my fragile body's struggle to recover from it. That necessary escape takes me from one prized memory to the next to bypass pain and this drag of time (and the fear that goes with it). I make ready to launch my tie-in of Wordsworth and Beckett with my cancer operation and pause only because I am forced to do so by last night's earthquake, which happened just after midnight. Lucky for me I was out of the hospital and back at home. Debbie and I woke to the house quivering in its fifty-six earthquake restraints, plates and bolts added to the foundation to keep the building on its moorings and steady it for just such an occasion as besets it now. And the shake passed in a couple of seconds. The cat bolted off the bed and disappeared in the dark. The pocket door to the bathroom appeared to be the culprit that made all the noise. It sits and is held in place by sliders of ball bearings at the top and bottom, and it disappears into the bathroom wall with the touch of a finger. As noisy as a vuvuzela, tonight the door acted like a Geiger counter.

I grabbed my glasses, my phone, my dressing gown, and my catheter bag and with Debbie we headed for the bedroom door, where our eldest greeted us with wide eyes and a loud expletive. Liliana emerged on that upstairs landing, dressed and with her contacts left in as she slept. I asked her to grab her phone. Christopher made the descent of the fifteen steps that connect the second and first floors in three bounds. I followed Debbie and Liliana, my six stomach punctures and catheter dictating my pace. We met the dog and Nicholas at the bottom of the stairs and we headed into the kitchen. We looked out and saw other house lights coming on. We waited for another shake. The plan was to run outside if another one began. We waited for the aftershock and as we stood in the kitchen near the door to the backyard, we told each other many times over about the first short burst of shaking as if repetition helped us account for the many layers of comprehension that are necessary around a dramatic event. Also, repetition settles the nerves.

Thinking that another rumble might follow soon and force us outdoors, I excused myself for a moment and ran to the bathroom a couple of steps away from the kitchen, where I emptied my catheter bag with a horrible singular focus. It took about eight seconds to drain a healthy straw-colored liquid followed by a low degree of pink in the tube that signaled the bleeding that the doctor warned me about. I sighed, flushed, skipped washing my hands, and rejoined the family in the kitchen. The cats were nowhere to be seen. Usually they hide under the dining room table or on a chair under the table in the open space that adjoins the kitchen. Debbie called, Clementine. We knew that Moonlight, the older and more skittish of the two, would never respond.

We ventured outside and Bengal the stray cat appeared, ready to eat. I petted him, two quick strokes along his back, and scooped out a handful of hard cat food kept stored on the deck in an air-tight plastic container, and dropped the portion into his bowl, which he settled in front of right away and started to devour. Bengal was blissfully unfazed, so it seemed. Or else he associated our appearance in the backyard after midnight and a shake-up of the earth as something he could not influence except to eat. Debbie remarked on his calm. I think back to the rigmarole of borrowing a cage from a pet center and following the instructions to capture Bengal for him to be neutered. He mewed all the way across the city as I delivered him for his overnight stay. I picked him up the next day and he greeted me like a long-lost friend. I opened his cage in the yard and enticed him out of it with a can of sardines in oil. He licked the bowl and refused to leave the backyard. That was eighteen months ago. Now here he was, teaching us how to behave in an earthquake.

That COVID-19 had swept all our gods away, and not for a day, week, or month, but for the foreseeable future. That the earthquake followed to make sure our gods could never be reassembled. Taken together, they make me wonder about the power of my cancer. To come for me and for the city, in which I live, and the state and the world, just to be sure it does not fail in its bid to capture me. To tell me that the San Andreas Fault runs through my heart. To shake that belief into my single body by shaking the entire city to ensure I number among the twenty million. I do not believe I am exempt from any suffering beset on the city. I believe I must fight what I can see and what I know to be numinously present.

The ruins of a life, like the ruins of the past, were it an abbey, say, once glorious, now defunct, might be a good place to begin a quest to find out how feelings prompted by vestiges of a place help recall and shape our life practices. The poem is about the impossibility of return, among other things. Wordsworth's "five long years have passed" and return to the abbey finds him no less predisposed to the sensory alarms and charms of the place. Away from the place and it offers the poet solace, quickens the poet's mind and blood, stirs feeling even in the absence of its stimulus. The memory of the place stirs philosophical inquiry in the poet, who is able to "see into the life of things" as a result of exposure to nature.

It is less the abbey and more its surrounding nature—the river, meadow, fields, trees—that carry the magic that Wordsworth celebrates. The poet's above the abbey, working out a poetics of the spirit that's embedded in nature, and there's a secular vision. Nature as a force we can benefit from by knowing about guides my recovery from cancer. What if cancer presents its ruins to me to see if I can benefit from them? Do I capitulate or is my survival contingent on my bringing all that I know to bear on my attempts at finding a cure?

As long as I keep the poem "Tintern Abbey" in my arsenal, my cancer weighs less on my mind. As the cancer pulls me, the poem helps me tug against that pull. In a way that only a poem works, by recall, insinuation, and out of contemplation, I learn from it how to approach cancer.

Driving to my post-op appointment—being driven, actually; I am not allowed to drive so Debbie is at the wheel—we comment on the gradual return of traffic, more cars, the odd mad driver as usual on an entirely private road of high jinx, high-anxiety maneuvers, and on our sense of feeling unhurried, almost unshakable in a new calm of COVID-19.

Debbie pulls into the hospital. We park. We don our masks as if to hide some supercelebrity status. We pass the door nurses with their thermometers and questions. We sit in the waiting room, where other people sit spaced out in alternate chairs as directed, though at eight thirty a.m. the place is mostly empty. The hospital is so close to my office on campus that it makes me wonder how I've managed to avoid it for the five years that I've lived and worked in Los Angeles. I could answer by saying that I've stayed healthy and I've cultivated an aversion to sick places. I've been running several times a week, at dawn, between the piers of Santa Monica and Venice. The beach has been closed for weeks due to COVID-19. I've changed to riding a stationary bike while I conjure my run on the beach:

Lavender hills light—high seas that harvest the last of the night—waves apparently broadcasting more news—yesterday's Twitter by this president that reads like an invitation to whites to murder Black people—yesterday's new levels of homelessness—police brutality—gulls in a mass on quiet sands—space trembles, star-heavy—sky fruit falls from branches for me to wish by—wish for peace, as dead mount faster than we can dig graves for them—where not even one star lands—where waves sound like grief and no two mourners the same.

I wait for my name. Debbie reads her phone. At some point in my recall I run backward, skirting foam signing the names of the dead in sand that the waves wipe clean. More of us ready to fall. More of us dead than living, slowed by cut tendons. For all the rose stems plunged into the vases of rifles, rifles aimed at thinking hearts. The nurse butchers my name, which raises a smile in Debbie and me. Sounds like she issued an order for us to evacuate the reception area. Only Debbie and I respond by following her. She takes me straight to a waiting room and asks me to take off everything below my waist and cover myself with a paper sheet and wait for another nurse. I ask if I can keep my socks on—the air conditioning is ramped up in these septic spaces—she says yes.

Catheter-removal time—yippee. A handsome male nurse walks in. He is brown, perhaps from the South Seas, I say his color due to my SoCal location, where a tan comes with a premium as the thing sought after and showcased, and he is buff, not as novel in a gym-driven culture of bodacious bodies, but something of a rarity in a nurse, our culture's emblem of selfless care. His thick black hair and a warm, toothy smile crown the picture of a perfect specimen of my gender, of where I need to be and may never again attain, less because of my cancer and more to do with my location on the chart of time, with me on its downward curve.

He asks me to stand. He remains seated, his head just above my crotch, his stool on wheels that he pushes to the sink and back to my waistline as he twists his body to attend to a giant syringe and fill a kidney dish with water. He spreads a few absorbent sheets on the floor and asks me to step onto the covering. He says he will introduce some water into my bladder to see how things are working with the connected catheter. He asks me to let him know when I feel an urgent need to pull over to the side of the road. He empties about four of these big syringes through the catheter tubing into my bladder. I can feel my bladder ballooning. Debbie asks what the record is for such fillings. I get asked that a lot, he says, the record is thirteen and the man who set it, to look at him you would not think he could hold that much water, a skinny guy.

The nurse (I wish I had the wherewithal to retain his name, said just once when he walked into the room and hidden from sight on his ID, which hangs on a chain turned the wrong way), whose face I shall never forget, looks serious, and says, Now comes the tricky part, that I need to be quick with the one-liter plastic jug that he hands to me. The moment he pulls out the catheter I should slip the holder in place to catch my urine. Will it hurt? I ask. No. Ready. I nod and I swear my head has not completed that gesture and the nurse pulls on the catheter and it erupts from the end of my penis and a flood of urine follows as I shove the jug in place. He is right about the lack of pain and about my need to be swift to catch the flow. Clear water, that I cannot control, escapes me at top speed. He asks me to contract my sphincter. I concentrate and the involuntary spigot closes off slowly as if reluctant to obey me. We do this count-and-hold routine until all the fluid that he pumped into me is gone.

He asks if I have padded protection for my clothes. I say yes. He hands me a chart and says that I need to practice the flow-and-hold regimen for the next three weeks if I am to regain control of my bladder function. I thank him many times over. His broad smile, quick nod, and You are most welcome are hardly issued by him before the bulk of him is halfway out of the door, where he stalls for a moment to add that the doctor will be in to see me.

I dress, with the pad adding a comical protuberance to my crotch. The doctor walks in with another doctor and the stenographer, who boots up the computer and logs in and starts typing even as the surgeon introduces his companion as a senior resident doctor. I thank him for everything. For his magician's touch with my prostate. For his calm during my storm. For his deep knowledge of a road that was new to me at the end of 2019 and is in 2020 still news. He smiles. Debbie thanks him as well.

And the drugs, Doctor, and my next steps? He looks at me, and he smiles. I watch his masked mouth, to add sight to what I hear. To affirm my feelings. To double up on sight and sound that's the equivalent of how a smell of cut grass triggers my childhood memories. For sight and sound to work like taste, say, a taste of copper. That brings me tongue-glued-to-winter-post up against the blemishes in my youth. I'm at the mercy of my senses. I'm lucky that they're forces for good in my life. They steer me away from trouble. They shape my thoughts. They string thought on a clockface that cuts across my life and compresses years into a day.

Stop it all, he says, the tamoxifen, the tamsulosin, the Lupron Depot injections, the bicalutamide, stop them right away, and come back and see me in three months.

I feel giddy hearing this. Somersaults-on-the-spot giddy. My head undergoes this surge of light and electricity that sends my mood from even-keel good to laugh-out-loud stupid. I say it over and again to Debbie. Stop all the drugs. Three months. All I have to do now is regain control of my bladder. The surgery turns out to be that big battle that decimates cancer's army and leaves it in tatters to regroup, perhaps with guerrilla activity in me to spread chaos and for me to mop up with more decisive medicine (chemo, radiation). I leave the doctor's office, after profuse thanks with my face fixed in a Joker extreme smile, not feeling my steps along the hospital corridors and not feeling the six glued holes in my lower stomach.

Happy, happy me, I sing Pharrell Williams's megahit of mindless abandonment to serotonin and dopamine. Were it not for the glued wounds across my stomach, I would jump and click my heels to the best news from the greatest source. The doctor tells me to stop all the meds immediately. No more bicalutamide, no more tamsulosin, no more Flomax, that first Lupron Depot three-month slow-release injection is my last, no more occasional ciprofloxacin, and it's hey ho the Jabberwock (Carroll) for I am drug-free, as in no longer taking them thar (Wild West gold prospector) poisons, me matey, aarrhh (though not free of drugs as they work themselves out of me, though no less buoyed by exhilaration, which brings out the Captain Hook in me). Instead I settle for a high five, fist dab, with Debbie, and a prolonged hug (though no kiss, not with our masks on). I run though the doctor's words several times with Debbie on the drive home. At the house we seek out the kids in their rooms and in front of their computers, and tell them the good news, as unconditionally good, rather than happiness on a ninety-day lease that may be revoked and cancer reinstated, or happiness renewed indefinitely, depending on the PSA test.

I want to go to a restaurant or the movies and celebrate with Debbie and the kids. COVID-19 has other ideas. With everything shuttered we settle for a special meal and dessert by Debbie and a home movie. Debbie cooks this jaw-droppingly tasty roast festooned with garlic and cayenne and black pepper, with roasted potato pieces garnished with parsley, and she bakes my favorite carrot cake iced all over with cream and sugar and with the same filling between the two pans of stacked cake. I help myself to a large slice and spirit away another slice in a sealed Pyrex storage container knowing that the cake will be gone by morning. The wee famished ones (big and burly in reality though wee to me for all time) come out in the small hours to feast, you see. We watch a feel-good flick about a couple who face adversity and set aside their animosity to combat the threat only to find their old passion for each other, and realize, as a result of their joint struggle, that their objections to each other mean little given a whole lot of love that they share.

A song looms, because I'm cancer-free, I walk on air, and with a bounce to my steps, taller by a couple of inches, chin up, shoulders back, head high, cause Doc says I'm cancer-free, if you catch me with a smile that I cannot help and cannot wipe away, whose beam I send to you to infect you too with a little bit of my happiness, that's 'cause I'm cancer-free, and I can do anything that only yesterday I would not even try, at least that's how I feel, giddy, silly, bursting with energy, seeing a shine in everything around me, and in the things that I cannot see, all because I'm happy, I want you to join my conga line and move like train wheels linked by looping arms—do the cancer-free.

I thank Debbie for her stellar advocacy. I tell her I love her. I tell her so, many times over, as if each telling is a new manifestation of that love, a new way for love to grow between us. Over the last five months she kept all my details at her fingertips and asked all the right questions of me before I met with the doctor so that together we formed a unified front of judiciously informed people, hungry for cure but cognizant of the routes open to us as we speed toward the end of a bad journey. Whatever years I have left to live I want to spend them with her. And be there for her when she needs me as she was there for me. Cancer turns me into a sixty-year-old, not forty-five or fifty, or fifty-five as I kept saying I felt, always the younger man in defiance of time's euclidean geometry of reckoning with my body, but all of sixty years.

The scars across my lower stomach change from raw to crusty to bright new outcrops on my skin, blemishes rather than avenues cut through my flesh. One cut is just one inch above my navel, another about three inches above that first one. To the left of the first cut there is a three-inch space before another incision and another three-inch gap for the outermost cut on the left side. To the right side of the first cut just above the navel, there is a three-inch gap before a fifth incision and three inches away, on the far right side of my lower stomach area, the biggest of all incisions, this one about two inches wide, out of which my cancerous prostate and other matter sullied with disease made their bloody exit. A camera occupied the highest incision, that second one above my navel. It provided the internal picture projected on a monitor to guide the scalpels inserted into the other openings. The robotic element addressed the mechanized prongs in my body guided by the surgeon, who worked with the picture provided by the camera and headed for the places earmarked by the radioactive chemical tracers from the self-financed PSMA test.

I could sit forward after two nights in the hospital and two more days at home without pulling on something to spare my stomach muscles and aggravate those incisions. Another couple of days and even the swelling around my midriff deflated. After a week, the surface glue started to peel off in the shower and really flake like glue on a finger or any surface. I have to shake my head to clear a picture of this sealant applied all the way along a cut that opened a lane into my body, six lanes. With the restrictions of COVID-19, I have ample time for the slowness of healing. No matter how fast I rush ahead mentally, my body crawls along mending at a pace independent of my mind. I hope my daily walks help. I nurse a picture of those cuts closing and my midriff's return to its former middle-aged glory—slightly puffy, under the slight inflationary grip of midline fat, and something to pull in with a breath whenever I think about it (which is several times a day.)

Where does the feeling come from that I have lost something and returned from a funeral with the air of a burial still fresh in my body? It surfaced, this bad feeling, of impending doom as if I am about to have a heart attack, on my first night in the hospital. As my head cleared from the anesthetic I felt famished. The nurse told me to order something before the kitchen closed. He gave me a four-page menu—very five-star! I picked fish and mashed potatoes with corn on the side and rice pudding for dessert, with fruit juice. An orderly brought in the tray and did not linger and tried to keep far from me as she positioned the food tray on the adjustable table across the middle of my bed. I tasted the food and expected the flavor of hunger, which is no flavor at all, just a contented ravenous impulse. Instead, I chewed on sawdust and had the distinct mechanical experience of shoveling carbon into a pit of a machine. I chewed and shoveled the food but I was not there in that experience. I was absent from my body, still finding my way back to myself and filled with horror at the prospect of what I was in the middle of discovering and how the whole thing might grind to a halt and leave me stranded outside myself and so lost to my body.

The feeling of emptiness stayed with me for days: empty and exhausted, and ready to sleep for weeks in a new hibernation of the depleted spirit. At home I could see roses galore on the bushes in the front yard and remark on their rich display of red, pink, yellow and orange and white as if looking at the experience from some distance away. The ebullient display of life on the nettled branches just an arm's length from my face nevertheless seemed miles from me in my flat mood. My tiredness suffused my skin and bones. If lethargy was in the blood, then my body operated on a transfusion of it. With tiredness came this sadness. Not tears. The feeling of being on the verge of a flood of them, that I could burst at any moment, keel over and pound the ground and pull at my hair and dribble in hysteria. Somehow I kept myself away from that precipice.

My first surgery rehearsed my death. I have come back from the dead. I tasted what it was like to be present and have my grip on that present relinquished by some force outside my grasp. I simply let go of my life. That was the anesthetic. To come back from that helpless condition of death thrust on my body and mind leaves me scalded by an encounter with fire that blazed all around me and made it abundantly clear that there was no escape, just surrender. I am back in my life after a baptism in this fire. It leaves me sad, another place that I find myself in without wanting to be there, as if dropped into its coordinates by a shepherding clock, a time I must obey at a pace I cannot resist.

I miss this thing that is my life and all the people in my life. I left it without much notice. Had I not returned to my life, I would have left behind exactly what I find waiting for me upon my return to my conscious life. Now that I am back, I feel sad for this absence and for the return to the same place and with the knowledge that I have another departure waiting for me at some point in the unknowable future. I should benefit from my rehearsed departure and return. Something in me should be ready for the next time. Perhaps my sadness derives from seeing how little I can do to bring about any reasonable effect that softens the fact of my death. The readiness that Lear declares for something that's in media res and that involves not just preparation for but acceptance of the inevitable. No raging against the dying of the light, since that too is a waste of effort and an investment of energy that detracts from some more worthwhile undertaking.

Which is what? At sixty, I could have stopped living. And what a stoppage! Projects half done, scripts in need of my attention, money matters, security matters for my children and Debbie, who depend on me. Sixty feels too early. I feel sad coming back from that realization and knowing that if I devoted every waking hour to a readiness for death that I may need another ten years to reach that point of saying yes, I am ready. And maybe continual deferral of being prepared is a condition of being alive, that my mind works with deferral as a permanent condition rather than a thing to be resolved. I feel like that character in Pinter's *The Caretaker*, who has to go to Sidcup (a suburb of southeast London) to get his papers so that he knows who he is and perhaps settle the question as well of what his life means for him.

In the productions that I saw, first in my midteens and then again in my late twenties in London, the way the character gazes into the future and declares the intent to go to Sidcup to procure those all-important papers means he never will make the journey and at any rate, the journey is not one to be made by him but by us, the audience, those of us lucky enough to be left with his bequest to ask a better question of life, or to realize the pointlessness of posing the same question that he poses. Even in a space that declares a lack of something, it seems enrichment comes from just knowing about the absence of any meaning, and is preferable as a state of mind to outright ignorance of it (though ignorance of it is often an excuse from responsibility for certain actions).

I wonder if it hurts to know this for a fact? That my sadness arises out of a working knowledge of life's journey as an interrupted activity and not a goal or task that we can complete to any degree of satisfaction. In place of Dylan Thomas's rage—fight, not surrender; active demise rather than passive compliance—there is a quiet sadness that fits the conclusion of a thing worth the undertaking. Not for any point or meaning but for the joy and excess of phenomena that bombard the senses and invite fabulous abstraction to do what it can with such a state of being.

My body shows scars from a battle that carries on wounding my mind. I left surgery with a note of success in the battlefield against my cancer, routed from its base and chased out of sight, and with scraps of it left in place that in three months I can target with chemo and radiation; as such, it should signal a war that is all but over with me as the victor over my cancer. I have the scars on my body to show for it. There is this continuing fight with my mood. Cancer leaves its physical moorings and takes flight from my body as I sacrifice parts of me that held the cancer. On the psychological plane the cancer wages another battle of attrition to see how tough I can be with the memory of cancer in my body. I am to cherish the rest of my days as a cancer survivor. Cancer showed the error of my sixty years lived with ambition, idealism, righteous indignation, and not a small degree of selfish and damaging decisions.

Cancer says to me that I should remember it daily as I live out these last years. I am lucky to have learned from having cancer and lived to tell the tale. Has cancer poisoned the remainder of my life? Made my life the thing that I live thanks to the death of cancer. Added a sour taste to the flavor of my life, the afterglow when a candle flame dies, that bulb that shines for a moment in place of the light just switched off. My days singed by the blue flame of my brush with cancer. Cancer blues for the rest of my days. And the flip side, the B-side of the A-side, may well be a version of my life that is enriched by my cancer experience. The A-side for conventional living and the B for the walk on the wild side of things.

Maybe cancer wants me to be the beneficiary of its postbattle charm, not lessons learned from my fight with it, but the remnants of it in me as a flavor added to the remainder of my life. Cancer is the extra- that is placed in front of ordinary. In this way nothing can be just what it appears to be when faced with me. I come to things having snuffed the candle's flame for its afterglow, with the bonus light that follows the light just extinguished, with the boom and its adjoining endless echo.

Not echo as in a weaker copy of the original, nor the sound that returns to you after it runs from you and hits a barrier that sends it careening back to its source. More something that starts from somewhere as a result of the seeds planted by the original sound that you made. More like an independent force derived from that sound though not indebted to it. Something with a life and rationale of its own. You live for this and cancer knows it and came disguised as that sound, some quality that you needed in order to be renewed, as if cancer can ever be about renewal. As if you were on a road and the only way to get you to take a necessary detour had to be this calamity of a wheel breaking off the axle, a tire blowout, some impassable block in the road. Some bang, and its diminishing echoes, that add up to more than simply copies to be viewed as lesser than the original.

I move with leg irons, slow in the drag of a tide of bodily repair after surgery. No room in my head for any furniture other than my body's cut and bruised parts caught in their rhythm and gripe of repair. Pain under the skin, deeper than flesh, pain between my bones. I feel a dull ache. I move to ease that mounting sense of pressure, move from my back to my left side (there is a big scar on my right side, the largest by far of the six incisions that does not countenance any degree of touch). The hours mock me. They pass as if running on the spot with all the pumping arm action and high kicks of legs to mimic rapid movement.

One hour I think it is midmorning and the next I am in the middle of the afternoon and all that happened in between was my body barking my age and disrepair at me. How to heal when I feel stitched back together by the second hand of a clock? All my abstract art dispensed with in an instant by this body physics. The prescribed narcotics scoop up about three of those hours each time I take a dose and fling those hours away. And sometimes the gesture of disposal is into an oncoming breeze that pitches those hours back into my face. So I relive them with the same pain. Am I worthy? To think that this pain can be a university; that somehow Martin Carter's poem "University of Hunger" could be a solitary venture with the same long march of despair as necessary for repair.

The landscape of Carter's poem, Guyana, is superimposed with the marks of British colonial history on that land. Is that what cancer has done to my body? Marked it for destruction? Those who march in Carter's poem are on a desperate quest. They wake in this hunger and their only option is to let the rhetoric of the questions raised by their experience become self-answering. The hunger of the poem's speaker turns out to be a teachable moment in a long history of such lessons of suffering. I take my lesson from the poem's social and political example: to build a bridge between the personal and the political. As Carter teaches me to align with the poor as a standard for my art, so I wish my postoperative pain to forge a link with my artistic learning.

My art is more than just fashion or a pose. It relates to how I move in my life. More than a gesture, my art is groove and a rhythm, syllabic slap and empathic rap of nerves and muscle and blood dancing my bones. Surely with this pain and limited body (harnessed to body by my mind filled with pain) I can co-opt the engine of my art to move me to less pain and a delimited sense of self as more than flesh and blood. So I breathe deep. That vase again, and a network of vines growing through breathing holes in that vase. Breathe in this rhythm and live by each breath. I am more body than mind. My thoughts relocate from my head into pure physical pain. A routing of my mind: from its station in the head to one devastated location below my navel and behind my bladder. Everything about my thinking now in that lower area across my stomach marked with six punctures, some untidy as if made in a hurry or torn at the edges under duress.

My body's claim of me through its register of damage and pain and repair fills my head to capacity and underwrites cancer's claim of victory by a show of these hours as its winnings over me. Cancer left my body through the biggest of these six portals. Cut away from my body and dragged out of me and into the open. A true extirpation if there was one. A solid eviction. And for the clearing away of cancer the remnants of this pain. My sixty years strapped to my back; no, more precisely, below my navel, where sixty years declare a weakness, a burden of time, and too little of the nonchalance of youth at my disposal. Sixty shots from a rifle salute, sixty bugle and trumpet calls for a body curled around pain and in the grip of pain and wanting nothing to do with life if it means more of this and all of it just for this cancer.

The trumpet salute should be for cancer's departure. A burial for cancer's rose dug out of me. And for whom I grieve after months of fear of what cancer would do if left to its own devices in me. That I feared surgery would fail and leave the cancer to march on in me. That after surgery I may hear in three months' time that there is more of it and just as rampant and in need of new medical strategies. So the hours in my body measure my mind, as one analysis and worry follow the next, generated by pain. Whose university is a longing for it to come to an end. Where the lessons that I extract from my immersion in pain take flight from me before I can grasp their meaning, catapulted from me by my pain. A university of perpetual loss.

Perhaps a miniature violin plays for me. Other people live lives of pain, and here I am in a matter of days in pain's arresting company and I am ready to declare defeat. My requiem is for the territory lost by my mind to the demands of pain. And in its realm with cancer absent and fighting by proxy, I'm distracted by it. I find I can't think a thought that is not flavored by pain as a devotee of cancer. Though I know all about the finite body and its short span in that long march of time and history that Carter would have us attend to and benefit from even in our temporality.

My father died aged fifty-three, supposedly of heart failure. He had a separate family life at that point after years of no contact with us. My brothers and I returned to England in 1972, from Guyana, having never known him as a father. I left London at two with not a single memory of him. While we were in Guyana with grandparents he separated from my mother while they were in London setting up the good life for us. It dawned on me that his heart failure might well have been prostate cancer. With no communication between the families, his news reached us secondhand and something was lost in translation. First, there was shame associated with prostate cancer. Second, if anyone asks, tell them heart disease, since he had a dodgy ticker from his youth and military service in the UK, where he took seriously ill with pneumonia and had to be discharged from the army.

I wonder about the binary of either heart disease or prostate cancer, that one or the other must be false for a single truth to prevail. Maybe he had both heart disease and prostate cancer and they brought a premature end to his days. With just one of them on my plate and with seven years' advantage over him, I take my cancer as his dubious gift to me, with heart disease as the less attractive of the two (in a beauty lineup of them). Or so I estimate from my pain, cuts, drugs, and prognosis. My father gave me nothing of use to me in my life except the fact of my life along with the baggage of his gene pool. I feel no hurt or rage toward him. He did his thing and he left early. Had he stayed in my life and lived to a cure or maintenance of one or both of his diseases, or if he had died and I knew what the cause of death was, I would have taken those preventive tests for diseases earmarked for those with family histories.

I neglected my health checks and I am to blame for allowing my cancer to fasten its hooks into me, making it that much harder to cure it. My father casts his shadow on me. His influence on me from his grave is that of a stranger whose bloodline I happen to share. And with blood comes the penalty of genealogies of want, those small deficiencies that undermine the largesse of a continuity of life. Some of this is about me shadowboxing with him. I have no wish to inflict harm. I seek merely to dodge injury from him. He lies dead as a passive figure, long gone, whose agency wakes as cancer in me. I wake him to shake him from me, shake myself free of his genealogical stranglehold. That his ghost can battle me as cancer awakened in my body from his genes dormant all through my youth and into middle age makes this a mini epic. Some lifelong endeavor in which I kill once more the father who died long ago but refused to go in peace. I uproot my cancer and I kill him so that he dies twice, to stop his parade in my body in the shape of cancer.

My mother loved him to the end of his days, as she will to the end of hers. He left her for another woman. She loved him and he walked away from her and from us and started anew, with a new wife and children. He left me his wobbly genes probably rigged with cancer DNA so I need to reach him the only way I know how—by memory and invention—see him at his best, early in his adult life, in order to lay his ghost to rest.

12

THE CITY IS DYING

I see his smile and bright eyes and hear him over and again, "The operation went really well. It was hard. I hope I got everything. Stop all five drugs right away and come back and see me in three months for a test to check your PSA." I start at ninety and hope that when I count down to day one I will see the doctor again and hear that the cancer is cleared from my body, that the PSA (prostate-specific antigen) test registers way below 0.5 and so frees me of the need for more tests and possible radiation and chemotherapy. That is my wish. For three months I hope that wish comes true. I count each day and take them one at a time and see what each brings and what I make of each of them, no two the same.

I conduct this countdown under the added duress of COVID-19. I hope each day lessens the pressure on my mind, loosens the knot of my shoulders, and helps me breathe with a little more ease. That is a lot to hope for. I place my faith in what exactly? What kind of charity do I practice during this ninety-day period? How do I tack a meaningful course between the cliché of cautious optimism and that of an abundance of caution?

My body continues to heal. The drugs diminish in my system. I am winning my fight over control of my bladder. Where is the specter of the cancer? Evicted from my body, has the cancer morphed into a state of nonbeing? To continue its fight with me at the level of the subconscious, working on the margins of my waking life, and the moment I fall asleep greeting me in full armor in my dreams?

I worry. I doubt. I second-guess the doctor—what if he is wrong?—and myself—what if this starts a life-shortening affair with cancer?—and everybody—they tell me I will prevail, what if I don't?—and everything—drugs, along with surgery, cannot stop cancer, only slow its progress. I cannot believe that the cancer succumbs to a six-and-a-half-hour surgical operation. Nor how zapping it with radiation or drowning it in chemicals can succeed where the first wave against it of a scalpel-and-meds combo failed (assuming in my gloomy outlook that the PSA test in ninety days will say as much and confirm that the beast within me lives on).

*   *   *

COVID-19 sails in the city air in search of naked faces and bare hands that touch things plastered with COVID-19 that then touch faces. COVID-19 smells of disinfectant and of decay. The two vie for dominance in the city.

The city sits on a crate in the entrance of a shuttered church and shouts gospel all day until hoarse. The city tries to keep to itself in a tent on the sidewalk. Shrink-wrapped food stacked untouched beside that tent.

Our masks resemble theater or a wrestling persona. Masks muffle speech and hide our smiles, and collect what we exhale. Our noses stream into them. Our glasses fog. We move slower and feel short of breath. We begin to fear the city air and the openness of the city. And each other.

The city is dying. Asking for distance and anonymity and vacating its soul in the process. COVID-19 moves in to conquer not us—for we run and hide from it—but the brick, cement, glass, and steel of the city that cannot get away. Once the city falls we all fall with it. COVID-19 dies with the death of the city. Those of us who survive occupy a ghost town and crave the countryside, and never seeing another soul six feet away in a mask with fear and rage in their eyes.

COVID-19 is the jumbo jet equivalent of the paper airplane of my cancer. Except that I do not fly it, it flies me: from early morning waking before the city cockerel crows to reading with my eyes picking up the words that bounce off my mind uncomprehended.

*   *   *

We are in the makeshift gazebo in the choked backyard in Mid-City eating dinner at sunny six o'clock and listing our various aches and pains—it starts with Liliana's crooked neck from sleeping awkwardly, it seems, and moves to Christopher's many joints inflamed from sitting too long at his computer, to Nicholas, who dug a hole for us to plant and peeled off the skin on his palms, to Debbie's dodgy lower back that aches from standing for hours while she concocts our delicious meals from scratch, when the conundrum of a friend from my high school days springs to mind.

He danced for a while and hurt his spine. He wore a body cast that encased him from his armpits to his crotch. He moved like a robot, turning his entire body in any direction he wished to direct his attention. He had to sleep on his back, and to pick up something off the floor involved bending his legs to the point of folding them under him in order to reach that thing.

One morning he woke with an erection that had worked its way up and under his body cast and was stuck there. The discomfort woke him. He could not free himself from that cast—he tried, it hurt—without inflicting some injury on his member. He had to speed to the fridge, as much as his robot incarnation allowed him to move quickly and find ice, which he applied to the engorged area to drive away the warm blood. His erection gradually disappeared and he freed himself.

For a moment we laughed so hard and long that our bodies

were perfect again and my errant bladder was prelapsarian (with my surgery as D-Day) in its efficiency. I peed myself a little, laughing. I report it to Debbie and she tells me that peeing thing happened to her a lot and for some months after the birth of each child. There is so much secrecy and shame around the complications of the body as it recovers from trauma. The challenges feel private and unutterable. The small failings of the body in a fight to recover control seem outside decorum. I wore a catheter for a week after robotic surgery hauled away my diseased prostate and my seminal vesicles and nearly three dozen lymph nodes.

I prefer that body cast. Something everyone can see and link to my robotic state. Something to collect signatures on that one day will be cut off to restore all of me, nothing given away. None of this trade-off with my cancer, my pound-of-flesh scenario that leaves me feeling incapacitated. As if in ninety days I should be ready for a new conflagration with cancer and from here on in I should not waste a minute of preparation.

This voice from my distant past is not the only one that wants to be heard in my cancer wars (plural because no sooner one is over than another presents itself as a distinct possibility). Another voice that belongs to cancer, that I shut out of my story as a defensive strategy, may have to be allowed to have its say if I am to present a full picture of the many dimensions to my battles. That voice should not be taken as a ventriloquist trick performed by me. That voice is my cancer.

*   *   *

I do not feel far from my cancer, post-op for ten days. That thing still rules my life. I repair from my fight with it. And I fear that it lurks just around the next corner not far ahead of me. I wonder about the form taken by a guerrilla action by cancer conducted in me. How long before medicine catches up with it? How long before I detect its sabotage of my biology and chemistry and physiology?

"Don't worry, be happy," as Bobby McFerrin's maxim goes,

although replete with wisdom about the need to simply chill, it just does not cut it for me at this time. I worry. I am not happy about it. Cancer has my attention. It's this nagging doubt about the success of the operation that occupies me as a thing that I must understand and live with or else suffer from. Understanding (over-stand, my brethren) comes with a price. I have to embrace the thing I fear if I am to come to terms with it. My impulse is to run in the opposite direction and not look back.

Instead, I must stop, turn, and confront cancer, what is left of it, or the ghost of it, if I am to live without anxiety riding me and dictating my days and nights. Ghost cancer is cancer that has lost its footing in me, its body coordinates in me, to become an absence that maintains a presence in me. This is Toni Morrison's "absent presence" that she applied to Blacks in a White world: we're present but Whites don't see us and use us only as relative bodies to help pin down their White coordinates, and refine their White being.

Who will blink first? My cancer or me? Fuck you, cancer, you blink first. My eyes are staying wide open even if they weep and then dry up. You won that first round that hospitalized me for two days and pummeled me with a cocktail of drugs and left me scarred and humiliated and stupidly grateful to have escaped your stranglehold. This next round is mine. Now that I know what I am up against—I call it many things, a fight, or dance, or a couple rowing a boat—I am ready (or as ready as I can be under the circumstances).

Doubt leads to worry, and worry is my enemy and cancer's friend. Doubt feeds my art, sure, and outside art takes on the personality of cancer. Worry is one of the shadows of doubt. Worry powers that ghost incarnation of cancer. Worry powers the disease around my mind until a sickness takes over my flesh and blood, and hijacks my spirit. How do I fight a ghost? The thing I cannot see that asks me to keep it locked in my sight? Its dimensions are worry. If I worry, cancer takes flight in my body. If I control worry, I keep that ghost trapped in a closet or jar or chest.

I might even have that ghost under a microscope for my inspection. Ghost experiment. I search for ways to examine an invisible and malignant force so that I can rid it of its influence on me, or worse, its recapture of my life to end my days. The lab is my mind. I have a ghost machine that operates inside me. My heart is its engine, my thoughts its velocity. I have to match that ghost stride for stride, lock eyes with it and pivot as it pivots in and around me.

*   *   *

It's one of those stay-at-home and keep-close days. Seeing the world beyond the front door as the deep drop off a continental shelf if we step over that threshold. We surround ourselves with familiars—each other, home furnishings, favorite finger foods, television, books, and online campouts. The most that we do is let the dog out the back door for his yard exercise and bathroom break around the side of the house.

Disease rages outside. The air carries the threat of contagion. We watch the news and feel panic seep from the screen and fill the room. We read our phones and that same urgency creeps up our arms and changes the light in our eyes. COVID-19 invaded the city. Reports of it circle in the air. To breathe, we must wear masks and avoid contact with others.

I read slowly, as if everything were poetry in need of my singular attention. Really it is because I cannot think outside ruminations about the pandemic. No room left for anything else. I retain even less. My eyes land on words and bounce off of them rather than picking up each, as if they were little shells on a beach, for closer scrutiny. The rhythm of the words stays with me, so I fool myself into thinking, even if their meanings slip from me. They chime in me like the sound of the sea.

*   *   *

As a child in Airy Hall, I fetched water with two buckets, one in each hand. We worried that just one bucketful of water carried with all the body weight pivoted to one side to keep the arm straight and preserve every drop of that water along the walk home would make that arm longer than the other arm. We thought that we would end up with our bucket-bearing arm inches closer to the floor than the arm thrown out for balance as we walked in that peculiar way of keeping the knees bent a little and no bobbing about in a movement as if in a short run.

Oddly, twice the weight did not translate to twice the work. The body could be straight with two buckets instead of tilted sideways as it was when you carried one bucket. That tilt kept the knee clear of the bucket as you walked home as fast as you could without spilling any of the gold.

Two buckets meant an even walk with a focus on as little up or down or sideways movement as possible. The key thing was not to spill any of that precious cargo on the walk back from the village standpipe. If water spilled over the side of the rim of the aluminum, the sand road gobbled it up. There was almost a sizzle to that spill. The watermark lowered a fraction and served as a reprimand until it dried. The walk kept your eyes just in front of you to avoid potholes or stones and to keep an eye on the buckets and make small adjustments to the limbs, so small that the water hardly registered them with a wrinkle.

My bladder is that single bucket that I fetch with me. The slightest move without proper forethought results in this little spill of urine. I have to keep my mind on the sphincter muscles that close the opening of my bladder. No sudden moves, no sneezing or outburst of any kind, not even laughter. Otherwise, that spill.

When we reached the house a grown-up helped us hoist the bucket with care up to the water barrels stored in shade under the steps that led from the kitchen. Pouring made this music of water tumbling onto water in a drum.

Then it was back on the road for the walk to the standpipe for another load, talking all the way about the glory or misfortune of the last journey, who spilled what, when, where, and why. How next time no such bad luck would happen.

I walk with my bladder halfway full and delicate in as normal a movement as possible to avoid drawing attention—no slightly bent knees, no wooden gait to advertise, there goes Fred with his dodgy bladder. Thinking about it all the time, the attention flicks from one thing to the next and I have to bring it back to focus on stopping any spill.

*   *   *

Year crushed by COVID-19. Make room for more blather about my rebellious and cancer-afflicted bladder. Underwear padded as though I have just graduated from diapers and although potty trained, still prone to the odd accident or two. Adds protuberance to my crotch area. Feels stuffed between my legs. If I sit with my legs folded and my equipment sidles to left or right, any leakage misses the pad and soaks through my pants to implicate my trousers as well.

I am so conscious that this might happen that I have taken to wearing black trousers to disguise the wet patch. I have become Pissy, the kid I knew in Georgetown, Guyana, who earned his nickname for the telltale wet stain at his crotch and an ammonia cloud about him. Pissy should have been a loner and teased to death but he was a gorgeous storyteller and unlike the rest of us ten-year-olds able to see adult movies, mostly westerns, since his dad worked at the local cinema and always let him in to see the matinees. Pissy relayed each plot complete with dialogue and shoot-out sounds. He drew two imaginary pistols from imaginary holsters at his hips and with index and middle fingers straight and the small and little fingers curled, and his thumbs tucked at the first joint of his index fingers he wielded those two six-shooters. He fired by parting his lips with a sneer and spitting quite a bit to produce a sound that was a cross between a gargle and a cat's hiss that tailed off in a tinny echo. He blew on the end of the barrels and thrust them back into his hips.

As Pissy relayed his story, complete with gunfights, a wet patch grew on his khaki school short-pants. The dark stain that began as an island in a sea of khaki by the end of his story had become a dark sea enveloping an island of khaki. Pissy made an excuse to leave school before lunchtime and rarely returned until the next day with another episode from a film to relay to us. And we were ready, even if we breathed through our mouths to avoid his ammonia and tried not to stare at his crotch.

Not to be Pissy, I change my black short pants and briefs (boxers do not work with pads) two or three times a day, shower once, add talcum powder to my crotch for that baby-sweet smell, and think Kegel and practice Kegel throughout my waking hours. My struggle with Kegel exercises centers on sneezing, or coughing, or a raucous laugh, each of which elicits leakage, as if my bladder in a festive mood has to mark those occasions with a splash. If my bladder fills up while I sit through a movie (sitting appears to reduce my bladder's capacity), that leakage just happens as though a bucket, left under a running faucet too long, simply overspills. I feel the warm fluid spreading in my crotch and must pause the film and rush to the bathroom.

How do women power through that conundrum? They bear children and must work at recovery of their bodies and with the memory maybe repeat the experience. It's a sobering thought for my one-off wrestling match with my bladder. I ask Debbie about it. She puts it down to benefit analysis, that she weighs the risks with the benefits and the latter far outshine the former.

*   *   *

I find out in a casual chat with Debbie that caffeine irritates the bladder and intensifies that sensation of needing to go to the bathroom. I love my morning coffee. I add a lot of almond milk to the two large mugs that I consume over a couple of hours from the moment I wake. I eat a banana and a palm of walnuts before I zero in on my coffee consumption. I warm the almond milk, about one third of a cup, in the microwave. If I add the almond milk to the coffee without heating it, the coffee becomes luke-warm from so much milk. I hate lukewarm coffee. I prefer that my coffee is too hot and I have to wait for it to cool a little before I can drink it than to drink it lukewarm.

I increase the quantity of milk from a third to half a cup to re-duce the amount of caffeine that I consume while preserving my habit of three big cups before eleven a.m. It helps. I pee less often and a lesser amount. I practice Kegel each time; that is, hold for ten to twenty seconds, two or three times during each visit to the bathroom.

A listener outside the bathroom, who did not know about my condition, might be forgiven for being puzzled at the burst of urine, then silence, and another burst followed by a longer si-lence, and again that burst and an even longer pause before that final emptying. They might think that I was conducting a battle to urinate: that the silences between short bursts of peeing were my buildup of musculature, or will, or pressure of some kind.

I refuse to give up my morning coffee. I need one vice to add to the enrichment of my life. So I compensate with cups of green tea in the afternoon—one every hour from two to five p.m. I brew it as instructed, with a little warm water added to the teabag in a cup, topped by water that boiled, or nearly boiled, and left to stand for a couple of minutes before I pour it. It takes about five long minutes before I can sip from that cup. Since I associate all my body's excretions as contaminated by my cancer, all infusions that I consume should mitigate against disease. I hope that caf-feine carries some uncharted medicinal effect that fights cancer. If all my medicines that I took came in this form of a morning cup of coffee, from that aroma that fills the kitchen when the machine brews, to that bittersweet taste of a roasted nut, I would have been a happy gladiator against cancer, instead of a neurotic mess, frightened of my shadow.

Do not tell me that coffee feeds my cancer. Do not go there. I can face the news in eighty-two days that it has returned, anything other than implicating coffee with cancer. Pl-ease.

*   *   *

According to the nursery rhyme, Thursday's child has far to go. So it feels today, two weeks after surgery: that I have far to go before I can feel anything like I felt before this trial began with cancer. I am an old man in a child's frame of mind.

The old man who has to cope with his postoperative condition quantum-leaps to a time free of any worries about the body as an escape from having to face too much reality. The old man cannot believe what is happening to him—that he has to wear diapers again to catch the production of a bladder out of his control.

One thing happened that made the diapers indispensable. I woke early in a pool of urine. Worse, I held Debbie in a gibbon-like spoon embrace, and she too was soaked, along with the bedding. I felt the warmth in my sleep as a dull register and instead of experiencing alarm I felt a deep comfort and so allowed the undisciplined spigot to flow at will. She felt it too and took it for sweat since we both sweat a lot at night these days. The pee soon turned uncomfortably cold and I woke with a start, which woke Debbie. I pushed back the bedding to see this darkened map. I apologized profusely to Debbie, who did her best not to laugh and was very understanding with her tales of leakages after childbirth as we pulled off our wet things and found dry ones and stripped the bed and remade it with fresh linen.

The child in me was mortally embarrassed, the adult bemused. Neither one wanted another second of communion with the other. Both had nowhere else to go if the two were going to pool their resources, so to speak, and take on cancer. The old man in the present needed that child from the distant past, given cancer's long history of engagement with the body. The two had to accept upsets and setbacks, and recover quickly from them, if they were going to stop cancer from regrouping.

Those stories from childhood carried, in embryonic form, the fortitude of the adult. A remembrance of an early episode of the child's, in theory, should assist the adult mired in difficult present circumstances, since this present is in part indebted to that distant past. We shall see how that turns out. We know that cancer is older than both of us. As the child in me eats dirt unwittingly so the adult must crave it too and embrace it with the sensibility of the child. With this twinning comes the formation of a resistance to cancer staged *through* time, performed as a continuous present to bring those healing powers of adventure and laughter from that past into the present.

*   *   *

If I laugh too hard, I spill a little bit of pee. If I cough, if I sneeze, more pee. If I move too fast, too sudden, I pee a little bit. If I walk too long, pee. My body in action is permission granted to my urine for it to spill. It's like I'm walking around all day with an egg in a spoon. Or I've filled too much water in a balloon and that water needs no excuse to head somewhere other than where it should be. I have my mind on my bladder and my bladder on my mind. If my attention strays from it for a moment, my bladder, balanced on a high wire, loses its footing and falters, and spills, and I wet myself.

My bladder is one of those mischievous spirits that need constant supervision. If you take your eyes off it for more than a second, it gets up to no good. Spillage. It reminds me of the cup that I have in one hand while I try to twist a bottle cap with the other, and the hand with the cup automatically mimics what the other hand is doing and turns as well and spills my cup. Which doth not runneth over. Which makes me feel inadequate and dotty. Or I try to look at the time on my wristwatch and forget that I hold a cup of tea and that twist of my wrist to see the face of my watch spills the rest of my tea all over.

Don't even talk to me about running. I may as well just be facing a urinal. My bladder runs things, not me. I feel like a pupil in school who needs a permission slip to leave the classroom and walk the corridors on an errand. No note, no guarantee of a dry spell, and the expectation that I will be detained by an accident. I need to be a ninja with my bladder. I have to find a way to laugh without laughing. And stifle a sneeze and a cough. No sudden movements anymore, every move calculated to please my bladder and no movement outside of this bladder economy.

It's as if the surgery has left this opening in me and my life is spilling from me, little by little around all my attempts at living. It is the calling card of my operation; the signature of the doctors who operated on me; my urine as ink for their illegible scrawl on my clothing. As if they are pop stars and their biggest fan, me, I meet them and let them sign the most intimate part of my clothing.

My Kegel exercise is my only friend, otherwise I'm at the mercy of my bladder, going over Niagara Falls in a barrel. Or I've walked behind the cannon of a waterfall, but to get there I've stepped through the waterfall, and I'm too soaked to enjoy the storeroom of quiet behind those falls. It's water, water, everywhere and not a drop to drink.

Do I imagine a cloud of urine about me as I navigate among others? A smell that makes people twist their noses and look me up and down, and take a step back from me? My clothes ablaze with urine, pungent as a primary color is vibrant, so that I consider washing and changing on the hour every hour to avoid that dilemma. I need to commemorate my bladder and designate today as national urine day. I can wear a badge that looks a bit like spilled ink on blotting paper. I can search the night sky for a new star to name after it. Or devise a meditation practice specifically to preserve my urine by maintaining composure. I would be as light-footed as a ninja and walk on rice paper and not tear it, and not spill a drop of my precious cargo.

PANDEMIC

A version of dear
Sylvia's *Bell Jar* covers
All of sweet LA,
All that LA sweats,
All the mayor's shame exposed:

Too many homeless,
Too much casual
Police brutality caught
On camera, left
Unsolved to fester;

Empty streets,
Shuttered shops,
Crowded supermarkets,
Pharmacies,
Traders of Guns;

Vendors at intersections
Stop selling flowers,
Traffic homemade masks;
Homeless numbers dwindle;
Smog peels from city air;

Our dog, Dexter, waits
By the door for us,
As we don protective gear,
His olfactory city map
Weighs on our mind.

The horror of Ahmaud Arbery's shooting—a modern-day lynching by three racists—overshadows my bladder, COVID-19, and cancer worries. I feel sick. The young man simply jogged through a neighborhood in coastal Georgia where he lived with his mother. He was shot on February 23 and were it not for the video recorded by one of Arbery's assailants, this lynching would have passed us by. It happened two and a half months ago. Ahmaud was twenty-five years old and Black.

Just as I start to think that my consciousness is full of cancer and its ramifications with no room for much else, this happens and it grips my heart and stops my breath and fills me with unquantifiable rage and hurt. Just as I wonder if the personal always disrupts the bigger picture I see that I am attuned to big events whose arc returns our world to the dark days of slavery and Jim Crow.

My cancer is not only my worry. My cancer runs this society as well.

13

I LISTEN AND HEAR MORE

My cancer tells me that my secret (that I have cancer) is safe with it. I need not divulge this fact to anyone. I can keep it just between the two of us. I get suspicious right away, that cancer is up to something if cancer is telling me that something or other that I am doing is supported fully by it. I decide to talk selectively to people who matter most to me.

I decide that it's time for me to call Geoff on WhatsApp. My early morning; his midafternoon. I have to wait for a few minutes as he settles back home after a thirty-mile bike ride with Peter. He says they are having a cup of tea and homemade Eccles cakes bought from a house in a village near Uffington outside Shrewsbury.

First, I run through my story—not the facts of it but the why of it. Why wait so long before I decide to confide in him? I did not wish to bother him with a thing that needed my full attention and of which I felt too preoccupied to spare anyone an ounce of extra effort to take care of their shock and concern for me. I did not want to involve others until I had definitive news about my struggle with the disease. I did not feel good. In fact, I was too depressed to talk to anyone. I felt too much anger at the world that I was dealt cancer's cards. I wanted to conserve my energy for the fight of my life.

I dial. He picks up. The grainy footage (analog, digital) of his front room notwithstanding, he looks fresh and animated. Sun

funnels into the front room and fills the space with charm. After
the preliminaries of how each of us is doing, I tell him that I have
some personal news. I relay the story of my diseased body.

I conclude by saying that I have these wounds that are healing and I'm battling with bladder control after the removal of a
catheter, and how I go back in three months for a blood test that
will give me the all clear, or else confirm more cancer, and put
me on a course of radiation or chemotherapy to resolve it. Geoff
nods and looks surprised. He plunges right away into a relay of
his experience with my symptoms among his patients when he
worked at the Shrewsbury Natural Health Centre as a massage
therapist. He is mercifully restrained in his offers of advice of
what I should be doing next. I have little patience for advice. Not
just from Geoff, but everyone. Perhaps the illness has curtailed
my patience. I think of Oscar Wilde's adage (that advice is an excellent thing not to follow, but to disregard) as a sufferer's dismissal of more things to think about on top of everything to do
with the disease. Though the advice may be good, it figures as a
distraction for the mind and body already locked in combat or
tango with the disease.

Geoff nods a lot, and I take his active listening as genuine empathy and love. He reminds me of his breakdown in the nineties—
he refers to it as when he cracked up—when he said he felt the
same things that I am telling him about, and that I wrote him,
from America, and called him too, though he could barely speak,
and it proved most helpful to him. WhatsApp freezes up a couple
of times while one or other of us talk on without realizing we
cannot be heard. We have to repeat ourselves quite a bit, which
wears me down. Nevertheless I feel elated that Geoff knows
about my disease. I feel that the disease might wish me to remain
locked up with it as a way to wear away at my resistance. Talking
with Geoff adds energy to my sense of a life that needs to be lived
with or without the cancer.

We soon stray to other topics. I say I've switched to online
teaching and lots of walks in the neighborhood. He mentions his

bike rides with Peter, who says a bonny hello (without knowing what Geoff and I are discussing) and he reports that a man is on a boat on the Severn, which runs past the back of their house, and the man's shouting at the houses through a megaphone that it's time to end social isolation. Peter then leaves and a moment later I see him on all fours crawling across the screen, around Geoff, to avoid being seen by me.

I tell Geoff how much listening to classical music and jazz helps. He is thrilled about that as an avid classical concertgoer. Classical, he says, enables the listener to work through complex emotional scenarios by providing a safe structure in which or by which you can explore quite challenging things. I agree. I find it quiets my mind and takes me away from my worry about cancer, and into these fields of emotion where I wander, or sends these huge waves through me that sweep me along with them so that I am lost to myself.

*   *   *

Coltrane's *A Love Supreme*, on a loop. A blank page with one line that starts in a corner at the top and wriggles, and writhes, and jives its way down that playground of white space to fill the place with joy. I chase after it and I seem to catch up and run along with it for a stretch before it zooms ahead of me and leaves me reaching for its coattails. Exhilaration pulls and pushes me to keep up with where Coltrane leads me, for even Coltrane appears not to know at times, as he forges ahead trusting in discovery as an impetus for breathing more notes.

Cancer, I wish to lose you now as I follow Trane. I hope my cancer cannot keep up with this flood of positive energy. Cancer finds that it is too much (like trying to drink from a fire hose), and I suppose that it burns cancer to touch it (like a red-hot brand), so cancer shies away from it. Me, I head right for that burn, that blaze that lights a path not seen before and one that beckons me onward to go, follow where Trane leads, trust what Trane trusts.

So it is that we (Trane and I) leave cancer far behind us, fallen on its face in the dust.

If there's a shape for the spirit housed in the body, Coltrane's exhalations embody it. That spirit emerges out of history. Pain shines in the architecture of that spirit. Coltrane works through his pain. He shakes off the shackles of his hurt and surges toward joy. He falls back into the pool of his punishment and treads there for a time before he jettisons out of that element into joy once more. His spirit is soaked in pain and joy. He douses us with the same mix of history as an instant enactment of the breath of the body in collusion with his saxophone.

Coltrane helps me in my fight with cancer. As long as he plays, cancer stays hidden and may even shrink, bombarded with the sound of Coltrane. He casts a spell with his sound. He picks me up and I fly with him in swirls and confident ziggurats. We veer toward objects and swerve from them at the last second so close we brush them with a sleeve. The flight begins in air with Coltrane. Air is only the beginning with him.

Once he wins my confidence and trust, Coltrane heads for the open sea. He takes me up to a cloud and dives in notes that add speed to gravity's pull on my body. I see the sheet metal of the sea racing to meet me as I zoom toward it. I brace myself and something in Coltrane tells me to breathe like him and work my body with those breaths and relax. Just as I obey Coltrane the two of us meet the metal skin of seawater and rather than obliterate us, it parts for us to enter its caves. I feel this closeness of moving underwater. I see the painted canvas of the inside of the sea being made with swirls and dabs. Some of it is my doing. The vast majority is Coltrane's breathing in twists and turns of meaning.

That is not all, though that may suffice. I listen and hear more and feel more and see farther. Coltrane dives deep with me in tow and makes a ninety-degree turn and heads for the shore. I think that Coltrane must know that he has to surface to make landfall. I think he must begin to head for the surface at any moment. I wait for the tug and prod of a change of direction and nothing like that

happens. Instead he accelerates. He means for us to crash underwater into the wall of the shoreline. I brace for impact.

Two things happened to me during my treatment for cancer,
which I'll relay because they remind me of two other things. The
first is a twang and puncture of skin that the doctor warned me
about in a test that broke through the wall of skin of one of my
organs, traveled across interior space and broke though another
wall of another organ to collect a specimen. The twang and puncture made me contract my body for a painful reaction that never
arrived. The second is a sensation that overtook me the moment
before I lost consciousness in the hands of the anesthesiologist,
that my tongue had filled my mouth and flesh had replaced everything in my head, my eyes, nose, ears, brain, and mouth, and all
the flesh, of me being turned inside out, nudged against bone as
if about to spill from my body.

Listening to Coltrane, that first crossover, from speeding underwater to tunneling underground, is the twang and puncture I
feel as one element, water, gives way to another, earth. The flood
of flesh in me that replaces everything inside and pushes gently
against bone and skin is what it feels like to move at high velocity
underground. The two things do not terrify me. I trust Coltrane,
my captain. I am a passenger on his craft built out of sound. I
expect us to turn at any moment to break free of earth and splash
into air and an expanse of light.

Which is where Coltrane trails off and cuts me loose, high up,
level with the top of a mountain. Which is when I free-fall. I do
not flail as expected. I stay calm and wait for what Coltrane has
in store for me. I breathe. Which is how I turn into what children
call a helicopter seed, one of those maple seeds with the prongs
that twirl as they sail from a tree seeking to become another tree.
I turn in slow motion and my descent follows suit—it too slows
to let me see that Coltrane brings me back to earth in one piece
though irreparably altered by my journey with him.

*   *   *

My body betrays me over and over. First, with time, my body leaves me stranded at a bar nursing our two drinks and walks out arm in arm with time. My body tells me I have to put up with it or leave. I shut up and put up. My body returns with bruises and scrapes and exhausted, the kind of exhaustion that results from masses of exhilaration. And my body sleeps for days. Or walks around with me, in a daze or like an automaton doing my bidding out of duty and absent from our shared routine.

Time is not the only outside partner with whom my body has questionable affiliations. Time is perhaps the least culpable of them. Time, after all, happens to all of us, and time shows its ravages on us all. My body goes one step further by inviting time to party with it. Doing time is one thing, biding one's time is another thing, but inviting time to do what it will with you and to show you the worst excesses of its pastimes, well, that is quite uncharted territory.

My body returns to me altered by the encounter with time at this reckless level of engagement and abandonment. Whatever the two were doing away from me amounted to a year or two of wild living squeezed into a night and day. I shake my head and throw myself into the task of getting my body back on track with me in terms of a good night's rest, healthy diet, and wholesome exercise.

I cannot wear a wristwatch anymore because of what time has done to my body. I look at wall clocks and see them as portals that open pathways into our minds and hearts, not with a routine to be obeyed and ordered by time, but as a chance to let all that go for this other way of living, as if on a short fuse that you can see burning out as it approaches you with its invitation to extinction.

Imagine a large jug of wine, decanted for the interaction of the grapes with the air; now pour that wine into six glasses and raise them in a toast. The time it took for those grapes to grow in the vineyard and mature and get pressed and bottled and left to stand again in a slow march toward maturity to end up in that jug is time not seen, whose surface is barely scraped in the brief duration of that toast. In similar fashion, the time that takes my body from me for an all-night party, one where everything goes, squanders all the time put into keeping my body healthy, all that preparation seemingly to prime my body for that night of adventure.

I work with a routine that invests in the time that is available to my body, the time that turns up and walks off with my body, goes on a spending spree with that investment. My body, built for living and marking time, even as time chips away at it, believes in abandonment to time and abhors my investment of a portion of that time in my bid to buy more of it for the body and me. My body and I tussle over this conflicting view of what the time given to us is for.

The second betrayal by my body is with cancer. I never saw that one coming. There was no bar in which I saw time saunter over and entice my body away from me. There was no jug of wine to measure out into glasses for a toast to our bacchanalian existences. Just this arrival one day of cancer rooted in my body and reading its dictate to me that this body no longer belongs to me but to cancer. The shock of the announcement stalls me. The willingness of my body to go along with it and give that cancer room and board until that cancer grows big and bold and launches its coup, that shocks me into stillness as well.

I cannot believe that my body hid this from me for so long. I marvel at the fact that it all unfolded as a plot right under my nose and before my eyes (in front of my inward gaze and awareness as insight) while I remained unaware of it. I ask my body why. Why do this final thing to both of us? What do you stand to gain from our mutual destruction? Do you hate me so much that you are willing to die to take me down? And so the questions pour out of me. Or they pour inside of me from my mind to my body. And they register as tears that I shed involuntarily away from others and alone in my office or the bathroom.

I try to let my body know that this latest betrayal cannot be slept off and showered away. That cancer is another matter altogether. That while we have a limited amount of time at our disposal to interpret it in different ways, and differ in how to put the amount of time that we are allotted to some good use (or not), cancer, by contrast, cannot be divided and parceled out in this way. Cancer is life's all-in poker game of boom or bust.

*   *   *

Boom, if you can gamble with cancer and win by securing a cure. Bust, if cancer takes over and cuts off the rest of time and takes your life. Boom, if the lesson that you learn from having cancer and being cured of it puts you on a richer and more meaningful path of spending the rest of your time on earth. Bust, if after all the taxing treatments to cure you of your cancer you end up dead from cancer anyway. Boom, if the love in your life multiplies and intensifies as a result of the threat of cancer in your life. Bust, if all that love just ends up as a witness, forced to watch you perish from cancer.

Boom-bust. That is what cancer brings, no in between. No flirtation with time for a chance at repair from the encounter. And perhaps another binge with time in some other future encounter. Not so with cancer. Once you strike the deal (cancer will promise anything to make a deal with you), cancer moves in and takes over. You might like the look of what you see initially, a blast of color, and lots of frenzied activity by your athletic cells to rein in cancer, since those cells view cancer as an invading army. You might feel the buzz of this turn in your body's chemistry.

All too soon all of that dissipates. What you are left with is the worry planted by the knowledge that you have cancer and all the side effects as it impedes bodily functions as a result of its intrusive and growing presence in you. By then it is too late to change your mind about cancer. Nothing can be done about that contract with it. The body becomes alarmed at what it has gotten into, and panics, and does what only the body can after a revolt against the mind: the body turns to the mind for help.

*   *   *

Our twoness is a oneness. Our division into distinct entities rests on the false assumption that one of us can live without the other. In fact, we are interdependent moment by moment: body on mind and mind on body. Mind made the move to separate from the body and rule over it. Mind seemed to think that regulating the body's hungers amounted to dominating the body, superior to it by virtue of acting the part of manager of the body's needs. Somewhere along the line the mind forgot that what the body consumes is also consumed by the mind, and that both body and mind need those nutrients.

Cancer thrives on this division. Cancer wants nothing more than to invade a body that operates as if it were independent of the mind. Independent-thinking bodies make for easy prey. Cancer chases that body that runs from cancer until exhausted and collapses and cancer lassoes it or sinks teeth into its neck. Or the body sees cancer as something enticing, as if cancer wore a disguise, and voluntarily goes with cancer, without asking the opinion of the mind. Cancer feeds the body to make the body lose its bearings and ability to resist what cancer does next.

What does cancer do next? As the body lays transfixed by disease, cancer opens a vein (not an obvious one, think between the fingers or toes) and secretes itself there, plants itself in the body. The body comes to its senses alone and wonders what happened to all the company that it started the night with, before the psychotropic drugs broke out and scrambled everyone's sense of time, turned time elastic like a clock painted by Dalí (time warps, time bends) that drips off the wrist as time runs out of my life.

Nevertheless, tomorrow is Mother's Day so I google what local florist might be open, locate one a mile away, and take off in the car solo and with a mask. How odd to drive on empty streets and see hardly a soul. I am the florist's first customer of the day.

The place is chock-full of arrangements from moderate to extrav-
agantly priced. They offer me a free balloon and when I pick the
arrangement that I like, balloon the price in keeping with my enthusiasm. I rush back to the house and ask Debbie to go upstairs
for a moment while I bring something from the car that she is not
allowed to see. I place it in the small front room beside the living
room and close the sliding door with instructions to the children
to keep out.

I take Liliana on a separate shopping run to the local CVS for
cards. Liliana wraps her order of earrings and a necklace for Debbie in a number of outsize boxes. (I mean those huge Amazon
boxes, one for each earring and the necklace.)

*   *   *

MOTHER'S DAY

In the first Superman movie, Superman arrives too late at the site
of an accident to save his beloved Lois Lane. She perishes. Superman operates among us ordinary mortals with one golden rule:
never intervene in time as experienced by humanity. His grief at
his failure to save Lois Lane soon turns to resolve: he decides to
break this condition of his cohabitation with people. He zips into
the space outside earth's atmosphere and starts these rapid rev-
olutions around the planet to reverse time and recoup the time
that he lost that made him late in Lois Lane's moment of need.

In true Superman fashion he arrives in time to save Lois Lane,
who is none the wiser: that she died and that her hero steals time
to reverse her fate and rescue her. What happens to the entire
planet gifted those precious minutes to relive? I see what I can
do to avert disaster with my body and cancer. In the bonus time I
tell my body the following: "Dear flesh and blood of my night and
days, you who drive my ability to see feelingly and feel with sight;
most bountiful bundle of nerves and bones and with a gorgeous
one-piece skin suit; hear, oh hear! Much has passed between us.

Much has been shared. We have tried to go our separate ways, though conjoined twins, and never managed for long or to get far. This is our one and only opportunity to do something together for our mutual benefit and to underwrite our shared time left for us to enjoy a life that may be our one shot at living (assuming religion to be Marx's 'opiate of the people,' and a contrivance).

"You see that shiny thing that catches your eye? It is the hypnotic glint in the eye of a boa constrictor. Walk away from it. You sip that condiment with sweet and sour, salt and pepper, cardamom and coriander inducements? Spit it out and toss that drink. You smell that rose that wants you to stuff your nose into it for more of its honeyed aroma? Pull away and run away from it, and do not look back at it until you are out of breath. You feel that silk against your skin that makes the hairs on your arms wave in its direction and incline toward it for more of that touch of delight? Free yourself from that touch and remove yourself from its vicinity, as far away from it as you can get and as fast as you can do it. You hear that music that makes you drop everything that you are doing to get closer to it so that you can hear more of it in unmediated and unadulterated ways? Cork your ears against it. Chant something nonsensical (*om-na-mah-sheva-ya*) or something principled (*no justice, no peace, prosecute the police*) at the top of your voice to drown out that magnetic music. As you chant move away urgently from its realm of sound to a safe, silent distance.

"Hear, oh hear. All those temptations are forms of cancer that if we can outwit in this borrowed time, granted to us by the luck of the marvelous, then we can be safe and free of cancer's untimely murder of us. Are you with me, brother, sister, comrade body?" It is a no-brainer for the body. There is no hesitant weighing of possibilities. The body knows what it must do before it finds the words to declare its intent. In the same way Superman sweeps Lois off her feet and to safety, the happy ending is that body and mind walk into the sunset in unity and at peace. Yeah, right. Wake up, Fred.

For Mother's Day I begin by serving Debbie. First, her cup of coffee, in bed. We wait for the children to wake and she opens her cards and I fetch the bouquet in a peacock fantail stuck in foam to keep that fan shape, mostly roses and some colorful brush and a few hydrangeas and lilacs as fillers. Debbie loves it. She enjoys opening those boxes and reminds everyone that it is a trick that I introduced one Christmas back in the early 2000s to disguise my gifts to her and the children, since she tended to guess pretty accurately what slippers or dressing gown or pajamas or underwear I would buy for her (perfumes only on Valentine's).

For supper I grill salmon decorated with olive oil and lemon and garlic, and a pinch of salt for the salt eaters in the family (the kids) and a couple of twists from the black-pepper shaker for the pepper people (me). I grill squash, onion, mushrooms, and tomatoes from the garden (the latter do not turn out so good). We eat in the gazebo. We watch a movie, a romantic number that makes us wistful for days long gone when the kids were wee and all three ran in different directions for us to catch them.

*   *   *

This is where I sit in a half lotus with my wrists flopped on my knees and breathe and retreat deep inside and as far away from the clamor of the present as I can bear to be at the moment. Is there such a place? Of stillness and quiet, so quiet I can hear the wings of a butterfly fluttering by (yak!), so still I see specks of dust afloat in a slant beam of light. Ah, to be one of those specks floating without a care. Take me there and leave me. Lose me. Confuse my cancer like fuck.

No balls, no ass, no brain, no heart, just this speck afloat in defiance of gravity, history. A complete escape and no prospect of a return, no passport to pass through the usual ports, no escape clause from the cause that captures this landscape, or cord to pull to show saturation, once I slip this time I do so for all time, for good. Watch me float off the ground in that half lotus on a flurry of breathing and lost to myself. History thief. Antiblack paint, spiked to thwart white supremacy's climb.

Bodiless like this I retain nothing of history's hurts; contain nothing other than this essence of sunlight that keeps me buoyant. *Nyabinghi* for me as I possess and am possessed by this flotation of all things good outside history, in defiance of linear time. Stay with me now. I dictate to you what is dictated to me in my condition of being nameless, bodiless. Do not take notes as much as soak up these notations by osmosis of your skin, eyes, nose, mouth. Drumbeat. Wavelength. Elastic. Porous.

Yet I bounce as if bound in flesh and blood. Not sure I want the divorce between body and mind just because my body is afflicted. I work with elevation and transport to lift my body out of the clutches of cancer to some kind of safety. Not to be free of it, since I cannot see anything outside my body that is not indebted to it, rather to help it toward a cure of some kind, contentment of one sort or another.

*   *   *

You can catch me with a butterfly net. That's me in a buttercup field, bobbing up and down and nodding into flowers. Heavily disguised and completely at home. Billy Cobham acts as a flotation device for my mood, making it lighter and keeping me airborne longer. His album *Total Eclipse* played in its entirety for his blast of drumsticks, liquid and multiplied into a dozen sticks and a dozen drums. There is this fountain that rises in the spigot and I am balanced on it, not sure how, but I stand on that rising tide as it lifts me higher and higher, powered by Billy Cobham and his drumming. And just as I think where can this go I find myself multiplied from one fountain to one dozen of me lifted and made airborne, balanced on water.

That butterfly satisfied me. This show by water from a drummer turns those buttercup fields into suns, their shine turned down for my eyes, their heat cooled to perfection. Billy Cobham eases up on the drums for the horn and guitar to build something new. Water fountain and buttercup field conjure a third force. Where does the sense of a spin take over, that sends me on a tight spiral so that I descend into my body? Cobham takes me closer to my heart. He pushes my nerves against that beat so much so that blood courses through me with my eyes and feelings mixed with it, rather than outside it, and so no longer separate or able to see myself as separate from it.

It is the same field and fountain in a vortex and plunged from outside to inside. There is this interior melee of disruption caused by a multitude of elements and emotions all conducted by Cobham. He does not allow the stirrings to settle and the spin to stop. He allows them to slow for a spell. He lulls the heart and mind into a slumber. Then he unleashes once more those sticks of tempestuousness. To send me on a head spin and tailspin, spiral and vortex at one and the same time in and through things as if to traverse a forest was to fly over and fly through it as well and under it if a tunnel could be made as fast as this flight.

Cancer cannot live in Cobham country. Cancer is a drag on such velocity. Cobham shakes off that drag and flicks it from him and sound marshals at his behest and drives away to leave cancer stranded in the middle of nowhere. Cobham is a cure for cancer. A sound wave mode of cure for cancer, whose bellow and hum is in the shape of Cobham. A body thrown behind that groove, sweat and breath with movement of hands and feet and spinal column.

Cancer shatters in the face of Cobham's sound. Cancer turns to dust pounded by drumsticks. Cobham eclipses cancer. I need the sonic equivalent of dark glasses to listen to Cobham. He does things to the ears that the ears have not come across before as the body's chief arbitrator of sound. He turns my pores into ears. I listen to Cobham with my entire skin. He gets under my skin to treat everything inside me as if all my internal organs were arranged on a stage for him to play on them. Heart batter, liver beat, kidney strafe, lungs echo, symbol-clash of stomach. They play Cobham and hear him too.

As the last note dies on *Total Eclipse* and his drum majesty rests, I emerge from his world weaved from sound and silence feeling giddy and renewed.

*   *   *

Ways to forget about cancer. Take a deep breath and dive and swim underwater from one end of the pool to the other. Recite Kamau Brathwaite's poem "Caliban" by heart; and Derek Walcott's LIX. i, from his book-length poem *Omeros*, also from memory. And lots of Grace Nichols's "I Is a Long Memoried Woman." For as long as these readings last, cancer cannot breathe, unless cancer grows gills, and can breathe unaided on the summit of Everest.

MEMORY AS INVENTION

DJ Cancer

I remember things that happened before you were born
I waited patiently looking in the distance to catch your arrival
I was passed from your father and your mother to you and they
Inherited me from their father and mother and that is why
I have the patience of Job and I bide my time for the right moment
To present itself to me when I know the time is ripe for me to strike
For I'm the foe inside of you and the one you least expected.

Guess what? You had me plucked out of you and now you wait
To find out if I'm gone for good. Guess again. This is my comeback
Song that I was gone but not for long and I return to wreak havoc
In your system and take you down, but this time it all happens
Before your wide eyes and there is nothing you can do to stop me.

*   *   *

I forget, so the adage goes, in order to remember at a deeper level. Forgetting is survival from trauma. Forget or perish under the pressure of the memory. Remember selectively and become strong and able to combat trauma. I forget that I had cancer. I do not have cancer. One addresses the past and my operation, the other my present and my consternation that it might be present in me. Can I really package the operation that removed the bulk of my cancer and place it in my memory vaults out of reach of my conscious mind? Or am I performing a trick of memory and a pretense at a coping mechanism?

During the moments of forgotten cancer I regroup my energy to combat the possibility that I may still be poisoned by it. Why do I find it hard to have a song for my troops to sing in my encampment?

I draw squares in the dirt with a stick for a game of hopscotch. Three stacked squares branch out to two drawn side by side, and continue with another one, stacked like the first three, two more side by side, and finally one stacked on top. The diagram of squares has a start and finish in the same place at the head of those first three squares. The rest of the diagram is a circuit. The player has to hop on one leg throughout and kick an object from one square to the next all the way to the top of the squares and back to finish at that starting place. All the while the player must maintain that hop and keep the object inside those squares without missing any of them. The player must nudge the object with the foot that hops: one nudge for each hop, no resting on the other foot, the leg of which must be kept bent at the knee to avoid touching the ground, all the way up and down those squares.

During that game, the only thing in the world is the object that I have to kick and the borders of those squares that I must stay inside to progress from square to square. As a left-hander I hop on my left leg. I call it my leading leg, not my strongest leg but my most accurate leg. For this game it must play the role of strongest and most accurate. Hop to burning point and beyond burning to outright evisceration at a cellular level and remain accurate with those jabs of what turns out to be a dry mango seed.

*   *   *

"Saturday night at the movies . . ." The Drifters' song pops into my head to remind me of what no longer happens in Tinseltown, of all places. Nobody in the neighborhood is getting dressed to be there, alas. We have drifted away from all things social for all things isolated. That song was nostalgic, even in my youth. As for most things that endure, it carries an emotional register for me. It is akin to what Walcott said, "Sometimes there's more pain in a pop song than in all of Cambodia."

That sounds corrupt until you concede that most people conduct their emotional lives far from the politics of injustice and shut out the news of another massacre somewhere on the planet and tune in to images of a neglected dog and cry inconsolably. History is my tearjerker. That song appeals to me as a sound that strikes a certain tone. I do not think of movie theaters at all. The tone takes me back to my childhood in Guyana's countryside, where the only movie that we saw was shown to the entire village in the open with a white sheet for a screen and two large spools of film that had to be changed halfway through the screening.

I don't remember the movies. They did not serve popcorn. It was a huge treat to meet up at night to see a moving image, larger than life. Could it have been *The Sound of Music*? There were no hills near us. The night air was alive with the sound of insects and peeper frogs, and mosquito coils burned all around us to keep critters at bay. The youngest among us fell asleep and had to be carried home from the village square after the show. Was there even a village square or was it just some field beside the church house? Most likely, the latter.

I was six or seven or eight or nine. I walked unaided in the dark with the others. I carried my sleeping cancer.

14

I WAKE WITH HIS NAME ON MY TONGUE

George Floyd, I add your name to a long and growing list of those killed by the police, though no less of a shock to see nearly nine minutes of an officer with his knee on your neck and you in handcuffs with two of the other three pinning your body and legs and the third standing guard. How long those minutes string out on my nerves and stretch to breakpoint my ability to bear that time and not succumb to damage of my ability to see with clarity. Who am I kidding? Cancer and COVID-19 together amount to less than what you had to bear in those nearly nine minutes of your murder.

George Floyd tied to a history of slavery. History that is as warm as Floyd's body. A history before the noose of that officer's knee consigned George Floyd to history. His body, robbed of natural breath, refills with the breath of history. A history that insists it must be for his flesh now, his flesh that looks like flesh back then.

It is this suit of history in the shape of George Floyd's skin that I wish to unzip and have him step out of it and walk away. Without this suit of history the police see a big man in good shape whom they must bargain with to find out what part if any he plays in their reason for being there. Without this suit, this black skin, with the naked appearance of whiteness, the police see a perfect specimen of themselves. They talk to him and shake his hand and wish him a good day. He walks away and lives to see his children and grandchild.

With this suit on George Floyd that cannot be unzipped, the body's biggest organ, the other option if George's black skin is nonnegotiable is to pluck out the eyes of the police, or have them wear lenses that see black skin without the negative connotations of history, skin as somehow neutral, as somehow freed from a history of enslavement.

If the police are blind when they meet George Floyd, they encounter another person, a stranger; if they can see, they meet George Floyd but do not see the individual, and register only the history attached to his skin that robs him of his humanity. By seeing, in effect, they are blind to him.

*　　*　　*

The city of Los Angeles is under curfew. For the first time in my nearly thirty years in the States I am living in a city under martial law. Debbie and I stop at the red lights to cross Venice Boulevard into the strip mall with our local supermarket. There along the cordoned-off three-lane street for each direction of traffic on Venice we see yellow police tape and two recycling trucks parked across the lanes to block all entry. We gawk at the desert fatigues of the National Guard and their sand-camouflaged armored vehicles. I utter an expletive out of shock and horror.

There's urgency in the crowd inside the supermarket. It feels as if something terrible is about to happen along Venice Boulevard that might include this supermarket. Everyone fills their trolleys quickly and heads for the checkouts. In the line a woman says her husband is armed and waiting in their car, guarding it. We shake our heads and look at each other a little disbelieving of what we just witnessed on Venice and what we hear now in the checkout line.

We cross Venice slowly and look long and hard at the soldiers and their armored vehicles. Venice Boulevard corrupted, tainted, infected. The air full of those spores able to permeate our masks.

COVID-19 takes second place to this emergency curfew response that brings the National Guard into our streets.

*   *   *

As the city burns so my heart bleeds for the minutes George Floyd lay handcuffed on the ground restrained by four officers with one of them pressing his knee to his neck.

As city streets fill with protests for George Floyd, who pleaded to his last breath to be allowed to breathe, I draw on this bitter air for him and all who died at the hands of genocidal anti-Black violence.

We walk our dog in a neighborhood that hurts all over. We talk uncompromisingly: this is the time to prosecute all police who have records of the use of excessive force; and fire prosecutors and coroners who have upheld brutal murders by police by not prosecuting them for first-degree murder and for declaring dead Black men who died at the hands of police as dead from a preexisting condition.

As the world reels from COVID-19 and this latest police murder, I want to see the police force reformed to protect and serve the community, not terrorize and brutalize black and brown and poor members of that community.

Today's society-cancer is the police—a force sanctioned by the state to control its citizens by violent means. My cancer is the police—a rampant disease in me that does violence to me. George Floyd's murder must result in a reinvention of the police force— defund them and put those funds into social and economic programs, such as mental and physical health care, education at all age levels, anti-incarceration initiatives, and youth employment training.

George Floyd's murderers must be brought to trial—no peace,

no justice, even if it means unpredictable violence. Thank goodness for the energy and outrage of the young, who take to the streets no matter the personal cost. They march and chant, "No justice, no peace, prosecute the police." They hold silent vigils for eight minutes and forty-six seconds, the length of time the officers pinned George Floyd to the ground with a knee pressed to his neck.

This has turned into a manifesto for radical change of our police force. The body count goes back to slavery in America. That a uniform protects a murderer is cause for shouting in the street. That George Floyd and so many others died because the police protect officers who practice racism to the point where they commit murder methodically or spontaneously, knowing they can get away with it, deserves community and wider public outrage.

As my city burns, my heart breaks for George Floyd. I mean my nerves feel this unbearable strain of another death of a Black person at the hands of the police. It feels too much on top of society's COVID-19 restrictions and my battle with cancer. It takes me back to '92 and Rodney King's beating and the acquittal of the police involved, longer still to '55 to Emmett Till's murder by Whites for his alleged whistle at a White woman, who retracted her story much later, saying that the whistling incident never happened.

*   *   *

Hurt strafes the air of Mid-City. Someone or something bruised this morning light. The light runs a gantlet, beaten with sticks. Or else squeezes like wet clothes through a clothespress. Trees, grass, wire fences, brick walls, buildings cower from that particular shine, which dents your eyes, makes them bloodshot. You walk the streets as though every paving stone were broken bottles with you barefoot. You wait to cross at the lights no longer sure cars will obey the red light and white-lit pedestrian walk sign. You do not trust the quiet kept by houses. Their curtained windows harbor surveillance and threat.

The city mourns for George Floyd and a long list of other names. We look somber, we move slowly. We breathe for George Floyd and many others who met a similar fate. We say some of their names, Breonna Taylor, Eric Garner, Ahmaud Arbery, Tamir Rice, Sandra Bland, Antwon Rose, Trayvon Martin. We recite as we inhale deeply, "This is for you, George Floyd." He stands for all those murders. We lend him our strength so that he frees himself of his three police assailants with their knees on his legs, his torso, and his neck, the fourth standing guard to cover them. They fall away from him, blinded by the collective power of his light, he shines above the road, unhurt, full of his restored Black being, and departs that scene.

REGGAE

DJ Cancer

Cancer comes to spoil your party
Cancer here to keep you company
Cancer play the part of DJ
Cancer plan to run things his way
Cancer going to put disease in you
Cancer going to turn your party blue
Cancer is the elephant in your headroom
Cancer is the merchant of your early doom

Everybody wants to avoid cancer
Everybody carries pieces of cancer
Watch how cancer walks human
Watch how cancer talks human
Don't stick your head in cancer's lion mouth
In the middle of your faith, entertain doubt

Back in Airy Hall, way back when, a posse of about six of us decided on a whim to steal out of the house before dawn and head for the village bakery for some free baked goods—the broken buns and cookies that no one wanted to buy that the bakers sometimes gave away to children on a first-come, first-serve basis.

The night was pitch. A thick darkness that the moon, half-full or half-empty, slipped from behind cloud to bathe the place in an eerie luminescence. We tiptoed through it in pairs, sticking close to each other. We whispered as if the dark were made up of thousands of ears, a few of them belonging to grown-up relatives who would catch us out so early and punish us for it.

We saw the bakery lights like beacons. As we drew near, the smell of the bakery, all sugar and flour sizzling the air, hooked us, watered our mouths, and reeled us over the tall fence and chained gate and into the yard. We trotted to the open top half of the half doors. We stuck our heads inside, those of us at the front, to catch the attention of an adult. Those of us at the back held on to someone nearby and craned our necks to see past the heads and shoulders of those at the front.

At last an adult appeared with bits of biscuits and pieces of the sweet buns caramelized on top with brown sugar. He wore his white baker's hat lopsided as if at a nightclub. He dished out something to every empty hand. He warned us to hurry out of the place because the watchdogs were still out somewhere on the grounds.

We did not have to be told twice. The dogs had a reputation for biting and they were kept in cages during the day away from contact with people. They rarely barked, which we considered the worst of all character traits, because it meant that the dogs preferred not to warn but rather to bite. Someone heard a growl rapidly drawing near and took off in a sprint for the front gate. We must have been about twenty yards from it. The panic spread among us in an instant and without looking back for confirmation and without hearing anything the smallest two (I was one of the two) of the group followed the bigger ones, already a couple of strides ahead and opening more ground with each step, leaving me and my cousin neck and neck doing our best to keep up.

I could hear the growl closing in and getting louder. It sounded like more than one growl, perhaps two, even three. My bigger cousins jumped up at the fence and cartwheeled over it and disappeared. I reached the fence at just about the same instant as the cousin my size. We launched ourselves at it, gripped, and as we clambered up I heard something tear and felt something that made me scream, and my scream spooked my little cousin beside me and made him scream too. I forgot about my bakery treats. I may have stuffed my bread and biscuit samples into my mouth or dropped them to free my hands for the climb. My short khaki pants were so old the pockets were ripped out. They were a hand-me-down. They did not even have buttons at the crotch opening (zips were a luxury). I pulled and climbed away from the yard and the dog whose teeth gripped my short-pants, ripped them, and sank into my bottom. I screamed so loud as I tumbled over the fence and fell to the ground on the other side that my cousins rushed to me. They helped me to my feet and brushed my clothes and straightened them. The lights from the bakery flooded the yard as the workers came out to see what the commotion was about. The dogs barked and jumped at the other side of the gate, rattling it, until they were called away with repeated whistles and names I couldn't decipher. My cousins all gave me a piece of their bread or bun or biscuit and I quieted. They looked at my rear in the dark and said it was only a scrape. We tiptoed over the rice-paper-thin moonlight and back into the still-sleeping house. An older cousin found a rag, wet it, and wiped away blood, and dabbed the offended area with cotton wool dipped in iodine and stuck on a plaster. The whole operation stung. I nibbled the extra treats that lasted long after everyone else's were gone.

*   *   *

Cancer plays hide-and-seek with me—hide in plain sight as COVID-19, hide behind the ramifications of the murder by police of George Floyd. The many always outweigh the few and so I bow in obedience to everything communal, and accept my lot, my fight with cancer, as a private matter. Cancer dares me to claim my disease as more important than the mass waves of COVID-19 and the uprisings over George Floyd.

I'm silenced by my situation. George Floyd died because of anti-Black racism. I am threatened with death by cancer. The assault on him, though unlike my slow burn with cancer, scalds my body. I hurt as a result of his murder. I wear a mask, and my cancer takes second place to my protection from COVID-19. If cancer wins as a result, then it deserves that victory, since there is nothing for me to do but honor the dead while I have the luck of my life.

Cancer cuts me loose in its maze. I wander around in search of an exit. Cancer keeps me busy as I bump into its closed spaces and must double back on myself and try a new avenue with the same dead-end result. Cancer laughs at my efforts to evade it. I keep trying, as I feel I must do if I do not wish to surrender. Flux on my part is everything.

I wake with his name on my tongue. I breathe on his behalf. I see him pinned to the road by three officers, the fourth standing guard, and I wish them gone and wish him to his feet. George Floyd splinters from his body into ours. We chant his name not simply out of a quest on his behalf, or in search of him, though both mean something—we say his name to count his presence in us.

George Floyd rounds street corners in long lines of marchers; his name echoes around the canyons of towers in financial and residential districts; he fills city squares worldwide; he blocks countless intersections, stops traffic on motorways, and bolsters our spirit with this multitude made of each of us alive in his name. We switch back and forth from grief to joy, grief *and* joy, from mourning his loss and that of so many, to affirming our

intent (the crowd drawn from all quarters of society) to stop further losses.

*   *   *

The tax of cancer attaches to my skin. I see fishhooks all over my
body donated by history and society. A history of transatlantic
slavery; a society built on racism. I do not bother to remove those
hooks, more trouble to try, best to leave them in place rather than
cause a flare-up at the sight of each one that I remove. I have cut
so many lines attached to those hooks. Worked against their tug
until each broke and set me free with its gift of a barb in my skin.

The bait that I swallowed to catch that hook came out of nowhere and headed directly for my body without my trying to
consume anything offered to me as temptation, or a trade-off, or
quid pro quo. The hooks sunk into me, aimed at my skin. I had
no option but to wriggle free of them, or flow with their pull as
they reeled me in. I opted to break free. Hence the hooks, enough
to fill a large basket, that decorate my body.

I say this knowing that I belong to a group all of whom wear
this evidence of someone or something trying to capture them
or exacting a toll on their body by virtue of the suit of Black skin.
There is a drag on the psyche of carrying so many hooks all aimed
at Black skin. People see the barbs so often and so many of them
there covering the person that they stop registering the presence
of hooks on a human being. They replace the hooks with an at-
titude or they put on dark glasses to obliterate the sight and they
see a Black body in history, as history, not human, more a string
of happenings that led to this relationship of White people with
fishing lines and Black people in the water.

*   *   *

Ghetto flyover of parrots—a banner made of color and sound for
this morning overcast with the threat of rain that burns off before

it amasses enough oomph to make it to land. I take the threat as a mood, somewhat bleak, for George Floyd, whose death lingers in the city that for all its mighty bluster cannot shake off the plight of the man. We won't let that happen, of course, for we are that city that refuses to forget and will not rest until we correct this gross wrong. As if a life once taken can be made good. It cannot. This is work for the living, who argue that George would not want another soul to go through what he did and so he would be the first to keep things stirring and keeping hold of a thing that burns to hold for long and staring at a place that threatens to blind us.

Writing this keeps me a stranger to myself. I do not have to look at what I do not wish to see that is in me. I gaze elsewhere and place the urgent far from me. This may be cowardice or a fair strategy, given the vagaries of my personality. Which is what? Not liking to be liked, not wanting the limelight and yet craving recognition. Not much in love with people, most of whom annoy me and most of whom appear to flip-flop on every conceivable front.

I feel rage and hurt rise in me out of dissatisfaction with my lot. Not happy to dodge cancer (assuming the op is a success) the way I did—last-minute rush to action and only after surgery and drugs steered me through its maze—I balk at the prospect that it may return after all that trouble and I will be left with my sour mood of too late and too little and always more to be gained and so much more to do and what little I have done I think could have been so much better.

No woulda, coulda, I tell myself. No point. That ship has sailed that proverbial sea. (Or some such inconsolable crap.) Hurt and rage make an odd cocktail. I resent it. I wish to dash it across the room. I need to drink it up and fast. Even this feels like a circle that I have to make for fear of crashing into something that I cannot handle, something dark and uncontrollable that will leave me stranded in despair. I think despair leads to madness, my last port of call, if there is a call to be made at that port.

I say all that and end up wanting to sit out in the makeshift gazebo in my Mid-City backyard and pick up the morning's industry of traffic and birds, with the dog and cat steering clear of each other in the yard. My ears zero in on each birdsong and I look for that bird. Small piece of life; small brown flick of momentum; eyelid flutter; pulse under skin. I gauge the light as if my eyes were scales capable of weighing the morning for its specific gravity. Specific gravity is a quality of the spirit, a charge emitted by light picked up by my eyes to add velocity to my day. Spin, as in the opposite of stasis. Spin, as in verve for this beat and breath, warmth and manifold hunger.

*   *   *

I am up against a deadline to submit a video recording of Kamau Brathwaite's "Poem for Walter Rodney." It is three a.m. I listened to classical and jazz for inspiration. The town sleeps, the house and all its people and pets. I do not want to be heard, so I set up shop in the movie room that is a space off from the kitchen. For white background I pull down the large screen and position a small armchair in front of it, and on a coffee table in front of the chair I prop my phone sideways.

The request arrived in my email about two weeks ago from an inspired collective curating forty nights of forty poems written by Kamau for his ninetieth birthday, and read by people with a connection to the Caribbean. They asked me to send mine in time for the June 13 anniversary of Walter Rodney's assassination by the then-government of Guyana, in 1980. I found Kamau's poem online. My copy of his *Middle Passages* is boxed up and locked away in my office at the university, where the building is being renovated after the flood. The online poem appeared in *Index on Censorship* in August 1981. It is in three parts.

I print it and arrange its four pages clipped to a folder. I keep a fifth introductory page to be sure I say the correct date—though I know it by heart. Rodney's death shocked everyone in London.

We could not believe that the government had placed a bomb in a walkie-talkie given to Rodney and detonated it and murdered the country's most promising political acolyte. We expressed horror at a regime that was willing to hurt its future politics as represented by a young Walter Rodney, for the sake of present power. I wrote a poem that I could do nothing with but had to write out of my grief and outrage.

Kamau's "Poem for Walter Rodney" is a sprawling exploration of a Black history that covers three continents. The spirit of the poem matches the life that it eulogizes. Composed in three parts, it recalls the majesty of Auden's "In Memory of W. B. Yeats" and the litany of Eliot's "Love Song of J. Alfred Prufrock." Kamau's poem is visceral, "to be blown into pieces" and elliptical, "for the sake of his *nam*," declamatory, "POOR CYAAN TEK NO MOORE," and imagist austere, "in my arms."

There are politics and economics in the poem, in keeping with Rodney's seminal study, *How Europe Underdeveloped Africa*, from his doctoral thesis at the School of Oriental and African Studies in London, and his political treatise *The Groundings with My Brothers* from his time in Jamaica before the government expelled him because of his radicalism. I say all this about the poem since it made me remember my view of Kamau at the time of Rodney's death, that he upheld the political voice of the oppressed at the cost of the personal (something I valued in a poem back in 1980 during the formation of my poetics in London). I was mired in the poem as first and foremost an act of autobiography that sought communion with other forces social, political, and philosophical. Always primarily focused on a single speaker who may or may not be the poet, the poem proceeded on the grounds that we believe the speaker to be in the process of thinking something through with the reader/listener as privileged bystander.

I loved Kamau's energy and invention and the way he brought Africa to the Caribbean and to Europe and North America. His historical awareness made me conscious of the poem as political intervention. Kamau made me think about the many ways that

ethics shape aesthetics. His performances electrified me. All of
which made me think of myself about to record his oral and lex-
icographer's rendering of his elegy as ideally unsuited to the undertaking. That is why I postponed making the recording until
three a.m. of the morning that it had to be delivered.

Of course I was wrong back then about Kamau. He was far
more complex than my understanding of him in terms of my art.
Throughout the eighties I embraced Kamau's music and story-
telling in his poetry, and shunned his overt orality, his voiceprint
(Stewart Brown's term) that called for much phrasal repetition
and lexicon inventions to highlight the sonic and visual multiple
registers of words.

His "Poem for Walter Rodney" was the culmination of all
these qualities (though the typographic experiments with vocal
and emotional representations are reined in). If ever there was
cause for righteous anger in art, this elegy for Rodney by Kamau
was it. You feel the artistic rage and hear the raised voice of outrage. The poem verges on disbelief at the murder and stops just
shy of despair. It predates by a couple of years his poem "Stone,"
for the startlingly original dramatic poet Michael Smith, who
was stoned to death at twenty-eight by a mob in Jamaica in August 1983. "Stone" amplifies all the representations of voice and
thought on the page that we see in "Poem for Walter Rodney."
This stone is nothing like the optimism of his earlier Caribbean
creation myth that can be sung, "the stone had skidded, arced and
bloomed into islands, Cuba, San Domingo, Haiti, Puerto Rico."

There is a side to me that wishes I possessed Michael Smith's
skills to render a poem in all its glorious multiplicity as a dramatic
device. To tell the story of a poem as a loudly declaimed thing
takes practice. To keep the listener locked into the emotion of a
poem, and the sense of its sound and its argument, takes talent.

I sat down and pressed Record and faltered time and again at
those broken-up words, broken to draw out their implied meanings as a simultaneous experience with what those words primarily denote. I felt lock-jawed. My neck muscles tensed. I looked and

stared hard at the lines to stay with their drive and sense as sound and argument and lament and legacy. It took me two hours of trying (and this is after many days of rehearsal) before I found success in one take. My reading lasted over ten minutes.

I received an email thanking me for sending the file and a second email saying that the file arrived okay in the file transfer system that I had to download. But then I received a third email that rankled me. The curators wrote this time asking me to shorten Kamau's poem to a usable extract and record and send the shortened version as soon as possible. I ignored the email. I fumed. I thought, A man was blown to pieces. The best of two poets from the region (Walcott is the other one) wrote an elegy about it, and this poet is being commemorated on his ninetieth birthday (had he lived) by my reading of his poem for that assassinated activist (my countryman) in time to mark the fortieth anniversary of the assassination: two big events in one. How dare they ask me to make it shorter!

Postscript. They posted my long reading of the unexpurgated version of the poem, made with my early-morning voice.

For those two hours I was free of cancer. Cancer vacated my mind and body for those one hundred and twenty minutes. Cancer left me alone and happy.

*   *   *

GEORGE FLOYD LAID TO REST

I keep such a tight grip
On my emotions that my knuckles
Whiten and I lose all feeling
In my hands, not even a tingling.

If I let go I would not know
The difference unless I stare
At how I feel with nothing
To hold me back or rein me in.

What happens next has always
Happened behind my back or else
Has never taken place in my life:

A salve of breath the likes of which
I have not felt, a surge of blood.

15

AS LONG AS I DRAW BREATH

That 2:45 a.m. sleep Mid-City, to the lullaby of a lone siren. To traffic lights regulating nothing but darkness bathed in business signs. As if these artificial colors called out to us in our sleep for us to wake and find them. Colored lights able to soak through eyelids and dictate dreams.

Cancer tucked in with my flesh and blood on its third or fourth dream with me keeping vigil. Now I know what it means to be burdened. Cancer stored in me and I know it and all I can do is walk on tiptoe so as not to wake it. For cancer is best left asleep. As cancer walks in its sleep that progress is slow. Almost movement with arms out in front measured by feeling. Small steps to avoid hitting the knees on the edge of furniture as my bones and nerves must appear—furnishings in cancer's home.

I shush my mind and heart for fear of waking cancer; index finger over pressed lips, eyebrows raised. I think in a whisper, which is thoughts lined up and made to pass through a turnstile in single file. I breathe evenly to keep the drum of my heart steady and low key. Even my eyes must behave in this purlieu of calm. My eyes take their time to alight on an object, assess it, and move on, none of their usual daytime zipping from one thing to the next with no mind for what they pick up and all those things piled up for later inspection as dreams.

If my noise—as rapid thought or sudden movement—stirs cancer and cancer opens its eyes, and sets out in all directions in me to explore which new site it might settle, that means I contribute to its spread in me. For now cancer behaves like the city and dozes almost at peace with itself and me. I almost fetch a blanket and cover cancer to keep it comfortably asleep, prolong its apparent lack of action in me.

*   *   *

As long as I draw breath I tell the story of my life and my death. Add my heart and my brain for that beat and thought. My automatic summons of air that I throw away when I exhale. That soul beats in my chest, neck, wrist, and groin. Those fleets upon fleets of my thinking dispersed. That my dreams gather, filter, and fling to the breeze. I share all three with cancer.

See that dandelion. I stoop, pick it, stand straight, and hold it to my lips and exhale. There goes my thinking, shorn from that dandelion stem in my grip. Each thought adrift on a raft of light, airship. Each thought strung with feelings that float behind it, attached as strings with electricity in them of a cluster of stings of a jellyfish.

I exhale onto a mirror, not to polish it, more to see the body of moisture of breath extracted from me. I pull deep on air, send air deep, as I see a pitcher that I must fill, hold for a second, then pour from me. And again, breathe, and again, until breathing slips the moorings of thought.

Beat of my heart and its pulse in various parts of my body. Fingertips pick up each pressed just below the skin. If I aimed the tip of a blade at that pulse and nicked my skin I would catch that beat as it escaped from my wrist or neck. A misshaped bubble of sound in a transparent skin of liquid that picks up colors in daylight, just as spilled gasoline shines rainbows.

Cancer insists on a portion of all expressions of life in me. It wields a knife that seeks its pound of my flesh. It casts a net and pulls what it captures from my lungs. There it is, once more adding lead weights to each of my thoughts to make them crash,

overladen. I polish my breath from the mirror for a clear view of
my cancer. That is why I nick the skin on top of my pulse. There
is cancer looking at me and wearing my face. And again, this time
my pulse drives it.

*　　*　　*

If memory serves me, the man who was famous for standing on
a cart while the donkey harnessed to it galloped along was my
cousin. Most other drivers would be seated and trying hard not
to bounce off the cart. My cousin rode that cart barefoot and I
thought of his toes as claws able to grip on to the wood cart and
keep him on his feet. He stood with a slight forward lean and his
knees slightly bent, and he clicked his tongue at the donkey, which
gave its best effort, perhaps to throw my cousin off that cart.

Maybe both were having fun. My cousin brushed that donkey
every day and always made sure it was well fed and watered. He
called the donkey "No Time to Lose." But the way he said the
name, fast and collapsed together, it sounded nothing like that,
more like "Nautilus."

My cousin crashed while fetching water from the village standpipe with his cart, packed with water barrels, roped together,
pulled by that donkey. The cart and its payload with the donkey
harnessed to it rolled into a trench and pinned my cousin underneath. The roadside trench was dry. Water from the barrels ran
along it. The donkey brayed and kicked and tried to stand.

My cousin could not speak. He vomited. His eyes turned in his
head. There were so many hands, digging away the dirt, cutting
the rope around those barrels and the harness, to grab him by
the armpits and pull my cousin free. The donkey trotted away
and brayed, apparently unscathed. My cousin had several broken
ribs, and bruises covered him. He could barely whisper. He spent
a week in bed. You had to lean close with your ear to his mouth
to catch his instructions about how to brush Nautilus and make
sure the beast had food and water.

*   *   *

No more niceness at the cost of truth. No more smoothing of the creases in the tablecloth to help with a pristine banquet out of gratitude that I am among the guests at the table. No more pause and fill in that awkward pause with humor to get past the reality of a hard thing to bypass and maintain decorum. No more belittling of that thing to stop stilted talk about it. No more explaining. No more couching in terms that are easy to digest. No more wishy-washy, namby-pamby niceties to preserve friendly falsities. No more let us do what business we can under difficult conditions. No more such accommodations for the sake of business as usual. No more the past is over and done with and nothing can be done about it to alter its nasty facts. No more in the present for its own sake. No more looking to a future free of a slave past. No more looking away from a thing that scalds the retina and begs me to look at it. No more, skin is not all there is about me, or skin is not the thing that you should be looking at as a condition for cohabitation. No more walking on history's broken bottles barefoot to demonstrate that it can be done by me so trust me. No more walking on history's hot coals on hands and knees. No more keeping calm to show control in the face of barbarism. No more that holding of hands all the time to get through a difficult time. No more setting that table for a feast. No more feasts. No more running on the spot to keep up with a present that moves without me as a part of it. No more running for the sake of keeping up with a thing that tries to leave me behind and lose me. No more. Enough is enough.

For you keep lynching us despite all that we do to make you feel at ease. You keep us in a second-class space. You keep using us and throwing us away as if we were not people and not alive and cannot feel and have no memories. Stop. The well is dry. I fetched buckets of peace from it until it ran out of peace to fill my bucket. You took each bucket and drank from it and looked satisfied and had that look of expectation of more from me. Stupidly, I returned to the well, thinking as long as you drank and looked contented I could find peace also and make progress with you. No more.

Yes to the safe zone of the streets of the city. Yes to the lion of authority lying down with the lamb of the citizenry. Yes to free health care and free college education for all. Yes to the call for closing all prisons. Yes to the demilitarization of all our military. Yes to the porous borders between Mexico and the US, as it is between Canada and the US. Yes to the lamb dictating to the lion what the lion can and cannot do. Yes to the bird path of all our travels as we fly over checkpoints and border walls and ports and stations. Yes to nonviolence in all disputes. Yes to the barrel of a gun as a vase for the stem of a flower. Yes to the power of the flower over the barrel of a gun. Yes to laughter. Yes to hugging a tree, a stranger (masks and social distancing notwithstanding), an enemy, such as my cancer.

I dig a hole for a plant in a pot in desperate need for room to spread its tight bundle of roots hemmed in by that pot. And that plant blossoms almost the next day. That tells me that all we need is a little stimulus to shine in ways previously unseen. I do not ask for someone to dig a hole for me. Just give me the ground and a shovel and watch me help myself to a better destiny.

My desert cactus has five spindly branches spread untidily in the pot. Each time I water that cactus I wonder why. I see no progress in how it looks; I water it all the same along with the other potted plants around it. It maintains a nonchalant brownish, greenish, and trace of yellow that appears anemic, as if on the verge of turning brown all over and withering up, if not for my regular water.

Once afternoon, I pass it and what catches my eye makes me stop in my tracks and look again at the source of that stimulus. There on the end of one of the five tentacles of the cactus is an enormous flower, yellow with dozens of bristling stamens, and layers inside like a catacomb in miniature. I take photos with my phone, I call everyone from the house to come and see the miracle of a flower where I thought no such thing could occur.

Thank goodness I kept watering that cactus after I dismissed it as ugly and unproductive or at least unresponsive to my care of it. The cactus flower proves me wrong. Nothing else in the garden comes near that flower's majesty. By evening it shrivels and lies limp on the end of the thin branch of cactus. Next morning I give it an extra drink and apologize to it, and encourage my dear, ugly, surprising cactus to keep on doing whatever it does and to ignore me. For all I know, water wants nothing to do with me. How I fetch water to a plant gets it from A to B, from where it stands to where it needs to be.

*   *   *

Friday served Crusoe in exemplary fashion, in a relationship that might be viewed as mutual role-play. Friday plays the servant to Crusoe's superior boss. Crusoe enjoys being in charge, and Friday accepts the childlike condescension with which he receives his orders from Crusoe. Friday continually defers to Crusoe's expertise. The cooperative relationship depends on their understanding of their roles of subservient and dominant for its success.

You would think this could last a long time given how clear the parts are defined, even down to black skin for the servant, Friday, and white skin for the boss, Crusoe, their parts color-coded for them, so it seems. What could possibly go wrong? This would not be an allegory if everything worked seamlessly.

Friday woke with the clearest understanding that his day would be much more enjoyable if he ditched Crusoe, if he did not wait for Crusoe to rise and begin to do things as directed by Crusoe. Friday did not harbor any ill feeling toward his boss. He simply saw his day going much better without being bossed around from sunrise to sunset. So Friday took off. He abandoned Crusoe on an island where he knew his way around and Crusoe was a stranger.

He felt that he had served Crusoe for long enough for Crusoe to serve himself.

The island was no longer a mystery or a danger. Both of them could thrive alone on it and be quite content. For Friday, his contentment centered on his freedom from servitude. What of Crusoe? To wake and find his servant gone; to think of himself as somehow needing to be self-sufficient on an island far from home. Crusoe cannot experience solitude anything like Friday's welcome of it. Crusoe calls for Friday. He searches. He curses. He plans revenge and punishments when Friday appears at last. He slumps in a hammock, woven for him by Friday, once he accepts that Friday has left him for good, and he cries.

I ask my cancer which one of us is Friday. I know who I want to be. (Clue—it ain't the White boss.) If, eventually, I could be free like Friday, I would gladly serve my cancer. The thing is, I play both roles, both Friday and Crusoe. My cancer takes the opposite of whatever I play. When I decide to run and take off without warning, I know that I will find myself abandoned at any moment. Cancer slips any part assigned to it. I end up punishing myself in everything that I do against cancer.

The Crusoe in me remains calm in the belief that Friday will see the error of his ways and come to his senses, and return as if he had gone for a stroll and forgot the time. The Friday in me walks around the perimeter of the island and ends up where he began, back at the camp with Crusoe. Both are wiser as a result of this day. Neither speaks to the other about it. Crusoe couches his orders in the form of suggestions. Friday obeys as if obedience were one of many options available to him.

*   *   *

Words fail me. I wish I could draw. My mouth seals its vault. My tongue swollen to the roof of my mouth. My head crowded with everything—music, images, things, smells, even touch and taste, but not one word takes shape in there for expression. I walk around the house numb and dumb, blind to the sparks that fly off the world all around me, that draw me into its ceaseless talk and flux. There is no word for this nothing that is a something all to itself outside description.

I may be exhausted from the protests over George Floyd and a host of other Black people killed at the hands of the police. The time for silent grief is upon me. To help me mark each death as a calamity, far outside routine existence. So that I face one wall and turn from it only to face another.

The volcano inside surrounding these killings that I keep gauging and sampling in poetry and prose and drama and essays may evade all my attempts to control it and erupt. What happens next? Will words rush to my aid? Another story to tell that staves off personal disaster. Who knows? There are no words for the deliberate taking of a life that satisfy me. There is the continual evasion of meaning in the moves made by my art to capture this police behavior.

I took cancer to be my challenge of a lifetime. I saw cancer as internal and a thing to be expelled from my body for my well-being. To see cancer all around me as the very history that I share with others means I can never hope for a cure, merely temporary relief from a scourge that is inside and all around me. Makes my cancer plural. Cancers. Hence its hundred thousand names.

*   *   *

I try to imagine a life and death for cancer and end up with my life and inevitable death under the microscope. All my attempts to grant cancer its independence from me fail and bring me back to the fact of a disease that has become part of me and insepa-rable from my being. When cancer dies—assuming I win this fight—something of me perishes with it. I need to make funeral arrangements for my cancer as cancer's only beneficiary and bene-factor. The casket must be closed after all cancer has gone through: the defacing surgery and medications. The ground is hallowed insofar as it belongs to a history of diseases that have dominated humanity before capitulating to scientific advances.

Here's the obituary: "Here lies cancer. Known to all as a rogue and a scourge to humanity, cancer made its name as incurable and unforgiving, as implacable and not amenable to the persuasions of positive thinking, crystals, aroma- and hydrotherapy, mantras, bells, incense, autosuggestion, hypnotism, chiropractic, gyroscopic, and magnetic therapies, acupuncture, meditation, hyperventilation, sauna, ice, fire, massage, and yoga."

The obit continues: "Cancer sought the death of every person whom it touched. Cancer was known as uncompromising and enriching of all those who survived it, even if survival meant a massive impairment of abilities due to the therapies undertaken to expel cancer. Those who have tried peace talks with cancer have complained of one-sided negotiations that end in deadlock with cancer walking out just as progress appears to be within grasp. Cancer remains humanity's most formidable foe."

There are no flowers, no poems secreted near the gravestone, no children's drawings. The site where cancer is laid to rest remains unmarked and plain as a waste piece of land that has to be cleared periodically of rubbish thrown there by those who do not care about public spaces. Cancer is encased in concrete to keep cancer from spreading in the soil and contaminating roots and water tables and finding its way back to the living through our fruits and vegetables and water supply.

Cancer flies the way of crows in a straight line from one point to the next. Cancer arrives late for its own funeral and sits at the back of the room in the funeral parlor, which is almost empty. Cancer answers to the name of the dead and the living relative and sole survivor of the deceased. Cancer digs its own grave of concrete casing and fills in that grave. Cancer marches from the site of the burial intent on living with double the energy devoted to the rest of its days.

Knowing all this, I nod in recognition of an adversary I can never underestimate. I count my days with cancer in tow as borrowed time to be lived as I see fit, regardless of the company I keep with cancer in my life. Among the long list of questionable therapies, I retain all the ones that make me feel good, regardless of whether their effectiveness against cancer remains proved only as hearsay, or whether science maintains that their efficacy with cancer remains unproved.

Call me stubborn, call me what you will, you can never say I turn away or avert my eyes, or look askance at cancer's full-frontal assault. I face that beast, lock horns with it, grapple and tumble, and want it to know I am engaged, a little fearful admittedly, but no way near capitulating to its bully tactics of me.

*   *   *

ON DUTY

DJ Cancer

I sleep on a bed made of bones with flesh for linen and blood for
    color.
I string nerves across that bedframe as if stringing an instrument.
When I sleep, which I rarely do, that instrument plays to my
    dreams.
The tune is a work song meant to conduct each moment on a
    chain gang,
Or down the shaft of a mine, or in the belly of a fishing trawler.

I work in bed as the best place to do my kind of work.
First I dig to gain a foothold. Then I grow roots, long tentacles
Able to grip any surface and climb and branch out. Last of all
I send miniatures of myself on exploratory missions to establish
New and independent colonies in the bone and flesh and blood
    world.

Those miniature selves if they succeed send back messages
That strengthen my hold on you and make it harder to uproot me.

*   *   *

BLOOMSDAY

My cancer. Janus-faced, molecular, and spellbound. Thief of my sleep, robber of my repose, pirate of my dreams, cancer. Bringer of night sweats, bearer of bad thoughts, bamboozler of my body functions, cancer.

Take my hand, cancer. Walk with me today. Imagine Mid-City is a theme park of economic deprivation and we plan to explore its every nook and cranny. You hear that rooster? He escaped from the farm for a better life in the city and ended up stranded here with nothing more to do than herald another morning of gross hungers. These earplugs block him since he can be heard all over the city at this hour. Several roosters spread across the city grid.

We pass tents set up beside walls, surrounded by shopping carts filled with knickknacks, plastic bottles, clothing, and old shoes. People asleep on cardboard arranged in the alcoves of shop doors. We say hello to a couple sitting on the roots of a tree, roots bulbous above ground pushing aside the paving stones. The couple chats as they drink from beer cans. They pause to return our hearty greeting with matching gusto. Street bins overspill rubbish scattered on the ground. Walls showcase graffiti by the same gangs or different gangs with the same territorial claims. And occasionally, a pristine garden with tended red geraniums, and yellow and white roses. The odd artificially grassed swale, oddly neat and tidy. Dogs bark and follow behind tall fences as we pass those guarded houses.

We step in rhythm and synchrony to the perimeter of the city where it meets the sea. As my constant companion you know how much I love to hear waves and every few steps look into the distance at the flat line of the horizon at the end of the massive sheet of galvanized zinc of the sea. You know me, how I cherish sand between my toes, and sandpapering my heels. Gulls threading air, gulls I can almost reach up and pluck. Baby sandpipers in clusters chasing after whatever the retreating waves turn over.

Race you up the beach. You may be faster than me. I can keep this pace longer. We stop and bend over to catch our breaths, or for you to catch my breath as I breathe for the two of us, doubled over, knees bent, hands resting on thighs, and peering into each other's faces with contorted smiles. This is where we might bump fists or high-five were it not for the nature of our communion, as opposites thrown together, irreconcilable forces heading in opposing directions with the one, indivisible life.

The key appears to be to do all this feverish living early in life, when it means twice as much and takes half the time, rather than late middle age's half-as-much meanings and twice-the-time undertakings. How deliberate and slow I appear to a younger self (at least ten years younger) that I retain, despite the vandalism on my body by time, a youthful alter ego through whom I view everything that I do with a tinge of wonder that borders on flabbergasted, mixed with a smidgen of disdain.

I decide to lose you on the coast and head home to Mid-City alone. You start to dig in the sand for something precious that you sniff out with your large nose and I walk away from you and break into a sprint and do not look back, and try not to listen to you calling my name. I run until I cannot take another step. I fight for breath. I recover and keep walking and do not stop until the sea switches off, and folds away out of sight, and the buildings sidle up all around me and portion off the sky, and I am back in rooster territory, at my front door with the key ready to plunge into the lock, and the door swings open leaving me with my arm outstretched, key in hand, and there on the other side of the threshold standing with head leaning to one side, and with an inquisitive expression and almost the play of a wry smile greeting me, is you.

All this because James Joyce and I share a birthday.

*   *   *

I hope I recall this next episode in a way that helps me with my fight with cancer. The hero of that past brought to bear on my present malady. My memory of struggle and how to overcome it steered toward my present dilemma as prescription, remedy, and salvation.

The shell pond . . . (Drumroll.) Not much bigger than an eight-person Jacuzzi, not much deeper than a roadside trench, the shell pond got its name for the bed of shells clear and wavering under fresh water. I think the adults dug it to store water from the rainy season for use in the dry season. We swam in it. The only stipulation was that we stay away from the bottom of the pond. We swam without ever touching the bed of shells. We dived for a closer look at them and after a quick inspection came up for air without kicking the bottom of the pond.

A wood-paling fence separated the house from the shell pond. The fence was six feet tall and as many feet from the house. The shell pond was another six feet or so from the paling fence. The fence ran from the road down the side of the house and away toward the back of the house, where pens for chickens and pigs filled the enclosure. We children sometimes found a loose paling in the fence to swing to one side and duck through headfirst to get to the pond for a swim.

The late afternoons were best for swimming, once the overhead sun dipped, its work of heating the water to a lovely cool on the skin completed. Even so we faked a shiver and dipped our toes before we dived and rose fast to avoid touching the bottom. This particular afternoon resembled all the others in the way the pond absorbed our bodies and polished our skin. A few of us wandered away and a few of us remained. The strong swimmers left the young ones to jump in feetfirst or dive and dog-paddle back to the corner of the pond or simply hold on to the tall grass at the edge and kick the feet for the splash and industry of swimming.

A cousin, about my size and six or seven like me, stood and looked at the water for a long time before she ran and jumped in far from the edge. Where was I? Holding the grass at the edge and paddling my feet as I mimicked a grown-up's agility in the pond. I assumed the usual downward plunge by my cousin succeeded by her surfacing, and then her dog paddle with hands underwater digging at chest level, chin just above the waterline, legs kicking in a sprint. I did not look back to check on her.

Apparently, my little cousin surfaced as expected and rather than paddle to the nearest edge, she sank out of sight again. Every child at the house had to drown a little bit first before they learned to swim in the shell pond. All of us had to dive down for ourselves and not touch the bottom and surface with a description of at least one of the shells that caked the pond.

I heard about this next part rather than witnessed it. A grown-up on the upstairs front porch of the house, catching some cool breeze in the rocking chair and watching us for entertainment, or for something to do, since our shrieks made dozing impossible, saw the young swimmer rise and disappear again. That grown-up climbed onto the porch wall and jumped from it and in that leap from twenty feet or so above ground he scaled the fence and covered all that ground from the house to the water and landed in the pond. He landed feetfirst and held his arms out to the side to stay afloat. He dived and fished my young cousin off the bed of shells.

I turned in time to catch him push my cousin out of the pond and climb out and begin to press her stomach and breathe into her mouth. In what seemed like an age, but could only have been a half minute or so, as he alternated between pumping her chest and breathing into her mouth. At last, she sputtered, issued a volley of coughs, and rolled onto her left side, coughed some more, tried to sit up and fell back, and the uncle who saved her and performed CPR caught her and gathered her up in his arms, and carried her into the house as she cried inconsolably.

For days afterward we looked down from the balcony at the ground below, and at the paling fence, and the land between the fence and the pond. We walked it and measured it by placing one foot directly in front of the next. We guessed how high a body had to propel itself to make it from the balcony to a safe distance into the pond. We threw stones to reconstruct the likely trajectory of the grown-up. We came up with all kinds of numbers and no one, not even the adult who made the jump, ever repeated it again.

People heard the story and came to see the place and upon seeing it for themselves asked several times if we were certain this was the place, and when we said that it most certainly was the spot, they asked to see the child and questioned her about it, and shook their heads continuously, and said aloud, in wonder, and to no one in particular, that no human could perform such a feat. And they left shaking their heads and they spread the story all over the village and beyond.

In my fight with cancer I want that grown-up by my side. I want his diamond certainty and shining conviction in a state of emergency. His sacrifice of himself, I mean with zero regard for his safety, in service of a good deed. I am willing to dive in and tackle my cancer head-on if I know that adult is there to lend a hand in case I find myself in deep water, and unable to reach safe ground.

*   *   *

Four a.m. catches me with my eyes open and in the middle of my itinerary for the day. I launch myself before the rooster and its Cape Canaveral of sound. I suit up to make ready for it: to ride that cock-a-doodle-doo free of the reins of earth and into outer space. There is something to be said for absolutes—absolute quiet, absolute stillness, absolute absence of relativity, absolute isolation, absolute dark, absolute time, absolute primacy of thought.

Just me, and my cancer for company, and the memory of my propulsion away from it all on the trajectory of sound provided by a cockerel. There is not much that I would change about the things I left behind. I look forward to an ideal in which I belong to no one and history has nothing over me.

Out in space, my skin does not have a negative, high premium attached to it. My skin denotes nothing unusual beyond its capacity to sweat and smell comfortable or not. I keep it undecorated by tattoos, though I have had Maori dreams of going wild on the canvas of my body for the sake of my biography. That day I arrived in Auckland stays with me. A line of warriors greeted a group of us artists. I was told to stand still and no matter what happened, not to move off that spot, and smile, no matter what. One of the warriors approached me. His body was covered in tattoos—a green and blue and black ink swirl and calligraphic canvas—he wore a short skirt and underpants that resembled woven tree bark. His feet were bare. He brandished a short sword or a cross between a sword and a spear. As he stepped toward me he poked out his tongue and shook it like a rattler. His mouth was very wide and his teeth shone brilliant white. He made the sounds of someone encouraging a horse to gallop, and someone who had just won at poker, and someone feeling a long injection in the rear.

As he met me and I almost fell as I rocked back on my heels, his rapid movements slowed to a crawl. He edged his head toward mine and I squinted, ready for a headbutt or worse. He drew so close I could smell pawpaw or jackfruit on his breath. He smiled. I smiled back. He leaned in more and more as I fought an impulse to recoil and run away. I widened my eyes in time to catch his nose as it touched my nose and he moved his head from side to side and rubbed his nose ever so gently against mine.

He stepped back with a broad smile, which matched my surprise. A woman stepped forward wearing a grasslike skirt and the mere hint of a bra, with bangles and beaded necklaces and earrings galore. She placed a garland over my head, which I ducked a little to receive. She smelled like apricots. She said, "Welcome to New Zealand." And she called it something else as well.

Space is the great equalizer. I float without gravity, the equal of every human who ever lived and every human as yet unborn. I am equal to my cancer. As I revolve, it revolves. We maintain the same undefined distance from each other, though cancer is inside me. My cancer is not equal to me. Not up to the task of ruling me. Not up here in space, where the coordinates of domination are scrambled for the coordinates of the sun.

Time loses dimension. There is no proper measure for it. I eat when I feel hungry and drink in answer to the call of my thirst. There is no sense that I have grown older or leaner or less able as a result of spending this currency called time. If anything, I may be getting younger with all the weight off my feet and distributed equally throughout my body. This lack of time robs cancer of its principle tool of incremental spread over measurable time.

The David Bowie song sounds a rising sense of alarm and panic coupled with isolation as horror—the farther from earth, the worse the feeling. Major Tom is lost to us and to himself thanks to alienating outer space, where none of us would want to be stranded. The chords are plaintive, there is longing in them, which is a condition of being earthbound. And the chords amplify their relationship to each other by introducing some delay between each as if space had opened up among them and each finally can stretch its limbs. Absent from the song is the exhilaration of discovery of something new. The listener is left with a sense of life on earth in need of some spiritual injection to cure it of its malaise.

Cancer must be confused up here. Cancer must wonder what it means to grip tighter onto a body part and spread around that body when everything weighs nothing and to grip feels the same as to release one's grip. To contract and disappear conceptually registers as no different from spreading and growing. I figure if cancer reverses its activity in me, then it should put itself out of commission. But only up here, where I shall remain until there is peace on earth and my body is free of every last droplet, particle, speck of cancer.

Aotearoa. Listen. That touch from the warrior who greeted me relocated all my senses to the tip of my nose. The woman who presented the garland to me said, "Welcome to Aotearoa."

16

JUNETEENTH

To help me to get past the shock of so many killings, I turn to the 1955 murder of fourteen-year-old Emmett Till. I place myself in his mother's shoes so that I may deepen my understanding for the history of Black suffering in our time.

"This is a photograph of my son, Emmett Till. My son. Emmett Till. I have to keep saying it to believe it. Don't avert your eyes. Keep looking at him. I want you to see him the way I must from this day to my last. Is that the face of a fourteen-year-old boy? Is that my son's face? I do not recognize him. Or I should not, but I do. That's him. I was the one who sent him to the place where this was done to him. I sent him there for him to have the time of his life with my relatives. I thought that if I gave him a break from the city, he would come back to me stronger and brighter and refreshed by his time in the country. But look what happened to him. Look what they did to my child.

"When he left me in Chicago for his summer holiday in the South he was beautiful to look at, warm to touch, strong. His face had a shine to it and his mouth and eyes smiled at you. I want you to keep looking at this photograph of the child I collected off that train, because your eyes added to mine will give me strength, and help me to look a little longer, as I must do to serve my son's memory. I still see traces of Emmett in there, there among the cuts and swelling. I can't help seeing his clean features—the face I told him to wash and dry, and the face I examined and touched, many mornings, before I sent him off to school. I see both pictures of him at the same time: this photo of him, broken like this, and the many others of my healthy child that I have in my mind. I want you to look with me and see both pictures of him.

"The day he left I waited with him on the platform for the long train. We stood close together and made small talk. Mostly my dos and don'ts, which he was quick to reply to, with a slight and growing trace of frustration in his tone, a tone I had to put a stop to, regardless of the fact that he was about to leave me for a long spell.

You must remember to be polite to my relatives.

Yes, ma'am.

Remember, whatever you do—good, bad, or indifferent—will reflect back on you, and on me, in just the same way you did it.

Yes, ma'am.

Don't lose your one good belt. You need it to hold up your church suit.

Yes ma'am.

You know "Please, sir" and "Thank you, ma'am" go a long way in Mississippi, much farther than in rude Chicago.

You worry too much, Mama.

And try to whistle less, and keep your hands out of your pockets.

Yes, ma'am.

Don't you "yes ma'am" me in that tone, Emmett. I'm not one of your friends.

Yes, Mother.

I just want you to be safe and enjoy yourself.

I'll be fine. Don't worry.

"I straightened his jacket one last time, though I did not know it at the time. I hugged him and kissed him, and by the way he pulled away from me, I guess he must have thought his mother was holding him a little too tight, and a little too long for comfort. I can hear him! After all, he wasn't a baby any longer. He was big. He was fourteen. I want to say to him, Emmett, you may be big but I am your mother and you are my baby and shall remain so always.

"Of course, none of that exchange was possible in that little embrace and quick kiss. It seemed to last a long time now that I look back at it, and as I stare at this photograph. Who would do this to a fourteen-year-old? You tell me. Look at this picture of my son with me, and help me to understand something about the men who would do this to my son.

"I watched Emmett board the train with his suitcase full of the things that I pressed and packed for him for what was to be a summer of fun with my relatives.

"He left me in the city for the countryside of the South, where time stands still for the body to throw off its cares, and renew, for another bout with the demands of the city. A child can play there. See more than concrete encasing trees. That was the idea.

"They said he whistled at a White woman who walked past him as he played cards with friends outside a shop. When does whistling become such a crime that it can cost you your life? Is it only in America in August 1955?

"Emmett liked to whistle. He whistled around the house as he did his chores. I made him help me around the house so that he would grow up to be independent, and make some woman proud to be with him, just as he made me proud. Who cares if he whistled as he worked? I didn't. But in the South adults think it's a precocious child who rinses his teeth with the air and hides his idle hands in his pockets while in the company of big people. I knew that, from my time growing up there, before I left for a better life in Chicago.

"Did I remind him not to whistle so much? I said so many things to him at the station that I may have missed the one important thing that could have saved his life. I should have saved him. I should have kept him safe here with me.

Don't whistle around, or at, White people. In fact, don't whistle, end of story.

Yes, ma'am.

Don't you, "yes ma'am" me, unless you hear what I say to you.

Yes, ma'am.

"His suitcase looked heavy but he said it wasn't. I made him pack too much. He had to have his best suit for church on Sundays, his good belt to hold up his long pants, and several summer cotton short-sleeve shirts and short-pants and a toothbrush and comb and polish for his church shoes. I sewed buttons onto two shirts and strengthened others that seemed to be coming loose. I didn't want anyone saying that my son was not well turned out. I put things into the suitcase and he took things out, and I put them back in again. To close the case he had to sit on it while I secured the clasps. He said he wouldn't be able to open it without help, or repack it on his own. As he carried it to the station, he worried that the lid might spring open and all his clothes burst out, and scatter, for all the public to see his private things. He complained about it but I said,

If that happens everyone will see what good care your mother takes of you.

"In the end we laughed about it.

"I worried about letting him go and imagined all sorts of trouble that a fourteen-year-old might get himself into. Maybe meet a boy who wanted to test his strength in some wrestling or boxing. Maybe meet a girl who took a shine to him and he to her. But I never imagined this. That's why I have to look long and hard at him, and why I need you to look with me, and help me to keep looking. They said that after he whistled at the white woman two cars full of armed men came to the house and demanded my boy. His cousins tried to plead with them to forgive the child. But the men were armed and they threatened the entire household with retribution. Emmett stepped forward, off the front porch, and said that he was the one who had whistled and that he was sorry for it, but no one else in the house had anything to do with it. He said he was the one they wanted. They must have seen from the way he was dressed and heard from the way he talked that he was not from Mississippi. He was from up north. They would teach an uppity Black northerner how to behave in the South. His age didn't matter. That he was a boy. They called all Black men boys.

They grabbed him roughly and drove away with him. And that was the last time he was seen alive.

"This photograph is what they did to him. I need you to help me look at it. His face is swollen to twice its usual size. He is missing one eye and many of his teeth. His whole head is swelled up and covered in bruises. His skin looks stretched, and underneath, just below his skin, it looks pooled with blood. I cannot help seeing those men hitting him again and again, grown men, hitting a young teenager, over and over again. They had to repeat this beating of my boy for a long time for him to look like this. I want to take his place. Have them beat me instead.

"Why didn't they just teach him a lesson? I wouldn't mind if they hit him for it. I would have given him a second beating for his rudeness. They could have used his belt and lashed him a few times around the legs and backside. They could have made him perform some community chore for breaking a code of the South. He whistled at a white woman. *For your transgression, boy, you cut this grass and pick up the trash along this street. You hear! And get out of town before nightfall!* And I would have made him do another set of chores for a long time. But not this . . . Those three men beat him and they wrapped him in barbed wire with a cotton gin fan to weigh him down and they threw him into the river. He was pulled from it a day later, and I ordered the undertaker to leave the casket open for my son's last ride home, and leave it open for the world to see what trouble a little whistle can get you into, in a place that needs to look at this photo with me, and with the whole world, and make sure my child is the last one to end up this way.

"Many mothers have told me that I should be grieving. They've asked me, How can I show him to the world in his condition? I tell them that before I saw him, saw what they did to him, that I cried when I heard, and I bawled, and pulled my hair, like any mother would who lost her son. But seeing him changed me. If they can do this to a child, they must never be able to do it in secret, without the world seeing what they do to children in the name of one race ruling over another. I thought, for you my son, who I keep locked in my heart, for you I'll do this last thing, and let the world know that I put my healthy child on a train, and this is what came back to me, and that is the condition between the races in this country at this time, and that must change for all our sakes.

"But some days, Jesus, I just want my son to come back on that train, with his suitcase stuffed with all the things I sent him away with, his one good belt, the clothes I sewed and ironed and folded neatly and packed tightly for him, come back to me, and with his skin darkened by his time in the open summer sun, and with him full and brimming with the stories of his time in the country. Not this. So help me to look a little longer. Help me to see how this might save other mothers from what I'm going through."

*　　*　　*

A SERMON BY DJ CANCER

Assume that I am everywhere and always. Among the killers of Emmett Till back then and George Floyd and so many others in recent times. Assume that I circulate in the air and take the form of ingredients in your food, drink, injections, tablets, and serums. Assume that I drive time as seen on clocks and as felt at wrist, neck, and groin. You store me under your fingernails and toenails, in the corners of your eyes, behind your ears, under your tongue, between your thighs.

If I show my face in one place, take that appearance in public by me as a sure sign that I am present in many other places in discreet ways. If you engage with my face, I mean turn your attention to the place where you see me, that would be your first big mistake. I want you to look at me and listen and reply to what you see in front of you.

My real work takes place behind your back, while you grapple with my appearance in front of you. You blast and lambast me. Pour scorn and invective on what you see of me. And though that may be as it should be, given the shock of my appearance in your body and the way your body registers me on all its senses, those responses are the exact ones that I need from you for me to thrive as an indispensable part of you.

How? Well, think about it. Who breathes and gives me life? Who puts food in your mouth and feeds me as well? Who sleeps and leaves a portion of your dreams for me to star in them? You are my main benefactor and beneficiary, the two rolled into one. I am mixed up with you to the point of being indistinguishable from you. The pieces of me that you cut from you are parts of yourself.

You see where this is going, don't you? Everything that you do to thwart me results in your giving me a helping hand in my conquest of you. I put out a part of me for you to focus on, and you focus on it while I work undetected and unobstructed in other parts of you.

You know those lizards that you trap and they relinquish a part of themselves, say the end of their long tail, and leave the trapper holding that part while those lizards wriggle away to safety? That's the two of us; that's me with you. You wriggle away from me and leave a part of yourself behind, thinking you have me fooled and that you are free, when in fact I am inside you and you have taken me with you.

*　　*　　*

Midsummer solstice and Father's Day. I delayed the former by one day to stack up the two to see what they might do for me with their unified strength. First things first: Will I live to see another of either or both of them? Honestly, I do not know. Everyone says that. My claim to a special relationship with temporality rests with the outcome of my cancer. Am I cured or has it recurred? I'll find out.

Until that day comes, let me live as that crab that Debbie and I saw this morning on our six a.m. beach walk with Dexter pulling me along. I handed the lead to Debbie and switched my phone's camera to video and stooped to catch that crab up close. It opened its pincers and raised them and walked toward me. Feisty. I thought of that crab in Walcott's *Omeros*, brandishing a pen, with the maestro imagining literacy as a trope for describing the unscripted tropics. (The Walcott of "We were blessed with Adam's gift of giving things their names.")

The tide was farther away than ever. We could walk around the outside of the promontory. I carried my flip-flops and loved the cool of the compacted wet sand, which widened a ring of pressure around my feet with every step. To look back is to see that print erased by the wet that rushes to cover where my foot lifts away. Soon the crab-like creep of a wave finalizes that erasure.

Enveloped by that sea sound, the walk is a float in a sea bath made of sound waves. I bank this goodness. It makes me feel rich. The reserves of this kind of rich help me in my fight with cancer. For cancer wants nothing to do with the sea or this crab. Both nouns verb their names and create this vibe of well-being. The crab, crabs along in life as life. The sea, seas. With the help of these two, and at my best, I, Fred, Freds.

To walk around the wrong side of the promontory on the springy bed of the sea left to air by the retreat of the tide on this longest day of the year.

I get hugs from Nicholas and Christopher, and open funny cards that I read aloud that make us laugh out loud, and a block-shaped balloon with an outlandish message about my greatness in the universe as a father, and two gift bags of summer clothes. If I could pray, I would say in a whisper to myself so that I can hear it for myself as I think it through, "Dear God, let this day last for as long as I draw air."

*   *   *

FATHER'S DAY ROOTS ROCK REGGAE

DJ Cancer

My digital self surfaces in a web sea
With my digital wife by the name of Debbie
We Bluetooth from phone to your inner ear
We come with a message plucked from thin air

If you see love on a flat screen
If you see it dressed to draw you in
Do not be tempted by that fast food
It lacks substance and brings you no good

My code is a function of your download
As you read me I want you to feel me
Allow yourself to be captured
By my lyrical digital mastery

I hope you have the bandwidth
To accommodate my message
Peace and love electricity
Free to you no tricks from me

My digital self surfaces in a web sea
With my digital wife by the name of Debbie
We Bluetooth from phone to your inner ear
We come with a message plucked from thin air

Peel your eye from the screen
Look all around you

What you see is not pixels
You see black killed by blue

You cannot believe your screen
Shows the same grueling scene
You grab your phone and run
To your first demonstration

Where you meet truncheon
Rubber bullets and teargas
Where you learn to chant slogans
March long and run fast

My digital self surfaces in a web sea
With my digital wife by the name of Debbie
We Bluetooth from phone to your inner ear
We come with a message plucked from thin air

*   *   *

Take my hand and trust me, for I come to lead you to the promised land of your extinction and to get there you must understand all things presented to you by me, for all things that roll off my tongue can be only sick and tiresome and fake guided as I am by the spirit of mighty pestilence and the spirit of all-powerful hate and understanding flowing in an everlasting fountain through me to you so listen and watch me now:

I'm going to say this once and once only
To those faint of heart and feeling lonely

I bring salvation from the treadmill of time
Stop putting up with life's dings and grime

Join forces with me I am the operator
Who can switch off that water torturer

Grant me permission I'll do all the work
I stick my spanner in the wheel of time's spokes

You don't have to do a thing just relax
Go with my swing and let me be your Ajax

Against time against boredom against longevity
For the short fuse of the little that's a lot of levity

For the promise of existence outside time's walls
For the quiet behind the cannon of time's waterfalls

*   *   *

Whereas love not hate is the compass needle that inclines my spirit away from despair, I reject you; whereas I cannot concur that time is a drag upon the soul and must be bided through terminal decline, I reject you; whereas the ails and travails of my body and mind in no way cancel the gifts of consciousness but work in affirmation of the good that follows the bad and the worse to come that gives way to relief and hope, so I reject you.

Your song leads not to salvation but damnation. You take us on a timespan devoid of all the good things in store for a long life. You speak as if your illness as an accelerant of my end represents opportunity and represents an escape clause from the misery, as you dub it, of a long life, when in fact to be sick with you is to be sick of you, sick of your mental pains and physical discomfitures; no ride with you can ever be smooth for the sufferer and those loved ones nearby.

You bring a bitter end. You sour the little of the life that's left in the body with your chemical infusions and poisons that cause confusion. You call that your way of ending things quickly when the time with you doing your work of sabotaging life slows time to a crawl of suffering. Your song deceives. You impel toward despair. You kill the spirit of the living, not just of those who must wait for their bodies to fail at your disposal but of the relatives who witness this suffering and must live with it. Sometimes I think our duel in words needs another response from me. What did the poet say about the response to an effrontery in his poem "The Schooner *Flight*"? "Some case is for fist, some case is for tholing pin, some is for knife—this one was for knife." I wish I could invite my cancer to meet me in the parking lot after work or after dark for us to duke it out, rather than this civil discourse of winner takes all by virtue of staying power, which has nothing to do with right or wrong, good, bad, or indifferent.

*　　*　　*

I am in it up to my neck. I wake early and my first thought as I transition from sleep concerns my cancer. Good morning, my foe. Let's get up and go at it. I do not need my first cup of coffee before I begin. It's three a.m. and by virtue of the fact that I am awake and thinking of you, that means things have started between us. What starts, exactly, apart from my worry about the spread of the disease in my body? I have no hard evidence that this is the case, just a hunch and a conclusion that my run of tough luck will continue with another piece of bad news that relates to the first piece about cancer.

I figured my fight back would have hardened into a regimen by now and not be as tentative and circumspect. I saw myself as equipped with chants, slogans, physical exercises (apart from Kegel), a robust diet, and a host of other intangibles to set up an army in my response to cancer and its possible return. And I'd be there at a battle site of my choosing ready to engage with it when it shows up. The mood in my camp tantamount to carnival as we arm-wrestle, wrestle, race, fence, target-practice, sing around camp-fires, dance, and ready ourselves to meet our foe and meet our fate.

By this time my fear would be tempered to suit my resistance to cancer and not the fear of a scrambled thought process and a body immobilized with it. The kind of fear that powers a sharp offense; fear kept under strict control and apportioned out to feed my strategic thinking made sharp by its controlled presence. Not the fear that makes you worried that you might pee yourself, or worse, shit in your pants. That's the fear sent ahead by cancer to do its nasty sabotage. That's fear beyond my control that floods my body like a heat flash I can do nothing about except breathe down the neck of my shirt, which I flap to cool myself, dry my forehead, and wait for it to pass.

There is no song and dance, or chant and prance, to rid me of this one. It could be that today I wake with vulnerability amped up in me, leaving me unable to stomach the smallest challenges. Taken one day at a time, my cancer is spread out like rice on a table for me to pick out the rotten grains. This is not something that I have done in the West. It was daily practice in Guyana and the rice was in a bowl and picked clean, washed, and then boiled. By casting my cancer as a bowl of rice whose grains are sorted for cooking, I make cancer one task in my day that ends up with me consuming cancer instead of being consumed by it.

This cannibal figure that I cast myself in allows me to eat a morsel of my enemy in order to learn what strategy my enemy intends to deploy against me. I am not really a cannibal who eats to his fill, more a symbol of conquest and ingestion as contemplation for insight. This sounds like an excuse for debauchery—tasting the flesh of the enemy—but I take it from certain indigenous practices to be instructive about overcoming subjugation by a powerful opponent. Cannibal is Caliban is me: three easy steps to form a triumvirate against cancer's unitary assault.

*   *   *

I feed all the animals in and out of the house: two cats in, two cats out, and a dog in the kitchen content with a biscuit treat. Now I qualify for my coffee after a banana and a palmful of walnuts. For my coffee I decide to add honey to the pot, as it were, which is a copy of the almond milk that I usually buy that I am out of, with its "hint of honey" as the label says. As soon as I sip the cup I think of feeding my cancer with a sugar treat.

The coffee turns sour.

You should see me peel that banana. It is curved to perfection and yellow and the soft flesh bears no resemblance to something I can eat without teeth. I bite into it and chew and both bite and chewing happen without my having to think about it, since there is not much resistance to the pulpy flesh and the taste is of a sugar distributed almost in concealed fashion, throughout the body of the banana. The moment I admit to the sugar as a register in the fruit I think of feeding my cancer with a favored candy.

The banana turns bitter like gall.

Walnuts are a sure bet. I chew with focused gusto to break up those compressed bodies broken into walnut halves for the most part, and some of the halves in accidental quarters. I bite and chew with some relish—the sort of enthusiasm brewed by overnight hunger and the prospect of the first engagement with sustenance. Those walnuts provide the right amount of resistance to my gums to make me bite into them and chew and feel how the pieces work into the crevices between my teeth. I catch the savory nuts and oils and begin to taste sugar, only a hint of it when I think of how this feeds my cancer (my cancer has a sweet tooth).

The walnuts turn iodine.

Why should I spit out my food each time I have the thought of aiding and abetting my illness? I finish what I am eating though only with a loss of my drive and enjoyment. How true is it that everything I enjoy adds to the body of my cancer? Not knowing for certain if it has returned to its nesting grounds in the area around where my prostate once resided means that I feed a ghost ailment. One that travels feet above ground with a flowing white sheet for corporeal sovereignty; a thing that haunts by virtue of its presumed absence and threat of imminent return. The terror, the terror. (My cancer is Mr. Kurtz from the dead-end conclusion to Conrad's *Heart of Darkness*.)

A part of me wants to refresh my morning and eat and drink those things all over again in defiance of my cancer orientation. Either that or I take up a water diet and host an online extravaganza, perhaps with a good playlist and thousands tuning in. A dance-off between my cancer and me. Would a raw diet hurt my cancer or just hurt me? Going raw means my poo will not smell. I will feel energized, fleet-footed, and giddy with the zealotry of the newly baptized.

*　　*　　*

Yeats said body built to pleasure soul as if the physical served merely to house and entertain the metaphysical. Now that cancer has me by the balls, I wonder if it helps me to embrace Yeats's viewpoint. Perhaps the castle is afflicted and worthy of abandonment for the true house of my being. To walk away from what I know for what I can only speculate about. Let the body rot with cancer and fool cancer into thinking that it has beaten me by winning my body when in fact my true self flies away to safety and bliss.

As I count the days, so I conjure the various ways at cancer's disposal of conquering me. The body of me. I view the two, body and spirit, as coterminous, in the fight against cancer. If that fight truly is lost, I figure that I can switch to a view of one aspect of my self as defeated and the other more enduring self as detachable from what is lost and able to fly to safety somewhere out of reach of cancer's sticky little fingers.

Why the pessimism? Each day should take me one step closer to conclusive news of my cancer's absence from my body. Instead, with each day that passes I feel a mounting sense of dread, that I will hear confirmation of what I fear, which is a return of my cancer. The negative thought has that much more traction in me than the positive one. My only evidence for this preferred mood of doom is my dread, some hunch that something is not quite right about my body.

I'm sorry to say that what comes next is not as ponderous in philosophical terms as what I have said about my body and its relation to my spirit. For this concerns my bladder and bowel functions. When they go low I am forced to go low with them. My bladder aches when I need to pee. The feeling is not as acute as what I felt before I registered my cancer in me. Precancer I felt a twisting of my nerves that was the equivalent of a high note on a guitar. Postcancer, or in its midst and postoperative, I feel the same nervous compulsion but stronger and with a lower note, if that same guitar is invoked as illustration. It is more like pain and less of the sense of a warning as before. If I do not pee right then or very soon after that first register, I face increased pain and immobilizing discomfort, as if the bladder were in the grip of a wave whose every surge means a heightening of its intensity.

Now I must go one step lower and deal with my bowels. (Let this serve as a trigger warning for those who need it.) I use the plural since I view my bowels as a cave with many twists and turns to it and a place where you might get lost spelunking. I know the route is singular even if contorted and I understand that matter includes pockets of air. My bowels were regular and attending to their demands once or twice a day at a fixed time or times of my choosing sufficed to placate them. I did not have to rush from a sudden urge. I felt that gentle and persistent notification of a task that needed my attention at some point in the near future. There was no emergency to the process, unless I ate something awful.

My postoperative bowels are another matter altogether. Indulge me for a moment as I turn Swiftian with the integument of my body. First, I feel this mounting pressure in my rectum as if a dial is being turned up on a sound over a handful of seconds. It is a weight as well, low in my body near my anus, and the only thing keeping that weight in my body is my clenched anus, that if I did not hold on to those muscles with all my might that weight would fall out of me. It feels disproportionately heavy to its actual volume. The sensation is magnified so that my image of it magnifies from perhaps some body the size of a baseball to a five-pound dumbbell.

I'm sorry to go on about this but there is more. And I persist only to paint the picture of why my outlook for my cancer prognosis is gloomy. If air is mixed up (as it so often is) with the feces, the sensation travels higher up my bowels and moves about rather like a nail scraped along a chalkboard but with a more devastating result and eliciting a more extreme response than a cringe. I bend my back to ease the pain and have to be careful not to topple over as I rush to the bathroom. I contract my anus with all my might and hope it holds for another thirty seconds. The pain pounds up and down my bowels as if in search of a weak point in the wall out of which to burst.

On the toilet the result is copious and immediate relief. I feel so good so fast that I wonder about the kerfuffle and think that it cannot be normal. (My norm is built around how I behaved before the operation.) It feels driven by cancer, by a foreign body at the controls of my usual mechanisms for evacuating waste. I think of a learner driver who oversteers, overbrakes, overaccelerates, indicates too late or too early and turns too sharply so he clips the sidewalk, or at too wide an angle and drifts into the opposing lane. That driver is my cancer with my bowel movements.

For years I used to enjoy a good, loud fart and a belch. I relished it. The buildup was innocuous and mild, the expulsion as a deliberate act by me loud and long, and disgusting if truth be told, since the kids and Debbie expressed mock and genuine outrage at my bad manners. It was not funny if on occasion when the kids were young I gripped the hand of one of my sons or daughter and thrust it to my backside and farted on it. They complained loudly and called their mother and called me a bad name or two.

I still belch though with a resigned capitulation to an inevitability rather than any relish of my pneumatic power. I dread farts. They are the cause of my consternation and pain. I think of cruciferous vegetables, such as broccoli and brussels sprouts, with some opprobrium. I love how Debbie prepares them with a touch of garlic and butter or olive oil and baked for a while. As I eat them I think of what they will unleash in my hapless body, and the thought tempers my enjoyment.

And why do I have to go three times a day? It feels overly efficient, as if I have lost my storage capacity and must move my products as soon as I make them regardless of what the market wants or needs. It is a new inner mechanism and it feels alien and I cannot alter it and so I put it down to my cancer working its ministry in me. This switches my mood from sunny to overcast. And it drives a wedge between my body and my spirit. I begin to see daylight between the two and I start to entertain the possibility of an independent spirit that, like a rocket segment, can jettison the body and soar away from the pull of gravity or the grave.

In my depressed mood I eat too much, I'm disinclined to exercise, I wake early and sleepwalk through the middle of the day, I crave sugar and chewing, I feel bloated, sluggish, the simplest tasks appear insurmountable. I'm easily irked by the most innocuous remarks from my daughter, such as, Dad I can't respect you if you say stuff to me that sounds trivial and if you don't take what I say seriously. And my sons' behavior of walking into spaces where I'm sitting and not saying a word of greeting to me though it is the first time that I have seen either of them that day. Or Debbie's habit of leaving things on the kitchen island's marble counter and my obsession with keeping it clear and clean, as if the clutter on the counter clutters my mind. Some of this has to do with COVID-19 isolation throwing us into close proximity for too long. Some of it rests squarely on my altered mood.

To calm myself I retreat into my office and read and breathe and try to write another installment in my calendar of accruing misery as I see this countdown diary. I did not expect to feel that the fight is lost so far away from the date of the PSA test. I wonder if I am weak. To so readily separate my body from my spirit when it is the two, as a unified entity, that presents me with my best chance of beating cancer.

*   *   *

I wake so early my eldest, living with me, Christopher, is still awake. I lie in bed and hear him bang about in the kitchen through no fault of his own since the cabinet doors do not have handles and the hinges are stiff. I see his glowworm lighting in his room seep out under his door on my way from the kitchen to the bathroom, what we call Nicholas's bathroom since it is just outside his bedroom, whereas Christopher has his own en suite (cramped, it must be said) bathroom.

The dog sighs in his bed and turns his face to watch me as I place water from the fridge into the kettle and peel a banana and help myself to a palmful of walnuts without slamming the door, a feat that takes extra care when closing the cupboard door. I warm almond milk in the microwave to drown my tea. I like it half and half: half water and half milk, which means I steep the tea bag in half a cup of hot water and add the hot milk a minute or so afterward.

I say all this to let my cancer know that I have not given it a single thought since it made me wake up abnormally early by playing on my dreaming mind. I decide to use the time to write, on the basis that my fresh brain cells are best for the task of invention even if my body needs more rest. This agitation feeds my cancer, of course. I am deprived of sleep and so the cancer ages me just a little bit, wears me down just a smidgen, as a result. It is clear to me that things could get worse: I could be awake and replete with worry about cancer, instead of awake and using the time to get work done.

It seems to me that I beat the cancer at its own game if I put the time to good use rather than ruminate over cancer's disruption of my sleep. There is no better use of my time than to write, second only to reading. As I write, sequential time alters. The usual clock face of seconds marching into minutes, and those minutes adding up to hours, fails to operate in that way for me. Time takes on elasticity and springiness. It seems to stretch so much that I lose track of those passing seconds. It seems to jump from its linear march so high and so far that one moment it is such and such a time, and the next an entire hour has elapsed.

How can that swift passing of time be good for my cancer? Time for cancer is treacle, stodgy toffee pudding, a thick onion soup, a frog march under the Florida midday sun, a wading into a strong sea, a stringy, chewy steak, old tuna in sushi, or tuna cooked into cardboard, a tight shoe on a long hike, an unquenchable thirst, a hole in the pit of the gut that food cannot fill, a nagging filling, executed poorly, that worries the tongue, a baby stingray flapping uselessly on the beach, crossing a muddy trench, crossing, on a windy day, a rope bridge strung ninety feet off the ground.

My writing time is marked by sips of tea from the giant teacup that I keep covered with a saucer to keep it warm, interrupted by bathroom breaks to pee. Between sip and pee, the two measure this exclusive time that is free of the tug of cancer. If I could stay in it I would live forever, with cancer at a standstill in me, frozen, waiting for linear time to resume, but it never does, because I leave my desk only to pee or refill my teacup.

Dream on, Fred.

*   *   *

Fireworks wake me. They've been sounding for weeks now in the lead-up to July 4. Behind the house on the isolated street that runs next to the school. And sometimes, all the surrounding streets seem to explode. How can people afford it? I chatted with Debbie and the kids about it and we came to the conclusion that someone sets an alarm especially for the task of exploding the ordinance at 1:30 a.m. to wake the entire neighborhood.

There is a door by the lazy Susan that keeps falling off its hinges. How is it hanging? I find it holding on by one hinge when I step over the cats, meowing for food, as I try to reach the kettle. As the kettle warms up I find a few tidbits for the little furry beggars and they purr appreciatively and squat and settle before the treats. Dexter stays put in his basket and watches. I pet his massive head and tell him he is a good doggie. I eat a banana and a palmful of walnuts. The usual Earl Grey teabag in a half cup of boiling water topped up with almond milk warmed in the microwave and I'm set for a spell in my office to moan about my cancer rising, or so I think as I head nearer to the date of that decisive blood test for PSA.

Debbie mentions some painting that we could do this summer and the deck that needs to be restained and a few odd repairs to our Mid-City dwelling, and I stop her in midflow to let her know that I cannot think about a single thing or undertake any projects, however menial, until I know what the upcoming test portends for my future. Good or bad, I can proceed with the knowledge either way. While I wait to find out—nothing doing. I float. I gestate, as if in a hellish version of that Floaters track from the dance-crazed and maudlin seventies, "Float On." (The extended twelve-inch version went on for a staggering twelve minutes!) It was all echoes and birth signs and ethereal, as a foundation for sentiment and its logic of hope, and magic of faith. Puke. Or, eew, as my daughter would say.

That feels certifiably diagnosable. That I have depression wrapped in rage. (This sounds like a fish and chips order, wrapped in newspaper, from the local takeaway.) That the cancer has splintered or diversified its portfolio of doom, and introduced its surrogate, depression (wrapped in rage), dawns on me. The rage part of it comes with the recognition of a virulent opponent in me. Still, the rage puzzles me. I do not understand it. I feel a surge of negative energy, say, impatience, or a gloomy outlook about the publishing potential of a book about my experience with cancer. I think what else is there if I cannot talk in public about cancer and show the beast to others who might benefit from hearing about my grapple with it.

Moreover, I view writing as my resistance to cancer. My understanding that comes from writing is nothing short of my troops sent in the field to meet cancer's army. I have a past that I access through writing, to deploy against my cancerous present. As I conjure imagined cancer-free worlds, I stem the flow of cancer's plunder of my body.

Dream on.

BLACK LIVES MATTER

brings us to this day on a dead-end street, face-to-face
with a young rabbit, no bigger than a tangerine,
blue jays pick up with articulate claws, fly four floors and drop,
but lucky nine lives rabbit lands, thud, looks hurt,
stays still for seconds, as if lost in dream space,
staggers away, and another jay grabs it, until we intervene,
shoo those blue jays into treetops, and wrap
the pulse of fur, with two dimes for ears, in an old T-shirt.

Too young for us to feed it carrots or lettuce, we know
that we must release the bright bulb of a creature back
where we found it, but not before we chase
those lingering jays, place shirt gingerly on dirt, watch that
fur ball flick away into tall, abandoned, lot grass,
as if that bulb lost its element and left an afterglow.

We wait as jays circle, then tip wings for another zone.
We retrieve that tee, its smell of game, and tiptoe home.

17

MY FATHER'S BODY

I know nothing about how my parents meet. She is a schoolgirl. He is at work, probably a government clerk in a building near her school. At the hour when school and office are out for lunch their lives intersect at sandwich counters, soft drink stands, traffic lights, market squares. Their eyes meet or their bodies collide at one of these food queues. He says something suggestive, complimentary. She suppresses a smile or traps one beneath her hands. He takes this as encouragement (as if any reaction of hers would have been read as anything else) and keeps on talking and following her and probably misses lunch that day. All the while she walks and eats and drinks and soaks up his praise, his sweet body talk, his erotic chatter and sexy pitter-patter, his idle boasts and ample toasts to his life, his dreams about their future, the world their oyster together.

Am I going too fast on my father's behalf? Should there have been an immediate and cutting rebuttal from her and several days before another meeting? Does he leave work early to catch her at the end of the school day and follow her home just to see where she lives and to extend the boundaries of their courtship? Throwing it from day to night, from school to home, from childhood play to serious adult intent? Georgetown's two-lane streets with trenches on either side mean a mostly single-file walk, she in front probably looking over her shoulder when he says something worthy of a glance, or a cut-eye look if his suggestions about her body or what he will do with it if given half a chance exceed the decorum of the day—which is what, in midfifties Guyana?

From my grandmother it's, "Don't talk to a man unless you think you're a big woman. Man will bring you trouble. Man want just one thing from you. Don't listen to he. Don't get ruined for he. A young lady must cork her ears and keep her eye straight in front of she when these men start to flock around. The gentleman among them will find his way to her front door. The gentleman will make contact with the parents first. Woo them first before muttering one thing to the young lady. Man who go directly to young ladies only want to ruin them. Don't want to make them into respectable young women—just whores. Mark my words."

My grandfather simply thinks that his little girl is not ready for the attentions of any man, that none of them is good enough for his little girl, and so the man who comes to his front door had better have a good pretext for disturbing his reverie. He had better know something about merchant seamen and the character of the sea, and about silence—how to keep it so that it signifies authority and dignity, so when you speak you are heard and your words, every one of them, are rivets. That man would have to be a genius to get past my grandfather, a genius or a gentleman. And since my father is neither, it's out of the question that he'll ever use the front door of worship. His route will have to be the yard and the street of ruination.

So he stands in full view of her house at dusk. It takes a few nights before her parents realize he is there for their daughter. Then one day her father comes out and tells him to take his dog behavior to someone else's front door, and the young man quickly turns on his heel and walks away. Another time her mother opens the upstairs window and curses him, and he laughs and saunters off as if her words were a broom gently ushering him out of her yard. But he returns the next night and the next, and the daughter can't believe his determination. She is embarrassed that her body has been a magnet for trouble, that she is the cause of the uproar, then angry with him for his keen regard of her at the expense of her dignity, not to mention his.

Neighbors tease her about him. They take pity on the boy, offer him drinks, some ice-cold mauby, a bite to eat, a dhal-pouri, all of which he declines at first, then dutifully accepts. One neighbor even offers him a chair, and on one night of pestilential showers, an umbrella, since he does not budge from his spot while all around him people dash for shelter, abandoning a night of liming (loitering) and gaffing (talking) to the persistence and chatter of the rain. Not my father. He stands his ground with only the back of his right hand up to his brow to shelter his eyes zeroed in on her house. She steals a glance at him after days of seeming to ignore the idea of him, though his presence burns brightly inside her heart. She can't believe his vigilance is for her. She stops to stare in the mirror and for the first time sees her full lips, long, straight nose, shoulder-length brunette hair, and dark green eyes with their slight oval shape. Her high cheekbones. Her ears close to her skull. She runs her fingers lightly over these places as if to touch is to believe. Her lips tingle. Her hair shines. Her eyes smile. And she knows from this young man's perseverance that she is beautiful, desirable.

She abandons herself to chores, and suppresses a smile and a song. She walks past windows as much as possible to feed the young man's hungry eyes with a morsel of that which he has venerated to the point of indignity. She rewards his eyes by doing unnecessary half turns at the upstairs window. A flash of clavicle, a hand slowly putting her hair off her face and setting it down behind her ears, and then a smile, a demure glance, her head inclined a little, her eyes raised, her eyelids batted a few times—she performs for him though she feels silly and self-conscious. What else is there for a girl to do? Things befitting a lady that she picked up from the cinema. Not the sauciness of a tramp.

Her mother pulls her by one of those beautiful close-skulled ears from the window and curses her as if she were a ten-cent whore, then throws open the window and hurtles a long list of insults at this tall, silent, rude, good-for-nothing streak of impertinence darkening her street. The father folds his paper and gets up, but by the time he gets to the window the young man is gone.

My mother cries into the basin of dishes. She rubs a saucer so hard that it comes apart in her hands. She is lucky not to cut herself. She will have to answer to her mother for that breakage. In the past it meant at least a few slaps and many minutes of curses for bringing only trouble into her mother's house. Tonight her mother is even angrier. Her father has turned his fury against her for rearing a daughter who is a fool for men. Her mother finds her in the kitchen holding the two pieces of the saucer together and then apart—as if her dread and sheer desire for reparation would magically weld them whole. Her tears fall like drops of solder on that divided saucer. Her mother grabs her hands and strikes her and curses her into her face so that my mother may as well have been standing over a steaming, spluttering pot on the stove. She drops the two pieces of saucer and they become six pieces. Her mother looks down and strides over the mess with threats about what will happen if her feet find a splinter. She cries but finds every piece, and to be sure to get the splinters too she runs her palms along the floor, this way and that, and with her nails she pries out whatever her hand picks up. She cries herself to sleep.

The next night he is back at his station, and her mother and father, their voices, their words, their blows, sound a little farther off, fall a little lighter. His presence, the barefaced courage of it, becomes a suit of armor for her to don against her mother and father's attacks. She manages under her mother's watchful eye to show both sides of her clavicle, even a little of the definition down the middle of her chest—that small trench her inflated chest digs, which catches the light and takes the breath away, that line drawn from the throat to the uppermost rib exuding warmth and tension, drawing the eyes twenty-five yards away with its radiance in the half light of dusk, promising more than it can possibly contain, than the eye can hold, and triggering a normal heart into palpitations, a normal breath into shallowness and rapidity.

"Miss Isiah, howdy! How come you house so clean on the west side and not so clean on the east? It lopsided! Dirt have a preference in your house? Or is that saga boy hanging around the west side of your house a dirt repellent?" The gossip must have been rampant in the surrounding yards, yards seemingly designed deliberately so people could see into one another's homes and catch anything spilling out of them—quarrels, courtships, cooking pots, music—and sometimes a clash of houses, a reaction against the claustrophobia of the yard, but not enough yards, not enough room to procure a necessary privacy in order to maintain a badly sought-after dignity—clean, well dressed, head high in the air on Sundays—impossible if the night before there is a fight and everyone hears you beg not to be hit anymore, or else such a stream of obscenities gushes from your mouth that the sealed red lips of Sunday morning just don't cut it.

My father maintains his vigil. Granny threatens to save the contents of her chamber pot from the night before and empty it onto his head. Could she have thrown it from her living room window to his shaded spot by the street? Luckily she never tries. She may well be telling him that he doesn't deserve even that amount of attention. If there is any creature lower than a gutter rat—one too low to merit even her worst display of disdain—then he is it. How does my father take that? As a qualification he can do without? How much of that kind of water is he able to let run off his back? Poor man. He has to be in love. He has to be wearing his own suit of armor. Lashed to his mast like Odysseus, he hears the most taunting, terrible things, but what saves him, what restores him, are the ropes, the armor of his love for my mother. Others without this charm would have withered away, like the proverbial Marxist state, but not my father, he smiles and shrugs at the barrage of looks, insults, gestures, silence, loneliness.

Watch my father's body there under that breadfruit and sapodilla tree (I do not see a repository of my cancer; I do not even see me). The shine of his status as sentry and his conviction are twin headlights that blind my mother's parents. They redouble their efforts to get rid of his particular glare, then are divided by the sense of his inevitability in their daughter's life. My grandmother stops shouting at him, while my grandfather still raises his cane and causes the young man to walk away briskly. My grandmother then opens the windows on the west side, ostensibly to let in the sea breeze but really to exhibit in all those window frames a new and friendly demeanor. My grandfather shouts at her that he can smell the rank intent of that black boy, rotten as a fish market, blowing into his living room and spoiling his thoughts.

But the windows stay open. And my mother at them. With the love Morse of her clavicles and her cleavage as she grows bolder. Smiling, then waving. And no hand in sight to box her or grip her by the ear and draw her away from there. Until one night she boldly leaves the house and goes to him and they talk for five minutes rapidly as if words are about to run out in the Southern Hemisphere.

My father's parents wonder what has become of their Malcolm.

"The boy only intend to visit town."

"Town swallow him up."

"No, one woman turn he head, stick it in a butter churn, and swill it."

"He lost to us now."

"True."

They say this to each other, often and interchangeably, but hardly speak to him except to make pronouncements on the size of foreign lands.

"Guyana small?"

"What's the boy talking about?"

"Why, England and Scotland combined are the size of Guyana."

"How much room does the boy need?"

"That city woman take he common sense in a mortar and pound it with a pestle."

Their two voices are one voice. Opportunity is here now. The English are letting go of the reins. A whole new land is about to be fashioned. And the boy is planning to leave! What kind of woman has done this to our Malcolm? The boy is lost. Talking to him is like harnessing a stubborn donkey. This isn't love but some obeah or voodoo or juju, some concoction in a drink, some spell thrown in his locus. A little salt over the shoulder, an iodine shower, a rabbit foot on a string, a duck's bill or snake head dried and deposited into the left trouser pocket, a precious stone, lapis lazuli, amethyst, or anything on the middle finger, a good old reliable crucifix around the neck, made of silver, not gold, and at least one ounce in weight and two inches in diameter. A psalm in papyrus folded in a shirt pocket next to the heart. A bout of fasting, one night without sleep, a dreamless night, and a dreamless, sleepless, youngest son restored to them. He wants to stay around the house, he shows them why he loves his mummy and poppy and the bounteous Guyanese landscape. There is no plan to flee. There is no Georgetown woman with his heart in her hand. And his brain is not ablaze in his pants. His head is not an empty, airless room.

My mother and father have one cardboard suitcase each, apart from her purse and his envelope tied with a string that contains their passports and tickets, birth certificates, and, for him, a document that he is indeed a clerk with X amount of experience at such and such a government office, signed "supervisor"—a worthless piece of shit, of course, in the eyes of any British employer. But for the time being, these little things are emblematic of the towering, staggering optimism that propels them out of Georgetown, Guyana, over the sea to London, England.

So what do they do? My mother is a shy woman. My father, in the two photos I've seen of him, is equally reserved. Not liable to experimentation. The big risk has been taken—that of leaving everything they know for all that is alien to them. My mother knows next to nothing about sex, except perhaps a bit about kissing. My father may have experimented a little, as boys tend to do, but he, too, when faced with the female body, confronts unfamiliar territory. Each burns for the other, enough to pull up roots and take off into the unknown. Yet I want to believe that they improvise around the idea of her purity and respect it until their marriage night. That they keep intact some of the moral system they come from even as they dismantle and ignore every other stricture placed on them by post–World War II Guyanese society: honor your father and mother; fear a just and loving God; pledge allegiance to the British flag; lust is the devil's oxygen. All that circles in their veins.

Over the twelve days at sea they examine what they have left and what they are heading toward. At sea they are in between lives: one life is over but the other has not yet begun. The talking they do on that ship without any duties to perform at all! My mother tells how her father, despite his routine as a merchant seaman, finds time to memorize whole poems by the Victorians: Tennyson, Longfellow, both Brownings, Jean Ingelow, Arnold, and Hopkins. The sea is his workplace, yet he makes time to do this marvelous thing. She tells how when he comes back to land he gathers them all in the living room and performs "The Charge of the Light Brigade" or "Maud" or "My Last Duchess" or "Fra Lippo Lippi" or "The High Tide on the Coast of Lincoln-shire" or "Dover Beach" or "As Kingfishers Catch Fire" or "The Wreck of the *Deutschland*." He recites these poems to his creole-thinking children, who sit there and marvel at the English they are hearing, not that of the policeman or the teacher or the priest, but even more difficult to decipher, full of twists and impossible turns that throw you off the bicycle of your creole reasoning into the sand. If any of them interrupts my grandfather, he stops in midflow, reprimands them in creole, and resumes his poem where he left off. When particularly miffed by the disturbance he starts the poem from the beginning again. Does my grandfather recite these verses before or after he gets drunk, swears at the top of his voice, and chases my grandmother around the house with his broad leather belt?

My parents are out on the high seas. They have only the King James Bible in their possession. They plan and rehearse every aspect of their new life.

"Children. I want children."

"Me too. Plenty of them."

"I can work between births."

"Yes, both of us. Until we have enough money for a house. Then you can stay home with the kids."

"We could get a nanny to watch the kids while we both work."

"What kind of house you like?"

"Three bedrooms. A garden at the front, small, and back, large."

"A car—a Morris Minor. With all that room in the back for the children and real indicators and a wood finish."

Neither has a notebook or dreamed of keeping one. They do not write their thoughts, they utter them. If something is committed to memory, there has to be a quotidian reason for it, apart from bits of the Bible and a few calypsos. My grandfather's labor of love, his settling down with a copy of Palgrave's *Golden Treasury* and memorizing lines that bear no practical relationship to his life, must seem bizarre to his children. Yet by doing so he demonstrates his love of words, their music, the sense of their sound, their approximation to the heartbeat and breath, their holding out of an alternative world to the one surrounding him, their confirmation of a past and another's life and thoughts, their luxury of composition, deliberation, their balancing and rebalancing of a skewered life. I imagine my mother benefits from this exposure in some oblique way—that the Victorians stick to her mental makeup whether she cares for them or not, that a little of them comes off on me in the wash or my gestation in her.

There is an old black-and-white photo (isn't there always?) of my father and fragments of stories about his comings and goings, his carryings-on, as the creole-speak goes, his mischief. "Look pan that smooth face, them two big, dark eye them, don't they win trust quick-time? Is hard to tie the man with them eye in him head to any woman and she pickney them. He face clean-shaven like he never shave. He curly black hair, dougla-look, but trim neat-neat. The man got topside." My father's hair, thick and wavy and credited to a "dougla" mix of East Indian and Black, in fact comes from his White father and his mother of African descent. The look exaggerates an already high forehead. Automatically, such an appearance, in the Caribbean and elsewhere, is equated with intelligence—"topside." And a European nose (from his Portuguese father), not broad, with a high bridge (good breeding, though the nostrils flare a bit—sign of a quick temper!). And lips that invite kisses. "They full-full and pout like a kiss with the sound of a kiss way behind, long after that kiss come and gone." He is six feet tall and thin but not skinny, that brand of thin that women refer to as elegant, since the result is long fingers and economic gestures. Notice I say economic and not cheap. A man of few words. A watcher. "But when he relax in company he know and trust, then he the center of wit and idle philosophizing. He shoot back a few rums, neat no chaser, with anyone, and hold his own with men more inclined to gin and tonic. He know when to mind his Ps and Qs and when to gaff in the most lewd Georgetown rum-shop talk with the boys. What chance a sixteen-year-old closeted lady got against such a man, I ask you!"

But most of the puzzle is missing, except for the big piece of my hereditary cancer, so I start to draw links from one fragment to the next. He begins to belong—fleetingly, at first—in my life. As a man in poor light seen crossing a road mercifully free of traffic, its tarmacadam steamy with a recent downpour. As a tall, lank body glimpsed ducking under the awning of a shop front and disappearing inside and never emerging no matter how long I wait across the street, watching the door with its reflecting plate glass and listening for the little jingle of the bell that announces the arrival and departure of customers.

Or I cross Blackheath Hill in South London, where I lived as a teen, entranced by the urgent belief that my father is in one of the cars speeding up and down it. Blackheath Hill curves a little with a steep gradient. It's more of a ski slope than a hill. Cars and trucks, motorbikes and cyclists, all come down the road as if in a race for a finish line. Going up it is no different. Vehicles race to the top as if with the fear that their engines might cut off and they will slide back down. Through most of my teen years of crossing Blackheath Hill, I want to be seen by my father. I have to be close to his car so that he does not miss me. I measure the traffic and watch myself get halfway, then, after a pause to allow a couple of cars to pass on their way up, a brisk walk, if I time it right, to allow the rest of the traffic to catch up with me, to see the kid who seems to be in no particular hurry to get out of the way looking at them. I step onto the sidewalk and cherish the breeze of the nearest vehicle at my back. Father, this is your son you have just missed. Isn't he big? Pull over and call his name. Take him in your arms. Admonish him. Remind him that cars can kill and his little body would not survive a hit at these high speeds. Tell him to look for his father under less dangerous circumstances.

I am searching the only way I know how, by rumination, contemplation, conjecture, supposition. I try to fill the gaps, try to piece together the father I never knew. I imagine everything where there is little or nothing to go on. And yet, in going back, in raking up bits and pieces of a shattered and erased existence, I know that I am courting rejection from a source hitherto silent and beyond me. I am conjuring up a father safely out of reach and taking the risk that the lips I help to move, the lungs I force to breathe, will simply say no. No to everything I ask of them, even the merest crumb of recognition.

"Father." The noun rings hollowly when I say it, my head is empty of any meaning the word might have. I shout it in a dark cave but none of the expected bats come flapping out. Just weaker and weaker divisions of my call. "Father." It is my incantation to bring him back from the grave to the responsibility of his name. But how, when I know only his ex-wife, my mother, and her sudden, moody silence whenever he crops up in conversation?

*   *   *

You ever have anyone sweet-talk you? Fill your ears with their kind of wax, rub that wax with their tongue all over your body with more promises than the promised land itself contains, fill your head with their sweet drone, their buzz that shuts out your parents, friends, your own mind from its own house? That's your father, the bumblebee, paying attention to me.

My sixteenth birthday was a month behind. He was nearly twenty. A big man in my eyes. What did he want with me? A smooth tongue in my ears. Mostly, though, he watched me, my house, my backside when he followed me home from school. His eyes gleamed in the early evening, the whites of his eyes. He stood so still by the side of the road outside my house that he might have been a lamppost, planted there, shining just for me.

My father cursed him, my mother joined in, my sisters laughed at his silence, his stillness. They all said he had to be the stupidest man in all of Georgetown, a dunce, a bat in need of a perch, out in the sun too long, sun fry his brain, cat take his tongue, his head empty like a calabash, his tongue cut out, he look like a beggar. They felt sorry for him standing there like a paling, his face a yard long, his tongue a slab of useless plywood in his mouth. "Look what Kathleen gone and bring to the house, shame, dumbness, blackness follow she here to we house to paint shame all over it and us. Go away, black boy, take your dumb misery somewhere else, crawl back to your pen in the country, leave we sister alone, she got more beauty than sense to listen to a fool like you, to let you follow her, to encourage you by not cursing the day you was born and the two people who got together to born you and your people and whole sorry village you crawl out of to come and plant yourself here in front of we house on William Street, a decent street, in Kitty, in we capital."

I should have thanked my sisters; instead I begged them to leave him alone. Ignore him and he'll go away. My father left the house to get hold of the boy by the scruff of his neck and boot his backside out of Kitty, but he ran off when my father appeared in the doorframe. With the light of the house behind him and casting a long, dark shadow, he must have looked twice his size and in no mood to bargain. Your father sprinted away, melting into the dark. I watched for his return by checking that the windows I'd bolted earlier really were bolted, convincing myself that I had overlooked one of them, using my hands to feel the latch as I searched the street for him. But he was gone for the night. My knight. Shining eyes for armor.

My mother cursed him from the living room window, flung it open and pointed at him and with her tongue reduced him to a pile of rubble and scattered that rubble over a wide area, then picked her way through the strewn wreckage to make sure her destruction was complete. "Country boy, what you want with my daughter? What make you think you man enough for her? What you got between your legs that give you the right to plant yourself in front of my house? What kind of blight you is? You fungus!"

As she cursed him and he retreated from the house sheepishly, she watched her husband for approval. These were mild curses for her, dutiful curses, a warm-up. When she really got going her face reddened and her left arm carved up the air in front of her as if it were the meat of her opponent being dissected into bite-size bits. That's how I knew she was searching for a way to help me but hadn't yet found it. Not as long as my father was at home. Soon he would be at sea, away for weeks, and things would be different.

That is, if my onlooker, my remote watcher, my far-off admirer, wasn't scared off forever. And what if he was? Then he didn't deserve me in the first place. If he couldn't take a few curses, he wasn't good for anything. If I wasn't worth taking a few curses for, well, I didn't want a man who didn't think I was worth taking a few curses for! I loved him for coming back night after night when all he got from me was a glance at the window. Sometimes less than a glance. Just me passing across the window frame as I dashed from chore to chore under the four baleful eyes of my parents.

It seemed like he was saving all his breath and words for when he could be alone with me. Then he turned on the bumblebee of himself and I was the hapless flower of his attentions. He told me about my skin, that it was silk, that all the colors of the rainbow put together still didn't come close to my beautiful light-brown skin. That my face, my eyes, my mouth, my nose, the tip of my nose, my ears, my fingertips, each was a precious jewel, precious stone. He likened the rest of me to things I had read about but had never seen, had dreamed about but had never dreamed I would see: dandelions, apple trees, snow, spring in England's shires, the white cliffs of Dover. In his eyes my body, me, was everything I dreamed of becoming.

That was your father before any of you were a twinkle in his eye. More accurately, that was my lover and then my husband. Your father was a different man altogether. I saw the change in him. I cannot account for it. A stranger occupied my bed. His tongue no longer sweet-talked me. All the laughter of my sisters, the halfhearted curses of my mother, my father's promise of blue misery, all came true in this strange man, this father, this latter-day husband and lover.

He simply changed. My hands were full with you children. He went out of reach. He cradled you as if he didn't know which side was up, which down. He held you at arm's length to avoid the tar and feathers of you babies. Soon I earned the same treatment, but if you children were tar and feathers I was refuse. His face creased when he came near me. What had become of my silk skin? My precious features disappeared into my face, earning neither praise nor blame—just his silence, his wooden tongue, and that bad-smell look of his. I kept quiet for as long as I could. I watched him retreat from all of us, hoping he'd reel himself back in, since the line between us was strong and I thought unbreakable; but no. I had to shout to get him to hear me. I shouted like my mother standing at the upstairs window to some rude stranger in the street twenty-five yards away. I sounded like my father filling the doorframe. My jeering sisters insinuated their way into my voice. And your father simply kept walking away.

Believe me, I pulled my hair and beat the ground with my hands and feet to get at him in my head and in the ground he walked on that I worshipped. Hadn't he delivered England to me and all the seasons of England, all England's shires and the fog he'd left out of his serenades, no doubt just to keep some surprise in store for me? The first morning I opened the door that autumn and shouted "Fire!" when I saw all that smoke, thinking the whole street on fire, all the streets, London burning, and slammed the door and ran into his arms and his laughter, and he took me out into it in my nightdress, he in his pajamas, and all the time I followed him, not ashamed to be seen outside in my thin, flimsy nylon (if anyone could see through that blanket) because he was in his pajamas, the blue, striped ones, and his voice, his sweet drone, told me it was fine, this smoke without fire was fine, "This is fog."

*   *   *

The first time I see my father is the last time I see him. I can't wait to get to the front of the queue to have him all to myself. When I get there my eyes travel up and down his body. From those few gray hairs that decorate his temples and his forehead and his nose to the cuffs at his knees, and at his ankles a pair of sparkling black shoes. He wears a black suit, a double-breasted number with three brass buttons on the cuff of each sleeve. He lies on his back. There is too much powder on his face. Let's get out of this mournful place, Dad. We have a lot of catching up to do. He has the rare look—of holding his breath, of not breathing, in between inhaling and exhaling—that exquisitely beautiful corpses capture. For a moment after I invite him to leave with me, I expect his chest to inflate, his lids to open, and those hands to pull him upright into a sitting position as if he really were napping because he has dressed way too early for the ball.

There are myths about this sort of thing. Father enslaves son. Son hates father, bides his time, waits for the strong father to weaken. Son pounces one day, pounces hard and definite, and the father is overwhelmed, broken, destroyed, with hardly any resistance, except that of surprise followed by resignation. Son washes his hands but finds he is washing hands that are not bloodstained, not marked or blemished in any way. He is simply scrubbing hands that no longer belong to him—they are his father's hands, attached to his arms, his shoulders, his body. He has removed a shadow all the more to see unencumbered the father in himself. There is the widow he has made of his mother. He cannot love her as his father might. While his father lived he thought he could. The moment his father expired he knew his mother would remain unloved.

I alight too soon from a number 53 bus on Blackheath Hill, disembark while the bus is moving, and stumble, trip from two legs onto all fours, hands like feet, transforming, sprouting more limbs, becoming a spider and breaking my fall. That same fall is now a tumble, a dozen somersaults that end with me standing upright and quite still on two legs with the other limbs dangling. Onlookers, who fully expected disaster, applaud. I walk back up the hill to the block of council flats as a man might, upright, on two legs. My other limbs dangle and swing high. Some days I will be out of breath, I will gasp and exhale, and the cloud before me will not be my winter's breath but the silken strands of a web, or worse, fire. Other days I might look at a bed of geraniums planted on the council estate and turn all their numberless petals into stone. A diamond held between my thumb and index finger crumbles in this mood, in this light, like the powdery wings of a butterfly.

Some years later I stare out of an apartment on the twentieth floor of a tower block overlooking the nut-brown Thames. That wasp on the windowpane nibbling up and down the glass for a pore to exit through, back into the air and heat, tries to sting what it can feel but cannot see. My father is the window. I am the wasp. Sometimes a helping hand comes along and lifts the window, and the wasp slides out. Other times a shadow descends, there is a displacement of air, and it is the last thing the wasp knows. Which of those times is this cancer time of mine? I want to know.

I don't want to know. I am not nibbling or trying to sting. I am kissing repeatedly, rapidly, the featureless face of my father. It feels like summer light. It reflects a garden. Whose is that interfering hand? Why that interrupting shadow? My child's hand. My child's shadow. My son or my father? My son and my father. Two sons, two fathers. Yet three people. Three entities: my father, my cancer, and me. We walk, we three, behind a father's name, shoulder a father's gene pool and memory. Wear another's walk, another's gait. Wait for what has happened to him to happen to me. Our bodies with this scar of cancer genes. His maladies that surface in me.

I want to shed my skin. Walk away from my shadow. Leave my name in a place I cannot return to. To be nameless, bodiless. To swim to Stevens's Key West, which is shoreless, horizonless. Blackheath Hill becomes Auden's Bristol Street, an occasion for wonder and lament. Blackheath at 5:45 a.m. on a foggy winter morning becomes Peckham Rye. There are no trees on Blackheath, but angels hang in the air if only Blake were there to see them. On the twentieth floor towering above the Thames, water, not land, surrounds me. Everything seems to rise out of that water. Look up at ambling clouds and the tower betrays its drift out to sea.

*   *   *

Night, cancer. You had me in a vice for most of this year of plagues. I bear six scars on my stomach from our encounter. Those are the ones you can see. The ones that you can't see, well, that's a song, "Me and the Devil Blues," that Robert Johnson sings better than anybody. Consider me one of the lucky ones. You turned up in me and we parted company, and, for now, I live.

ABOUT THE AUTHOR

FRED D'AGUIAR was born in London of Guyanese parents. He spent his childhood in Guyana and returned to the UK for his secondary and tertiary education. He has lived and taught in the US since the 1990s. He is a professor of English at UCLA, where he teaches literature and creative writing. He lives in Mid-City Los Angeles with his family and spends some time with his wife, Debbie, rescuing stray cats. Dexter, the family dog, doesn't mind since two of his house pals, Clementine and Moonlight, are cats.